The
Bradford Bishop
Murders

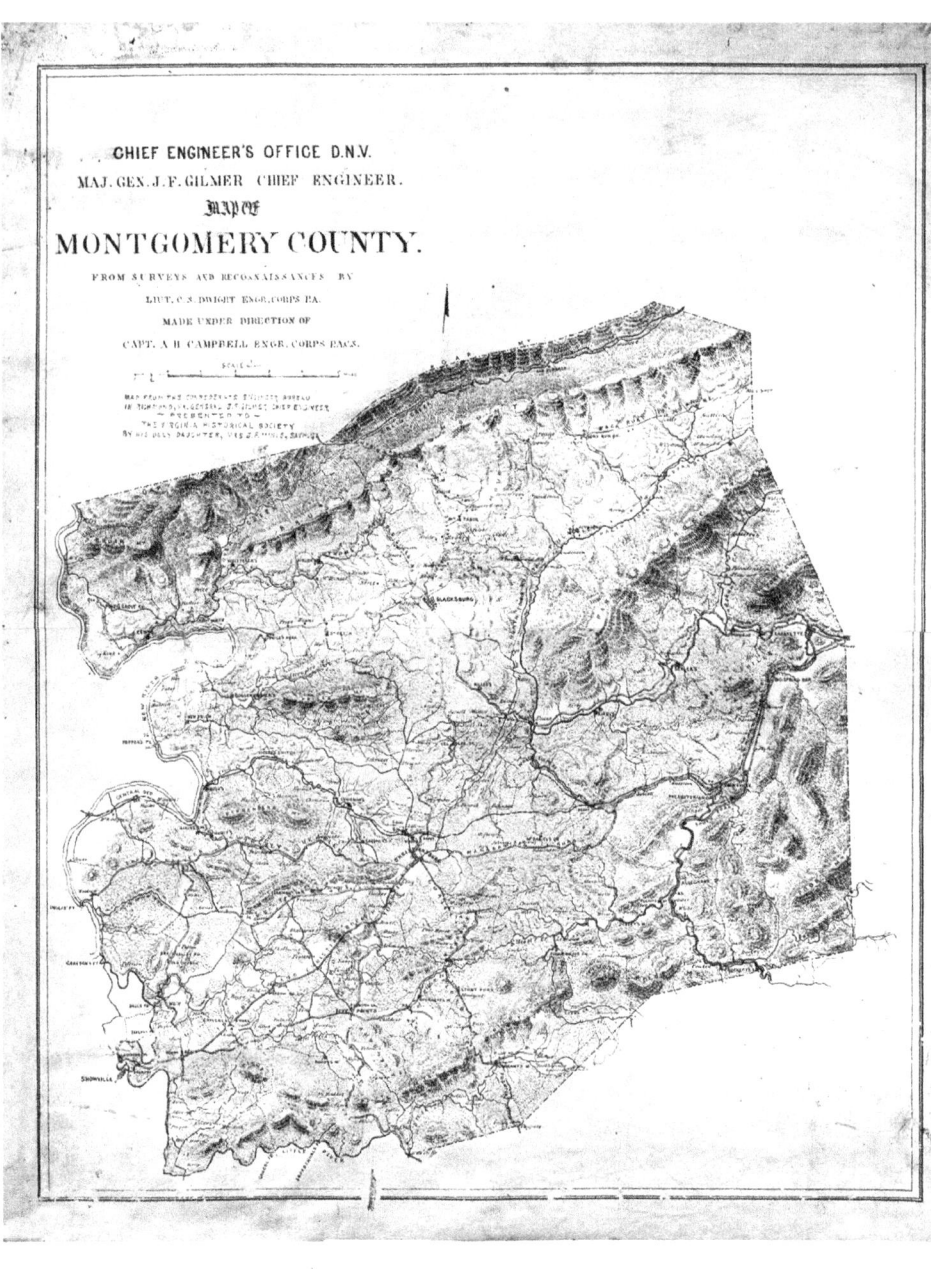

The Bradford Bishop Murders

Their First Loyalty is to their Careers

DAVID CASAVIS

DEEPER LOOK BOOKS

Copyright © 2018 by David Casavis
Copyright Number: TXu002071695
LCCN: 2017915496

All rights reserved. No part of this publication may be reproduced, distributed, or transmitted in any form or by any means, including photocopying, recording, or other electronic or mechanical methods, without the prior written permission of the publisher, except in the case of brief quotations embodied in critical reviews and certain other noncommercial uses permitted by copyright law. For permission requests, write to the publisher, addressed "Attention: Permissions Coordinator," at the address below.

Deeper Look Books
122 East 83rd Street
New York, New York 10028
www.deeperlookbooks.com

Ordering Information: Quantity sales. Special discounts are available on quantity purchases by corporations, associations, and others. For details, contact the publisher at the address above. Orders by U.S. trade bookstores and wholesalers. Please contact Ingram Distribution: Tel: (800) 937-8200; Fax: (800) 876-0186 or visit www.ipage.ingramcontent.com.
Printed in the United States of America

Cover by Daniel Middleton | www.scribefreelance.com

Publisher's Cataloging-In-Publication Data
(Prepared by The Donohue Group, Inc.)

Names: Casavis, David.
Title: The Bradford Bishop murders: their first loyalty is to their careers / by David Casavis.
Description: New York, New York: Deeper Look Books, [2018] | Includes bibliographical references and index.
Identifiers: ISBN 9780985652548 (hardback) | ISBN 9780985652555 (paperback) | ISBN 9780985652562 (eBook)
Subjects: LCSH: Bishop, Bradford, 1936---Career in diplomatic and consular service. | Fugitives from justice--United States. | Diplomatic and consular service, American. | Murderers--United States. | Work-life balance. | LCGFT: True crime stories.
Classification: LCC HV6248.B57 C37 2018 (print) | LCC HV6248.B57 (eBook) | DDC 364.1523/092--dc23

Dedicated to Annette, Lobelia, William,
Brenton and Geoffrey Bishop;

And to those who seek to unravel the psychology
of the US Department of State.

"One day we will send you missionaries."
49th Parallel: 1941

William Bradford Bishop III, Brenton & Geoffrey Bishop

Annette Bishop   (Grandma) Lobelia Germain Bishop

Contents

The Principal Characters in this Book 9

Preface 11

Notes and Acknowledgments 14

Introduction 15

    Life Beyond Shady Grove 23

Part One 31

    The Glittering Prize 33

    Only the UDBA Kills Like That 49

    Balkan Revenge 63

    The Great Smoky Mountains Search 68

Part Two 77

    The Golden Life 79

    The Bitch Goddess Success 89

    Sneaky Pete 107

    The Incursion 117

    The Best and the Brightest 127

    The Fair-Haired Boy 134

    Coffee Ranks Tea 149

    Milan 159

    Status Anxiety 167

    Gaborone 174

    The China Card 186

    The Corridor Reputation 197

    The State Department on the Couch 204

 God as a Verb 213

 Molasses 218

Part Three 227

 Bishop Seen Everywhere 229

 The Migrant Trade 233

 Petroleum 236

 Sightings 240

 The Bankston Letter 247

 Gunrunning 260

 Legend, Myth, and Brief Encounter Signaling 264

 John Doe 272

 The End Game 279

 Epilogue 287

 Afterword 295

 Notes 297

 Pictorial and Graphic Materials 299

 Glossary of Terms 301

 Addenda 314

 Index 351

ALSO BY DAVID CASAVIS
•
The Thomas Carroll Affair
Murder at the Embassy

The Principal Characters in this Book

William Bradford Bishop, Jr.	*A Foreign Service Officer and fugitive*
Annette Bishop née Weis	*Bradford Bishop junior's wife*
William, Breton, and Geoffrey Bishop	*The three sons of Bradford and Annette Bishop*
Lobelia Amaryllis Bishop	*Bradford Bishop's mother*
William Bradford Bishop, Sr.	*Bradford Bishop's father*
Charles Bishop	*Bradford Bishop Senior's brother, and Bradford Bishop Junior's Uncle*
Leo	*The Bishop Family Golden Retriever*
Charles Peterson	*Intelligence Operation Specialist at the ASA*
Albert Kenneth Bankston	*A bank robber incarcerated in a Federal Prison*
Dan Dugan	*An inmate jailed with Bankston*
Edward Korry	*American Ambassador to Ethiopia*
Charles J. Nelson	*American Ambassador to Botswana, et. al.*
Vjekoslav 'Maks' Luburić	*Former Commandant of a Death Camp*
Ante Pavelić	*The dictator of Croatia 1941 – 1945*

Josip Broz Tito	*Head of Yugoslavia after World War Two*
Rheinhard Gehlen	*Chief of FHO, the German Army's military intelligence unit on the Eastern Front, 1942 – 1945 Working for US Army G-2, until 1947, for the American CIA*
Kwame Nkrumah	*First President of Ghana (1960 – 1966)*
Kenneth Kaunda	*First President of Zambia (1970 – 1973)*
Hailie Selassie	*Emperor of Ethiopia (1930 – 1974)*
Jacques D'Amboise	*A dancer and friend of the Bishop family*
Roy Harrell	*A State Department Employee*
Friedrich Nietzsche	*A German philosopher*
Albert Camus	*A French philosopher, author, and journalist.*

Preface

"Beware that, when fighting monsters, you yourself do not become a monster. For when you gaze long into the abyss, the abyss gazes also into you."

— Friedrich Nietzsche

What no one understood was that he was bringing a bit of Cold War Eastern Europe to America. Cold War Eastern Europe was the real world. Distant and put away, it was like fire on the other side of the water. The murders were bringing terror to a place where terror was an abstract concept. The upshot delivered the people of the US State of Maryland a nasty shock. That shock reverberates still.

There are those who think he will return. To some he is the boogieman under their beds. Some think they see him in every suspicious twist and turn. False sightings abound.

Who is he? He is William Bradford Bishop Jr., the murderer who beat the life out of his entire family with a hammer: his wife, mother, and three sons. The chill that persists is because no one understood the why of it.

America had settled into a world of barbecues, network television, and the quiet enjoyment of suburban homes. America had put the world's misery behind it. The raw world of dictators and the mass movements of armies was outdated. All of it was largely sanitized: concentration camps, summary execution, and genocide. Profoundly disturbing film footage of the recent carnage and horror was sequestered.

Herein is an explanation. The why of the murders can only become clear once all the pieces - properly assembled and sorted - form a coherent picture. The Bradford Bishop murders can only be understood in the context of a vicious world beyond prosperous shores.

The carnage was part of the evil that emerged in twentieth century Europe and Asia. When the horror unexpectedly appeared in Maryland and North Carolina, it tore into the tranquil and tidy world of postwar bureaucrats; and the contented humdrum routines they enjoyed. This candid and unsettling account will close the book on an episode the US Department of State prefers to forget.

This is because, in part, the Foreign Service ethos too often leads to outrage and despair. With a background of frustration, violence, and obfuscation, career-driven Foreign Service Officers can turn deadly. Insofar as any decades-long, open case remains unsolved, and can be brought to a conclusion, this is it.

This is as complete a record and accounting of one of the worst family annihilations in American History, as can be assembled. It is a story with many twists and turns. The key to understanding it is that it is out-of-this world (Or at least out of America's world). The cotton candy world of eloquence and protocol, presented by the US Department of State to an unsuspecting America turned raw. This book is about how a monster appeared.

It was not just a monster; it is *the* monster. To many, the "Ballad of Brad Bishop" rang true. "There is a little of Brad Bishop in me and you," the band Coup de Grace, crooned over Maryland radio stations in 1979.

Perhaps. William Bradford Bishop Jr. was everything the State Department wanted. In retrospect, he was elevated to someone who lived the most enviable of American lives. Journalists, at a loss to describe his life refer to him as, someone who 'had it all.' Most of the world would have seen him as a member of the elite. This much is true.

Perhaps he had it all. Perhaps he was a mirror, a figure the US Department of State would neither look into, nor contemplate. Bradford Bishop wanted more, just as his fellow Foreign Service Officers wanted more. Ultimately, that same monster may have been in all of them, just waiting to come out.

The monster is smiling. The monster comes up to them all, smiling. This is because evil is casual at first. It masquerades as good. It gives every excuse for vile and contemptable deeds. It is no use pushing it away and saying that everyone has a monster within. The monster wants to hear that.

Therefore, and so... The pieces come together. What was once hidden is now revealed. The monster steps out of the shadows. And it is smiling.

David Casavis
New York, New York
June 10, 2017

Bradford Bishop proposes a toast at a party

Notes and Acknowledgments

My thanks to Rebecca Arthur, and Elliott Brown Jr. for design and mapping assistance. My heartfelt thanks to Kathy Smith, for her references to the psyche. Additional thanks to her husband, Joseph Smith, for his council on shipping oil overseas. Heartfelt thanks to Ed Golian and Fred Burton, two rookie police officers of the Montgomery County Sheriff's Office in March of 1976. I salute Don Baker, who faithfully followed the story for the *Washington Post*, and kindly took my phone call while in retirement. Many thanks to DeWayne Patterson of the *Daily Sentinel* for his photograph. Thanks also to Joanne Fitzgerald Bryant for her testimony. Special thanks to 'Yami Ecstasy' who has been so generous with her permissions.

The author sends his best regards to James Bruno, a fiction writer specializing in thrillers. Mr. Bruno provided an important service in the furthering of the Bishop story. Dayton Lummis was a great source as well. Without Mr. Lummis' recollections, those who dug deeper into the story would be without a clue.

Special thanks to Dr. Stuart Koschade for his diligent doctorial research. Thanks also to Mauritz Naude, for his paper on rondavels. The author sends his best wishes for his continual success in his doctoral research. Thanks to Bryan Jung for his encouragement, and to Reid Lonergan for his independent research. Thanks to Nancy Lyon of Yale University's Manuscripts and Archives section of Sterling Library. Thanks also to Judith Schiff for her archival references to the History of Yale and to Mike Zumbluskas for being my beta reader. Many thanks to Dan Carr and Randy Harris for the picture, "Tract C." Thank you also to the South Pasadena Local History Images Collection for the use of their photos. Thank you to the National Cultural History Museum, Pretoria, for the use of their picture of a rondavel.

Introduction

The ancient Greeks did not have all the answers. They did, however, get all the questions right. The author does not have all the answers. What the author can offer is enough background, by asking the right questions, to further the ongoing investigation. It is the only way to tell the story as it stands at the time of this writing.

I mulled through many possible true stories about crime at American Embassies abroad. Choosing a true story is important. Books of this sort can take years to complete. I was urged to take on this mystery by those at State still curious as to the whereabouts of Bradford Bishop. Like all State employees who know of the murders, the curious wanted to know the *why* and the *how* of the alleged perpetrator's actions. The police simply wanted to collar him.

It soon became evident that this book would be a monster to complete. There were three crime sites in three different states, and a trail that led to Europe and beyond. Planning this crime scenario typifies the busy mind of a Foreign Service Officer. The trail went everywhere.

Thus, I found myself plagued by false trails and reluctant police officials. This, the first open case I have ever researched, posed problems I did not anticipate. Now I better understand why fictional private detectives have contentious relationships with the Police. After a few months of this, I started to refer to this work of investigation as 'the Monster.'

When I first arrived at the Montgomery County Police Department, I had arranged to speak to an assembly of county police officers. They were eager to meet me and hear me out. I had been researching the case and had some ideas.

What surprised me was that everyone at the Sheriff's Office wanted to meet me. When I inquired as to why, I was told that every rookie police officer trained on this case. As the night of the murders was March 1, 1976, every active duty police officer either had trained on this case or had been on the force when it transpired.

Therefore, it was with equal surprise that, when I arrived at the Sheriff's Office in Rockville for my scheduled visit, that the place was nearly empty. Indeed, upon my arrival, an officer with a K-9 emerged from the office. He wore a bulletproof vest. Even the dog had body armor. I took my seat and waited.

When the lieutenant invited me in, only one officer was in the back of a very large room. He waved from the distance. Then the lieutenant said that there had been a jailbreak. The rest of the force and the dogs were out to track the suspect down. The suspect had a ten-hour head start. He could be armed and dangerous. "In Montgomery County?" I asked in astonishment.

The lieutenant pointed to pictures on the nearby wall. He said there were 34 gangs in Montgomery County, some of them armed with military weapons. (I had learned from my research on an earlier book that police weapons were not as formidable as military weapons.) If the escapee had taken refuge with one of those gangs, they would have the police outgunned. Needless to say, the meeting was off.

I hasten to add that the lieutenant then on duty was kind enough to direct me to the cold case officer in another building some distance off. As a New Yorker and a pedestrian, I took the bus there. I was one of only four passengers. For the first time in my life, a bus driver thanked me for taking his route. (He was concerned that his route, in the middle of the day, would be cancelled.)

Cold Case files are usually housed in the bowels of police operations. An officer close to retirement often staffs the office. This was fortunate, as the officer I met was a serving officer at the time of the murder. He was then a rookie police officer.

The big surprise was when he asked me where my car was. He was astonished when I said that I had taken the bus. It seems no one noticed that there was a bus stop in front of the auxiliary station.

This is suburban logic. In a world of cars, a sleuth on foot brings most people up short. I understood. What struck me as I proceeded was the compartmentalization of local law enforcement. A crafty Foreign Service Officer could easily think his way 'out-of-the-box' of rural/suburban authority.

The enduring lesson is that someone familiar with the dark corners of the world will act accordingly. Which is to say that, for Foreign Service Officers, it is not so much about outwitting the police, it is only that the 'box' for them is so much larger.

This should have been the logic in unraveling the crime. The flight went beyond local law enforcement. It was beyond the prevue of the States of North Carolina, Maryland, and Tennessee combined. This was a Federal Case. Then an international case. Ultimately, the FBI turned out in force.

The initial assumption (that the suspect fled into the Great Smoky Mountains National Park) was sensible. Indeed, had the suspect not made mistakes, he and his family would have been considered victims of unknown assailants, their bodies missing along with Bradford Bishop's. Conspiracy theories would float the crime into myth and legend.

The suspect did make mistakes however. Some were followed up. Others were left as loose ends. Ultimately, I in my research came up with enough clues to stir interest. It was with great surprise that I received a phone call from a reporter writing for an Italian newspaper about the murder. He asked if I knew what had just happened. I did not. He said, "Your boy," (When you are researching a true crime, the fugitive suddenly becomes 'your boy.') Just made the FBI's ten most wanted list."

Of course, there was a great deal of hoopla. I gave the FBI whatever I had and offered to keep in touch. A writer's life is a lonely one. Therefore, I was glad to have a confederate in the FBI to pass along any useful research and theories I came across. Unfortunately, some of the information – so closely guarded by the police – was snatched by WIKILEAKS. In my defense, it was not I who was hacked. It was the authorities. Indeed, I urgently called the FBI to report the leak. That was when I lost my confederate.

I took the fall for the leak. Suddenly I was persona non grata. It hit me hard and I did not approach my research and writing again for another nine months.

Later I derived comfort in, and insight from, rank and file

psychologists. I learned that the term *'Family Annihilator'* is a morbid fascination among many who study the motives of such awful people. William Bradford Bishop Jr. is one of the foremost cases. I believe I can shed a little light on the phenomena. If I can, it was worth wrestling with this research and writing monster.

Only authors with two background types could write this story. It could come from either an author with a Foreign Service background and knowledge of military intelligence; or an author with military intelligence background and familiarity with the American Foreign Service. The former would heap praise on Foreign Service Officers. The latter would see them as 'Embassy Pukes,' and keep any relevant, operational details out of the story. As a neutral party with no one to please (other than the reader) and nothing to keep secret, I humbly present my findings.

Here then is the most thorough rendition of the Bradford Bishop murders available[1]. I remind myself from time to time that my job is as a historian writing narrative non-fiction. My job is to write about William Bradford Bishop Jr., not to apprehend him. I, and investigative reporters worldwide, would love to interview the elusive Mr. Bishop. If, as I suppose, I never meet or speak with him, that is just fine with me.

Finally, my best wishes go out to FBI agent Steven Vogt. He heads up the FBI's hunt for Bradford Bishop who is, at the time of this writing, on the FBI's top ten most wanted list. I recommend that he take two aspirins read this book; and call me in the morning.

David Casavis
September 2016

---

[1] The author cannot know what law enforcement is withholding. It is common in any open homicide case for the authorities to withhold information, so as to positively identify the culprit upon apprehension.

State of Maryland

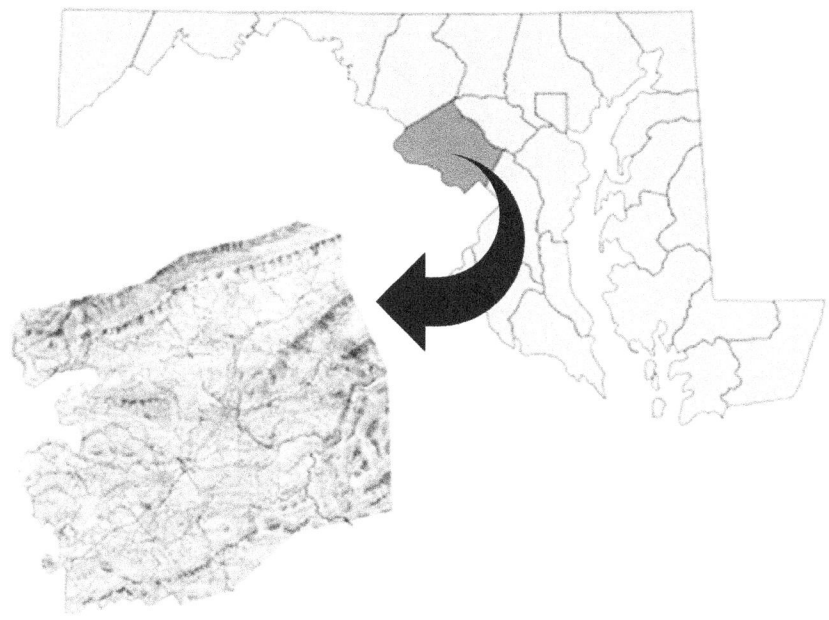

Montgomery County, Maryland

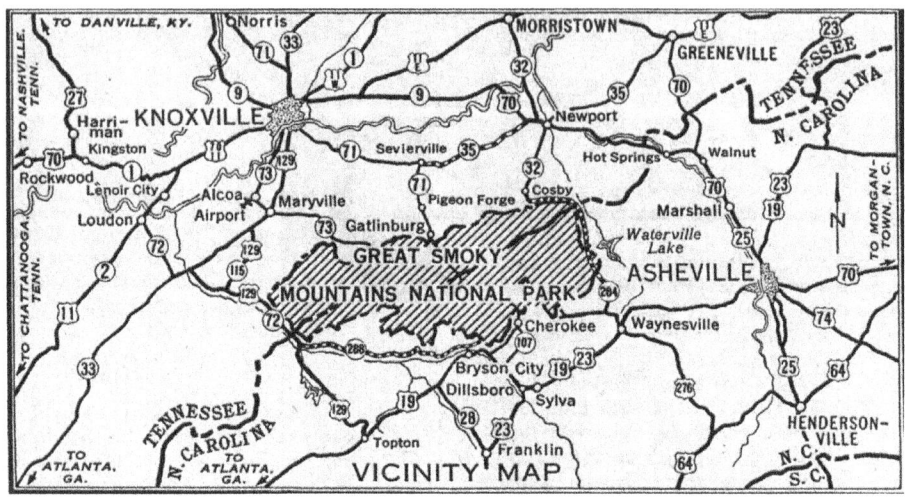

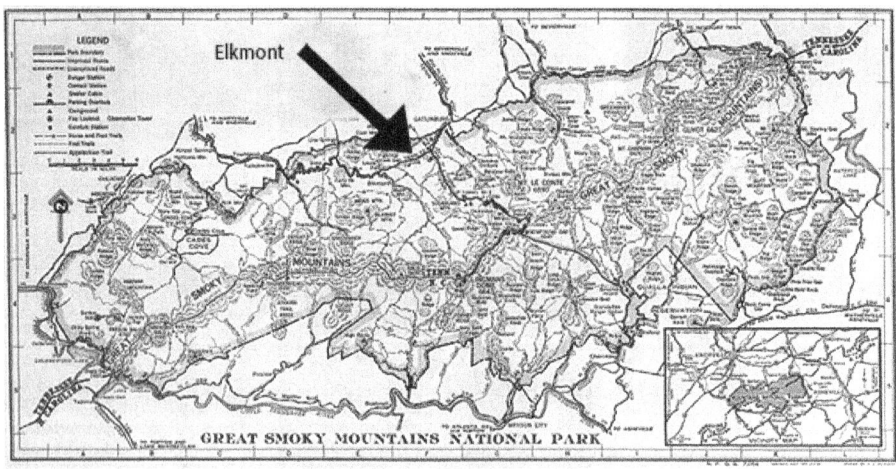

Tyrell County, North Carolina

22 | The Bradford Bishop Murders

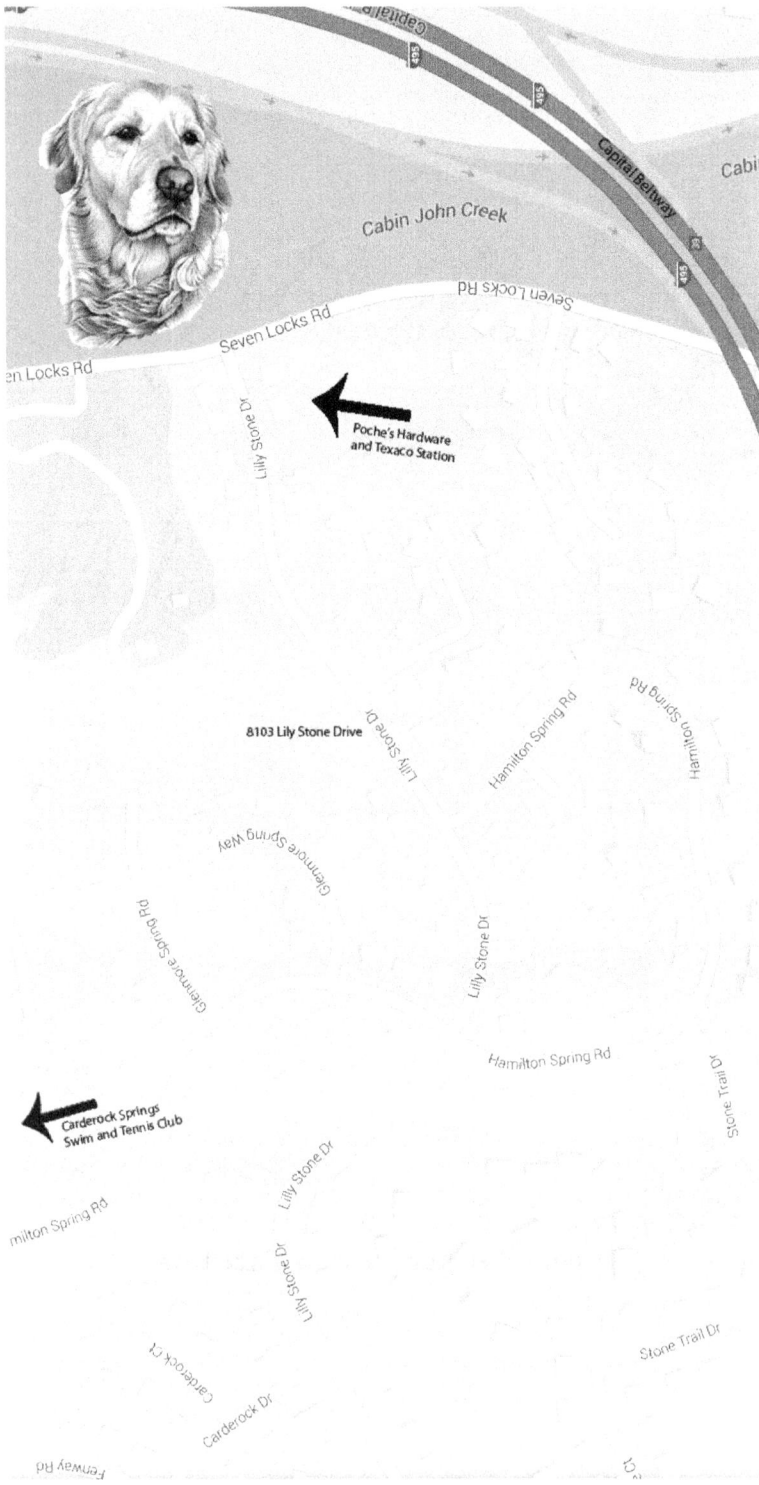

Life Beyond Shady Grove

It started with a little boy. Huge events are usually triggered by small things and small people. In this case, a small boy came to see his friend.

His friend lived at 8103 Lilly Stone Drive in Caderock Springs, a part of Bethesda, Maryland. That was the home of the Bishop family: Bradford and Annette Bishop, Bradford's mother Lobelia, and their three school-age sons. It was a contemporary frame house set back from the public road. The house was in a forested area with a shared driveway. No one approached the house unless the visitor was looking for the Bishops.

The boy walked up the shared driveway, proceeded up the steps, and rang the bell. No one answered. He waited.

The boy looked down and saw dried blood on the doorstep. He did not notice the days-old fliers in their protective plastic covers nor last autumn's windswept leaves. He hurried home to tell his mother.

The neighbor went over to the house to check on the Bishops. The side door to the kitchen was open. There was a pot on the stove. It appeared to have food in it. So, she closed the door and quietly returned to her home.

Still she was uneasy. The Bishops had been absent for about a week. They had been known to take off on caprice. Sudden excursions were not unusual for the Bishop family. They were particularly fond of ski vacations. If they were catching the end of the skiing season, they could be away for some time. Yet there was dried blood on the front doorstep, and not just a few drops. Perhaps she should call the police

When she did, Detective Cady was cruising past the neighborhood in his patrol car. The United States was in recession, yet it hardly affected the bedroom community[2] of Caderock Springs in 1976. The county he patrolled was filled with successful Federal Bureaucrats like Bradford Bishop. Life rolled on as it had before,

---

[2] Also known as a bedroom suburb or dormitory town, often distant from the place of employment

even while the rest of the United States was suffering. Caderock Springs was like the still surface of a lake without ripples.

It was a clear March day. When he got the call, it was all in a day's work. He turned his car past mailboxes and suburban driveways to Lilly Stone Drive. Someone had not seen a neighbor for a week, and a police officer was needed to check the house. It was routine.

Bishop House, 8102 Lilly Stone Drive

* * *

In 1976, Montgomery County was horse country. Montgomery County is north of Washington DC. It runs along Virginia's northern border. Light traffic turned the drive to Washington into a cruise on the open road.

In the nineteen-seventies I-270, which feeds into the capitol's beltway, was sometimes referred to as S-70. When you said that, the locals still knew what you were referring to. It was a time before COSTCO and other wholesale outlets. People shopped for bargains at the "Super Giant."

Super Giant was once part of a novel, nationwide trend: independent 'big box' stores. The old *Montgomery Sentinel*, founded in 1860, was still available. More prevalent was the Gazette newspaper chain, captained by the *Gaithersburg Gazette*. There was plenty of open space too.

There were farms. King Farm was not the operation it is today. It was huge and agricultural. Going beyond Shady Grove was a trip to the boon docks. The time and place combined to make it a quieter world for Detective Cady and others to patrol. Indeed, for a rookie officer, the main task during the Sunday shift was directing pedestrian traffic across the highway to a local church.

Life beyond Shady Grove drew urban Whites. The city of Washington is hot in the summer. Poor living conditions, discrimination, and unemployment sparked the riots of 1968 and 1971. It was not a place window-mount-air-conditioning, or a cold Miller High Life out of a Philco refrigerator, could make a lot better.

The new suburbs had been built on rocky or hilly parcels. The good, flat land had already been taken or farmed. Hilly and rocky land was heavily wooded, and cheap. Caderock Springs had been cut out of the forest.

There were large, mature trees aplenty. They made the new neighborhoods cool. Breezes billowed over the recently paved roads and onto the grounds of the newly constructed elementary schools. It was a place Annette Bishop and her mother-in-law, Lobelia, fell in love with. It was a basket of dappled light. It was a place one could have trust in.

The Bishops had lived in many remote places with few conveniences, such as Ethiopia and Botswana. They had lived in places without as much leafy green. Here was a place where the children could be safe, healthy, and venturesome. It was a place where a couple could gently settle into middle age.

The contemporary ranch-style houses let in the light while keeping the woodland character of the landscape. Families filled those new homes with Butterfly Chairs, shag rugs, and Danish Modern furniture. The new suburbanites entertained at home. They served wine chilled in their new GE refrigerators with icemakers. They mowed their lawns with John Deere two-cycle mowers, which featured an aluminum deck.

Caderock Springs was one of the nineteen-sixties many, new bedroom communities. It was serviced by a community center featuring a Texaco gas station and local businesses, like Poch's Hardware. The center, then referred to by the grander name 'Montgomery Mall,' was a pit stop on the way to I-270 and return.

The silence at day's end was broken by the occasional bark of a neighborhood dog. House lights winked off. They were replaced by a shower of whispers that lit up Caderock Springs' window frames in blue. Late night television filled living rooms.

* * *

It was into that community center that Bradford Bishop Jr., Foreign Service Officer (FSO), Yale Graduate, former deputy chief of mission, former chargés d'affaires, etc. etc. parked the family station wagon to shop. He usually worked long hours, but this day he did not.

This day he had left his office at the US Department of State in Washington early. He complained of what the office took to be the flu. Before leaving the office, he said that he 'felt weird.' Inside he burned.

He contained his fury. He stopped at Washington area's Sears Department Store where he purchased a two-and-a-half-pound sledgehammer with his credit card. As he was walking away, another thought came to him. He returned to pick up a two-and-a-half-gallon gas can.[3]

He then proceeded to Poch's Hardware, at the intersection of River and Falls Roads. There he purchased a shovel and (possibly) a pitchfork[4]. He filled up the can with gasoline at the Texaco station. He then finished his commute to his comfortable home along Lilly Stone Drive.

His wife Annette, aged 37, his three sons William aged 14, Breton aged 10, Geoffrey aged 5, had finished their day. It was late. Dinner was on the stove. (This was a time before microwave ovens.) Bradford demanded a neat environment: child toys away, living quarters spotless. It was one of the few ways he exerted control over his household.

---

[3] This second thought, was perhaps one of pure spite or of simply not knowing what it takes to cremate a body. It was the first of many mistakes that would set the police on his trail.
[4] It has been postulated that the pitchfork was old and was in Bishop's possession long before the murders. He may have brought it with him as an afterthought.

It was late for a State Department employee; perhaps 8:30 PM.[5] The children were in their pajamas. Annette was still in her jeans and denim jacket. He waited.

He concealed the short sledgehammer in his briefcase. He climbed the stairs with it. He stowed it away in his bedroom, not far from his father's 38 Revolver. He left the pitchfork and the gas can in the family's 1974 Chevrolet Station Wagon. Later he would retrieve a hatchet from the garage as well.[6]

Not all the children were in bed. Bishop's eldest son, Bradford Bishop III, was on the phone with his girlfriend. This was an age before call waiting or flash. The house phones were all connected on one line. His son's conversation was upsetting the timetable.

Brad Jr. got on another house phone and interrupted. He sternly told his 14-year old namesake to get off the phone. Brad III hastily got off the line. He scurried off to his room. It would be the last time anyone would hear from him or the rest of the family.

The agitated FSO had waited until his mother Lobelia, aged 69, took the family's dog, a golden retriever named Leo, out for his usual evening walk. It was a Monday. It was very dark. Leo usually spotted at least one rabbit or a fox crouched behind a bush or a tree along the way. The creature's eyes might light up for a moment, reflecting a full moon or a distant yard light. Leo would stop, point at the quiet and nearly invisible forager. He would then gruffly 'woof' and move-on.

Lobelia walked the dog every night. As with everything beyond Shady Grove, the walk was always the same. The night was still. The lights along Lilly Stone Drive winked off.

Bradford Bishop waited. He put on his pajamas. He waited while his mother put on her Saks Fifth Avenue coat, the one with the fur trim, over her pants suit. He waited for the door to close behind her and Leo.

Now that Brad III was off the phone, he slipped back upstairs to get the sledgehammer. With all the children now settled in their bedrooms, his wife turned to her college reading. She was reading on the shag rug in the den, while perusing an art book for school.

---

[5] Estimates range from 7:30 PM to 9:30 PM
[6] As part of burial, he might hit a rock and/or the bodies might have to be dismembered to fit the grave.

Her back was to him with one leg in the air. She was engrossed in her studies.

He crept up behind her. Taunt. He held the hammer handle in a white-knuckled grip, as all of the days of intense frustration and rage broke. He saw red.

This was the culmination of that one day all Foreign Service Officers at the US Department of State anticipate with hope and dread. It was the spark. It lit the fuse. And on this day every year at Main State, the fuse is short.

The list of promotions was out. Like many others, he saw the personally disappointing results. Unlike all others he reacted by purchasing a sledgehammer.

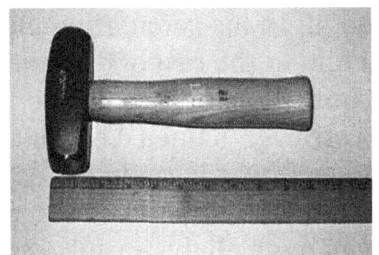 

The assumed murder weapon   W. B. Bishop Sr.'s 38

Shovel from the crime scene

The Bishops on a Ski Vacation

Part One

Main State in Washington, DC

Injustice and filth they throw after the lonely one: but, my brother, if you would be a star, you must not shine less for them because of that. And beware of the good and the just! They like to crucify those who invent their own virtue for themselves—they hate the lonely one.

Friedrich Nietzsche

The Glittering Prize

"One should enjoy success late in life in order to compensate for lost youth."
—Harold Nicholson, *The War Years*

"I quite agree. One is reminded of Daisy's husband in 'The Great Gadsby': all his life smacked of anti-climax."
—Bradford Bishop,
Diary - August 13, 1967

Impossible! William Bradford Bishop Junior was stunned. He stared at it. He stared at the two-page State Department Publication. He had anxiously anticipated it for weeks. He hustled to the office, left his things at his desk at Main State, and hurried downstairs to get it.

The State Department press was on the lower level of Main State, where Bradford worked. The two-page promotion list would be distributed throughout the building on that day. For those at diplomatic posts abroad, it was sent by cable. (So as to avoid the stress of waiting a week or more, as the list took that long to arrive by pouch.)

Foreign Service Officers' careers were at stake. The follow up, a congratulatory message from the Undersecretary of State, came as an accolade extending the glow of promotional glory. For a brief moment, the flush of victory animated the recipient. Those not on the list took their disappointment with varying degrees of assent.

Thus, for the anxious Foreign Service Officer (FSO) waiting at the publication's door that morning, the promotion list was quite literally hot off the press. It was a public announcement. His coworkers could see who was promoted and who was not. He gaped at it for a moment, but only for a moment.

Poise and coolness under fire was Bishop's calling card. They were virtually his middle name, that and protocol. Poise and protocol were at the heart of Foreign Service operations; and Bradford strove mightily to fit into them. Like all Foreign Service Officers, he tried to melt himself into the mold. Bishop knew how to deal with anything: diplomatic formality, precedence, etiquette.

Anything that is, but this.

He clawed at the still warm promotion list in his hands. This had to be a mistake. Surely, after all he had gone through, he could not have been overlooked. Yet, as incredulous as that awful moment outside of the pressroom was, his name was not on the promotion list.

This was final. He was finished. He had come to the end of the line. His rate of promotion, so stunning and promising when he started out, had petered out. The rules were plain, indeed etched in stone. An FSO could only serve so many years "in class." (The Foreign Service terms a 'rank' in the Foreign Service as a 'class.') Bishop, like every FSO, could only spend so much time "in class." On this day, he was three months short of his five-year deadline. After that, he was out. It was career death.

He was the Assistant Chief, Division of International Trade Activities and Commercial Treaties, Office of International Trade Bureau of Economic and Business Affairs.[7] He had a lengthy title intended to impress, but also a dead-end office insofar as promotions are concerned. He walked upstairs to his office dead to the world, and to the trumpeted glory of his State Department post.

Officially, it was about international conferences and economics. The State Department had yet to discover the importance of Economics in the Post War World. Protocol and Old-World honors were fading, but still vibrant for FSOs reaching for the gold ring. Bishop, whose star had shined so brightly, had suddenly flamed out. His career had, billiard ball-like, rolled and halted into this position. Though cleanly placed for a shot at a pocket on the US Department of State's English-green pool table felt cloth, he did not move. His present position was a promotional holding pattern.

There were many such posts at Main State. Washington is a place where a good officer could, after a successful tour or two abroad, ingratiate himself. Networking with a solid reputation in the field, superb education, and social credentials creates the opportunity.

---

[7] EB/OT/STA 3531A (Telephone 20641)

Bradford Bishop devoted himself to climbing State's pyramid with gusto. He reckoned that all the stars had aligned for him. In his own mind, he was a star. Now, as he climbed the interior stairway, all that was ashes. Tomorrow's late winter wind would blow the ashes away. It would be as if he never existed.

He was quiet at his desk. Fellow Foreign Service Officers knew to keep away. They could read the signs, though the promotion list had not made it to their inboxes. The promotion had not gone well for him. The system that he rose in had now dealt him a crushing blow.

For any FSO, annual rankings and promotion lists are the result of years of preparation. It could be said that as much as half of what a Foreign Service Officer does in the course of a posting leads up to this day. There are two parts to it. The first is the all-important promotion. The second is an assignment on that level to fill. This is to say that one can be promoted without a job where one can function.

It survived into the Twentieth Century with surprisingly few changes. There have been additions and extensions of course, such as the section Bradford Bishop then worked in. Yet state was modeled on the fledgling US Navy of two hundred years before.

This made sense in 1790. The US Navy delivered the diplomatic pouch. The pouch is filled with mail and sensitive documents for American embassies abroad. The drawback is that the Navy had an 'up-or-out' system of promotion. Similarly, embassies promoted and discharged their Foreign Service Officers in the same, 18th century, manner. It has been painfully obvious to many at State that what worked for the US Navy wasn't adaptable to State.

To accommodate a civilian service and bureaucracy, State developed its own discreet way of telling officers that they had outstayed their usefulness. In accordance with 'selecting' Foreign Service Officers for desirable assignments, State decided to combine charm with consistency in firing them. The officers who were cut away were 'selected out.'

That is what the promotion list was all about. As with so many, Bradford Bishop had not made the jump to the next class (rank) up. Neither gunfire, nor bombs, nor poison gas stresses a Foreign

Service Officer out more than this. His housing allowance, his job, his status in Washington and the world would evaporate if he or she were not on that list. It is no wonder Bishop's fellow employees at State, those who had survived the annual promotion list, continued processing their work around a plainly shaken Bishop, albeit at a quicker pace.

For Brad it was over. The situation can only be compared to active military service, as when a soldier who has lost both his legs is being shipped to a rehabilitation hospital stateside. The Sergeant stands to attention, -as the legless man is sent off - saying, "Good Luck in Civilian Life."

The stark difference between the Military and the State Department in 1976 was that there was no support structure for those 'selected out' at State. When he got the news 'hot off the press' Bradford Bishop Jr. wasn't just out, he was on the street. There was nothing for him; and he had a wife, three sons, a mother, and a mortgage.

His 1974 mortgage was at about 9.5 %. Thanks to his mother, Lobelia, the house was largely paid down.[8] Yet the family had only $400 in the bank. Brad did the math, though few others did.

* * *

The Bishop family did not make it any easier. The adults, Bishop's wife and mother, had been stubbornly against another overseas posting like the previous one. At that time there weren't any "unaccompanied posts." An unaccompanied post (workstation) was a posting overseas. Such a post was located in places, which were so turbulent or destitute that family life would be critically disrupted. Besides, the rest of the Bishop family liked it where they were.

This was going to be the worst part. Nothing was as soul-deadening. As he saw it, and as he got into his station wagon to make the half hour commute back to the bedroom community of Caderock Springs by Bethesda, Maryland. Nothing could be as

---

[8] An important element of the story is that his mother controlled the family purse strings. Not only did she pay for the house, her income largely supported the family.

bitter as the Promotion list had been on that day. He was finished.

Years of career service, from the joyful start to the 'sense of becoming,' was now gone. Like so many Foreign Service Officers before him, he had wanted to "be an Admiral."[9] Now he was out. He did not want to tell his family. This was especially so as he knew that his wife and mother could not be happier to hear the news.

His mother, Lobelia, never understood what TIC'd out (Time-In-Class) meant. He tried to explain that it did not matter how well he did his job, or how comprehensive his knowledge of the region of the world he worked on was. It was as if he was hired on as an aging able-bodied seaman. For Bradford, as for a seaman at middle age, it was promotion or to be permanently beached.

Lobelia simply could not understand State Department reasoning. (Let alone the US Naval background.) If her son did his job well, why would the State Department fire him?

His wife saw their wanderings around the world, courtesy of the US Government, as over. Moreover, she could add, after their last posting to a poor, newly independent African nation, good riddance. His children were just embarking on the craziness of their teenage years. Brad the third was becoming like his younger self, with Lobelia enabling him. She even drove him along his paper route when Brad III didn't feel like working.

Brad Jr. stoically walked up the sidewalk to his split-level contemporary house. By his brusque manner, his family knew that he was separated from State. In the middle of the greatest economic downturn since the Great Depression, mother and wife said nothing. He entered his suburban house like a wraith.

He mechanically sat down as dinner was placed before him. His youngest boy toddled up to his leg. He took no notice. No one spoke.

His wife and mother had anticipated the news and had made plans. Perhaps his wife would go to work for the while he stayed at home. She was already at Maryland State College and enjoying art courses there. She was so keen on it that she appeared on campus every day, including Sundays. His mother would further slip into the role of family matriarch.

---

[9] The Service to this day is still modeled on the US navy. So, an Ambassador ranks as an Admiral.

Bradford Bishop had made plans as well. He snapped out of it as he drove home. He had a long night and day ahead. The family had served their purpose. Family life at State is often used as an excuse to get things and go places. There always was - and always will be - a soft spot at State for an FSO pleading for something: a posting, housing, appliances, and schools for children. Now that he was TIC'd out, he no longer had any use for his family. His family was, as it had been with so many officers, an adjunct to his career.

As he pulled into the shared driveway to his 8103 Lilly Stone Drive, he coldly noted how the long driveway kept the house secluded. He had tried to use that seclusion to forward his career. He had tried to hire two contract killers to pose as outdoor leaders, downspouts, and gutter cleaners, for when he was away. They were hard men. They were convicts. Not four weeks before he had been certain that, they would do the job well.

He had planned it flawlessly. They were to kill his entire family. They would make it look like a robbery gone wrong. He would be away on an official State Department visit to Switzerland. When he got back someone from State would meet him at the airport and solemnly break the news.[10] Then he'd perform.

Of course, he would act distraught, stunned. In a polished scene, he'd break his impeccably cultivated veneer. He'd play the thunderstruck victim. Bishop was already an accomplished practitioner of eliciting sympathy. (Many in the Foreign Service were, and some still are.)

His plane landed at Dulles Airport on February 8th. His youngest, Geoffrey, would turn five on the 12th, Geoffrey's death prior to the planned birthday party was perfect timing. The shock of the murders, and sympathy elicited, would overwhelm the promotion board.

That was six weeks ago. Then he was stunned for real. No one from State was at the airport to meet him. He waited. Then he returned to the house.

As he motored up the drive, he knew it. He just knew it. The killers had backed out at the last minute.[11] He returned to hear that

---

[10] There was no Family Liaison Office at State at that time.
[11] One of the two, now in the witness protection program, said that it was against his code to kill children.

the maintenance men had not appeared as scheduled. All his plans, the sympathy, then the sudden shift in the evaluation process, a widower sent abroad to a faraway post to mend, came to nothing. Not for the first time did he conclude that he had to be his own pillar of strength.

Unlike his father, Bradford was demanding. The children's toys had to be out of the way, the house had to be clean and neat. Since his mother moved in with them, it was a way of asserting that he was the head of the family.

His mother and his wife strove to keep their house that way. There was a reason of course. And it wasn't the usual routine formed during his service in the army. It was far more.

Bradford Bishop wanted to be in control. He wanted to be the head of the family. Indeed, he wanted to be the head of something. When his widowed mother moved in with them, this authority was undermined. This was further complicated because his psychiatrist told him that he had a mother complex. Now that he was ejected by State, he no longer needed the family image.

When there was discord at home, he would whisk the family away somewhere. While they were in Africa, and his mother in California, he could get the family away cheap. That would keep them from complaining about or interfering with his career. He got Annette pregnant three times over the years. That preoccupied her while he was intensifying his 'mental powers.'

Now there was no longer a career for the family to boost. Now they were a burden with no upside for him. His mother was running his life, and once she moved in with them Annette sided with her. If he was now nothing, and they expected him to continue enabling them, they had another thought coming. It was time to settle old scores. His entire family would have to go.[12]

It would be best if they all died the next day. The day after would start the weekend. It would appear as if they had all left for a long weekend. He could kill them all and take them out of the

---

[12] Why did he kill his family? Why not just abandon them? The simple answer is that, if they could not get him what he wanted by dying at the hands of contract killers, then he'd finish them as an act of vengeance and distain. He killed his mother and his wife for steering him away from his deepest desires. He killed his eldest son for being as wild as he once was; and his second son for seeking attention with jokes and gags. The youngest son, Geoffrey, was murdered as part of finishing the job. Geoffrey was a loose end.

house under cover of night. First, he would have to arrange for an accomplice. He had a place in mind to ditch his station wagon. He'd fake his own death. He couldn't do it all alone. The risk factor increased that way. It was far better to get someone to assist in the escape part of his plan.

His mind was racing. He'd start with the plans he had made for the two convicts who backed out. He pondered it. He would have to start from scratch.

At first, he thought of distant sites where he could dispose of the bodies. Then he considered Phelps Lake, in North Carolina, as an isolated place to dispose of the bodies.[13] Just a few more touches to make the plan foolproof, just a few phone calls. After that, he would mail a hasty letter to the prison inmate who had procured those two weaklings who failed to do the job in the first place. Perhaps the convict could assist him. Bishop would have to bide his time until things were in place. It was five days before the murders.

* * *

Phone bills are traceable. In 1976, long distance calls appeared with the destination numbers on the monthly bill. Brad was mindful of this. He used the State Department telephones. With a root line (tie-line), the calls went all over the world. Tracing who called whom would be nigh on impossible. Another option was to call for operator assistance. He could use the service to place the vital calls he needed to without being detected.

He had always been secretive. Ever since college, he sought to be his own source of inspiration. As his mind raced at his desk, it came to him. All he had to do was pick up the plan and adapt it. There was enough fury in him to carry it out alone immediately. Yet he held his temper and his tongue that day. He had to plan the details.

He went home and ate supper sullenly. He showed no emotion when his five-year-old, Geoffrey, once again, was directed to come up to him at the dinner table. The family was appealing to him. He

---

[13] The letter recovered years later is better understood if the reader considers that it was written at the planning stage.

would not pick Geoffrey up. The meal was a wake.

Most of all he needed to find the woman he knew he could trust. She was in North Carolina, far enough away from where he planned to dispose of the bodies; but not too far from where he could ditch his car and fake his death. He would make her an offer she could not pass up. He would offer her something worth more than gold, something more valuable than platinum.

What is worth more than gold? What is worth more than precious metals? The one thing that America, in 1976, did not think of, as worth more than the fee any American would pay for it: A genuine US Passport.[14]

Therein lay the road to United States Citizenship, and to a rock-solid future on the lowest rung of the American ladder. With a legitimate US Passport, such things as an immigration raid or a police spot check at a busy intersection were mere annoyances. Without documentation, any minor infraction could erupt into catastrophe. Driver's licenses, ID cards, and all sorts of official papers would flow from there. No citizenship tests. No waiting periods. Green cards for relatives could also appear.

For emigrants from remote and troubled regions of the world a passport, a genuine US Passport was more than that. For those emigrants fleeing from starvation, epidemic, and revolution it is life itself. Bishop had access to blank passports. Like all Foreign Service Officers, he was trained in assembling them. His signature further legitimized them. More important than that, he was not searched when he left the building where they were stored.

There were mass killings just 15 months before in Ethiopia, a post that after 9 years was still dear to his heart. He needed to find someone he could trust. If that woman was out of jail and in a federal halfway house, he could offer her a new identity. He could rescue her family members from slaughter as well.

Forget the contract killers. Forget the thugs in jail. He had the world's best currency in hand. He was in the driver's seat now. He could be his 'real' self, footloose and fancy free. He would go on to a better job opportunity. It was time to cash in on favors bestowed in

---

[14] "You know a blank passport is like a blank check – its value is without limit." General Romeo Popescu, of the Romanian Secret Service, *Red Horizons*, page 103

secret. Just a few more calls, some contraband no one would report, a little prep work, and he'd be on his way. It was four days prior to the murders.

* * *

Bishop had put the new plan together quickly. As part of the process, he shot one last letter off in haste to Albert Kenneth Bankston, a prisoner at the US penitentiary at Marion, Illinois; Bishop needed to locate a reliable accomplice. He had someone in mind. When planning he considered that it was better to communicate with someone he knew who would keep a secret, than deal directly with thugs on the outside who failed him once already.

Bishop had written three letters to Bankston, setting up the hit on his family while he was away on State business. Bankston had come through with the two contract killers. Bishop was wary that any search for an accomplice might create a trail. Perhaps Bankston could locate the accomplice he had in mind.

After the shock of returning to find them all untouched, Bishop frantically called Sonny. David Paul Allen knew Sonny in Atlanta and had vouched for him. What happened? Why was the Bishop family still alive? What went wrong? Bishop, in spite of exposing himself, canvassed for the woman he trusted. She was now an important part of his plan.

Twice Bankston wrote to say that she was in the North Carolina State Penitentiary. Sonny had said so. Bankston was perplexed that his correspondent at State did not check it out. After all, it was public record. (It is likely that Bishop did.) Why else would he write Bankston again to ask if he was sure, she was in jail?

In the three letters after the failed murder attempt, Bishop's busy mind was working out the next step. He had written to Bankston about Phelps Lake. Dumping the bodies in the lake under cover of darkness presented complications. After the failed attempt to wipe out his family, he was consulting Bankston as a coconspirator, where Bankston only wanted to break out of jail.

After mailing the letter, he thought of the lay of the land, as he could recall it, not far from a CIA training site near Columbia, North Carolina. It wasn't far from the lake. 'The CIA doesn't like the local police nosing around,' he thought as he pretended to work at his desk the day before.

'Creswell,' he thought. No one there readily answers police questions. The people there are sympathetic to a fugitive from the law. They'd even been known to clothe fugitives, feed and hide them. It was a good place to blend in and wait if things got sticky. David Paul Allen had assured him of this. "How far was Creswell from the lake?" he wondered as he wrote Bankston, during the planning stages, in February.

* * *

Every Foreign Service Officer has his "go bag." It is more of a kit that one uses repeatedly when traveling. Even for many who do not travel, excursion kits with toiletries remain on a shelf unopened for years. Sometimes Foreign Service Officers open them up upon settling into a motel only to discover a long-lost bottle opener or trinket acquired on their last vacation.

Thus, it was not unusual for Bradford Bishop to prepare on a Saturday. He laid out his best suit and packed as he had for his recent trip to Europe for State. This time, however, he packed things he valued. He packed his father's thirty-eight pistol, a memento he kept after his father's affairs were settled. He tucked away his Yale Graduation Ring. Then he strategically placed a shotgun where it would not be noticed. He had plenty of ammunition too. Altogether, it would be at the ready should things get out of hand.

Bradford Bishop went to his office at Main State now that he made his plans. Few would be present to observe his preparations there. His section was nearly empty on Saturdays.[15] He accessed the blank passports.

He had the time and leisure to fill them out properly. Not only did he have access to the passport typewriter, he could well have

---

[15] Bishop worked on Saturdays. He filed an extensive report on the US International Trade Commission on Non-rubber footwear on the Saturday before. Filing a report on a Saturday was one way of proclaiming, 'I was at work over the weekend.'

taken one with him.[16] With his signature, they were even more valid. The passports alone could bring him more than the sale price of his house.[17] Indeed this day they were worth more than life. They were worth five lives.

The children went through their planned Saturday morning activities. Lobelia was up early as usual. She had set the breakfast table and prepared breakfast with Annette. As always, they were happy - often cheerful - in each other's company. This was especially so in the kitchen.

Sometimes their neighbor would stop by in the morning. The kitchen had a side door to the outside near the neighbor's house. They shared a driveway and in good weather, the neighbor would open the unlocked door to the kitchen and greet them.

Yet Bradford Jr. was not happy there. He behaved as if he were just a boarder in his own house. He was not a recluse, but he had no real friends in Caderock Springs. All his energy was focused on his career. Leo, the family golden retriever, was the only member of the household he seemed to care about.

Yet the atmosphere seemed to improve that morning. Annette drove him to the State Department that day. She ran errands with the baby as he busied himself with the passports. He carefully noted the series numbers. He made it look like the large numbers of missing passports were a simple typographic error. These he packed into his briefcase.[18]

Annette picked him up in the State Department garage. His second level supervisor, Karl Schmidt, saw them as Bishop approached and got into the car. Karl said nothing. At State, greeting the condemned man is never wise on the Saturday after the great disappointment. Wounds need time to heal.

---

[16] The Romanian Government, it is now known, claimed to have a US Passport typewriter not long after Bishop disappeared.

[17] It is also notable that the ink used to stamp passports varies. Different inks can be used on different days of the week. Visa issuing countries also shift and vary ink colors. A bottle of ink for a foreign power to analyze and reproduce is worth quite a bit as well.

[18] Although there is absolutely no proof of this, Bishop could have replaced the genuine blank passports with fake passports using the same numbers. This could have resulted in serious mischief as many retirees, perhaps going abroad for the first time, could have been detained at foreign airports when flaws in the fake passports issued by State were detected.

It was two days before the murders.

* * *

On the morning of the murders Bradford Bishop, Assistant Chief Division of International Trade Activities, etc., etc. drove to work with the next two days planned out. He rose at the usual time, dressed in his customary clothing, and ate the usual breakfast his mother had prepared for him. He left the house without any display of emotion.

He took River Road (Maryland 190) to I-495 and the beltway. He pulled into the State Department garage as usual then proceeded to his office. There he performed his usual duties, for a time. He had long ago learned to compartmentalize his life. Yet his rage was so all encompassing that he could only just keep his temper under control.

He had worked hard for this 'promotion.' It wasn't even a promotion. It was a 'stretch.' A stretch, in Foreign Service language, is an assignment above pay grade. Therefore, an O4, as Bradford Bishop was ranked, could 'bid' on a vacant 'O3' post.[19] He would get O4 pay[20] to do the O3-ranked job, but would demonstrate that he could perform at that level. This would buy him time and add another credential. This would give him another chance to get to the next level without being 'selected out.' For any FSO at that time, it would be a stay of execution.

This in itself was not notable. What was notable being that Bradford Bishop had three months left before State terminated him. This added bewilderment to his rage. He had touched all the bases, while working under great personal strain. This post was part of the scuppered plan of four weeks before, to be sent somewhere faraway with sympathy after his family were found in their house, dead.

With this posting he could, as he had in his African posting years before, prove that he could take on the responsibilities expected of an O3. Perhaps then, after performing for two years at

---

[19] Foreign Service Officer classes run O-5, O-4, O-3, etc.
[20] He was an FO-4, step 5 being paid an annual rate of $25,952

an O3 level, he could get a promotion and then plan the next four years to the next move, O2.

Foreign Service Officers inhabit a shame and honor culture. Most Americans live in a guilt culture. That is to say, people who make mistakes in a guilt culture feel guilty. People who make mistakes in a shame culture are, themselves, the mistake.

Bishop, now at the bottom end of the shame culture, looked around at those who received the glittering prizes. He felt he had earned his prize. Snatched away by people who were inferior, or as he put it, *people with less brains*. He would growl, just audibly and under his breath, about *putting people in their place*.

Now he was the odd man out, surrounded by his section of 'winners' and survivors. He sat uncomfortably at his desk. To perform his usual duties as if nothing had happened was humiliating. To his self-satisfied co-workers he was now a corpse.

After shock, the stunning realization set in. He, who strived for the goal so often, who had so often stood on the threshold of success, was once again tossed from near the pinnacle before he could grasp it. It was beyond unfair. He had been cheated out of his life.

What transpired next was perplexing for the army of complacent federal employees of March 1976. The situation was common knowledge elsewhere. Detroit's auto industry was experiencing layoffs. (Alternatively, as the British use the term, redundancies.)

Nearly 213,000 were out on indefinite layoff for the last week of March 1975, due to the Recession. New York City nearly went bankrupt, and layoffs on the city level ensued. Yet none of them became homicidal. It was later that industrial psychologists and industry analysts began to approach the problem.

The Post Office, the United States Postal Service, prompted the question. Why did workers in comparable industries, such as autoworkers, not pick up firearms and start to kill where Postal workers did? After lengthy study, the consensus focused on ownership.

Postal workers of that time had a lifetime employment guarantee in their contracts. Autoworkers did not. Autoworkers were disgruntled at losing their jobs, but they did not feel that they owned them. Postal workers did. This sense of taking something away that was theirs was at the bottom of the extreme violence.

Bradford Bishop felt that he had earned his promotion. He had done everything any review board would require to move up to the next level. He had endured Foreign Service Officer Egos and dealt with dysfunctional people who never should have been in the Service in the first place. He had dealt with pesky congressional representatives and ambassadors, who were out of their depth. He had criticized himself in private more than anyone would in public. Now this. Something that was his due was taken away from him.

He burned. He dwelled on it. Foreign Service Officers have busied enough minds as it is; when they start dwelling on their bitterness there is no telling what will happen.

By Monday he had, it all worked out. He had disciplined himself for years: in protocol, in statecraft, in timing, in discreet behavior. He had done it *their* way. Now he was going to do it *his* way. He used all that discipline tempered with rage. Now he would turn it on them. On or around 5:30 PM on March 1, he exploded.[21]

As he told the Foreign Service Officers in his section off, they let him vent. It was disturbing only because this could have happened to any one of them. The Foreign Service is a tightrope to be walked with care. Explosions such as this were only possible at the end of a career.

Enduring the bile and frustration of so many disparate (and disappointed) personalities for years is part of a Foreign Service career. Longevity in the Department is about tiptoeing around mediocrity and working with failure. Endurance is *the* essential quality in a Foreign Service career. Bradford, like so many of his colleagues, wanted to shine despite the system. No one should have been surprised when he lashed out. Indeed, on that day, no one was.

Thus, when Bradford had unleashed his rage with name-calling and invective, it was with patient relief that his section heard him suddenly stop. He said he was feeling 'weird,' and that it could be

---

[21] The eruption was so ugly that none of his coworkers could bring themselves to recount it in detail. Suffice it to say, Bishop signaled out each of his co-workers for flaws and disgusting behavior, either real or imagined.

the onset of the flu. He said he'd probably return on Thursday.

In the seventies, a case of flu was a common excuse for a day or two off. His section was happy to let him shove off with a boiler engine full of steam. Perhaps he would return in a couple of weeks with the news that an old college friend got him a job at a bank, or that he planned to open a restaurant. It isn't unusual for those FSOs whose culinary experiences abroad combine with necessity.

He left winded. Yet the sting of 'career disappointment' further prodded his desire to 'put all of them in their places.' No one dreamed that Bradford was using the system once again. He knew his section would give him plenty of time to cool-off. Others would carry the workload. It was Monday and saying he might be back on Thursday would give him the time he needed. The State Department is habitually lax. He estimated that they would not expect him back at his desk for at least a week.

Only the UDBA Kills Like That

> "Remorse. Never yield to remorse, but at once tell yourself: remorse would simply mean adding to the first act of stupidity a second."
>
> — Friedrich Nietzsche

Annette was taken by surprise. She never had a chance. Her skull was crushed. Bradford covered her up with one of his jackets.[22] The timing, however, did not come off as planned. His 14-year-old, William Bradford III, caused the delay by making a phone call to a girlfriend.

Then his mother returned with the dog too soon. She sensed or saw that something was wrong. She rushed to the family room with her coat still on. Annette was on the floor, under the jacket, in a growing pool of blood.[23]

Lobelia instinctively ran upstairs after looking up and seeing her son splattered in blood, wet hammer on the floor. It is likely that what ran through her mind at the time was protecting her grandchildren. They were in bunk beds upstairs. She headed for their room.

She got up the stairs with her enraged son close behind. She ducked into the bathroom and locked the door. Bradford smashed at the hollow core door. Lobelia was no match for her 6-foot 1 inch, 180-pound son. Trained in hand-to-hand combat, he quickly tore a hole into the door. He got his hand through the door and onto the interior lock. She may have screamed, but any call of parental authority would only have fueled her son's rage. The coroner would later state that the hammer blow to her head was not enough to kill her. He concluded that she died of fright.

The sound of the bathroom door smashing apart alerted the 14-year-old. He got out of bed and confronted his father. With renewed rage at the boy who had ruffled his perfect plan, the elder Bishop attacked his namesake.

Though smaller and weaker, it has been purported that

---

[22] The blood evidence points to his putting her on the bed afterward.
[23] The sequence of events is based on what evidence that was released at the time of this writing.

William Bradford Bishop III put up a fight. If he did, it wasn't much of one. This time parental authority was working for the attacker. Further enraged, the sledgehammer smashed into the boy's skull so violently that Detective Cady and others would later find a piece of the boy's skull on the floor.[24]

Bradford Bishop then proceeded to his two youngest sons' bedroom. They were still asleep. He dispatched his sons so violently that baby Geoffrey's face was unrecognizable.[25]

Afterward Bradford Bishop wrapped the bodies up and put them in the Station Wagon. He wrapped the boys' heads in towels to staunch the massive bleeding. He carried them on the grisly trip to the car and back, followed by Leo. Leo was a good survivor. He'd never talk and, if need be, could be dispatched of with the .38 later.

Bishop then went upstairs to his bedroom. There he left his bloody pajama top on the top drawer of the dresser. With spontaneity and exhilaration, he balled up his pajama bottoms and tossed them onto the closet shelf. He washed off the blood. He pulled out a pack of matches and pocketed them.[26] He took his favorite suit. Then he took his go-bag, into which he put his diplomatic passport. His father's Smith and Wesson M&P 38 revolver was loaded and concealed. Where he was going, it would be a warning to those he would deal with not to cross him. The shotgun was something he hoped he would not have to use.

A blast of the shotgun would slow his pursuers down. He didn't have to hit anyone; he just had to make the point. He packed extra ammunition just in case he had to make a stand. He wasn't going to be taken quietly.

The Station Wagon with Leo in the front seat pulled out of 8103 Lilly Stone Drive. It passed Poch's Hardware and the stores of the community center. The Texaco station closed at 10:00 PM. All

---

[24] There was so much blood that pieces of bone were found in the shower, where Bishop washed after the murders.
[25] The blows were delivered with such fury and intensity that there were hammer marks on the ceiling above the upper bunk.
[26] He had written a phone number on the matchbox he left behind at his desk. It was a CIA phone number at Langley. The author proposes that Bishop called on a State Department telephone to confirm that the burial site he had chosen near the CIA facility was still in place; and that it was still a mile or less from the CIA fence.

of the stores in Montgomery Mall were closed. It was 1976, and 24-hour shopping had not yet caught on. The night before was the second night of a new moon. He had the dark of the night working for him.

Putting Leo in the front seat was a good idea. It is likely that Brad Bishop knew that he was jammed for time. If he planned to take the back roads, he would not make it to his destination before sunrise. To make up the time he would have to pass through the tollbooths on I-95.

There were tollbooth operators in those days. Stopping to hand over a coin might draw attention to the load of bodies he had in the back seat. Leo would deflect attention away from that. Any curious tollbooth operator in the middle of the night shift would appreciate a Golden Retriever balanced on a front seat; and only glimpse at the blanket covering the load of bodies in the back seat.

The police would later plot a likely course down I-95 over to Suffolk, Virginia and down Route 32. From there Bradford's flight could merge onto Highway 64 East. That would avoid all but one tollbooth. Of course, that would be a longer, time-consuming route.

As the miles passed on that moonless night, Bishop was still anxious. Step 1 was completed, yet there was a lot more to do. He considered the plan he had devised.[27] It was perfect until the two hirelings backed out.

Americans! They backed out because they were reluctant to kill children. What did those two convicts know about the world? A hammer to the head was nothing where he once worked. Hundreds of thousands were killed that way.

The goal now was to dispose of and destroy the bodies, so that he would be counted among the missing and presumed dead. Perhaps the postcard his second son, Brenton, allegedly sent him while on temporary duty, would work for the bloody

---

[27] This would have been costly. The FSO could have offered the two hirelings new identities. In 1976 the cost of two contract killers might have been two-thirds of an FSO's yearly pay. The State Department's insurance payout might have covered the cost, but that would have taken time. The available evidence suggests that at least one of the two contract killers and Bankston, the presumed intermediary who referred the service, intended to get out of the United States. The author proposes that payment would have included new passports and new identities to get them to Mexico, as well as some cash and jewelry. (Telling the killers where to obtain Annette's jewelry would be part of the payment and bolster the robbery-gone-wrong narrative.)

disappearance scenario. Originally, it was intended as part of his first attempt at family annihilation.

Indeed, after the murders a fellow employee at State went on the record saying, "He was a great family man... My kids love me too. But State Department kids don't send postcards every time their father takes a trip. He had some special relationship."

In view of the rocky relationship he had with his family, there are two possibilities. Either his second son, Brenton, sent the postcard at the behest of Annette and Lobelia (Who might have been trying to keep peace in the family) or it was Bishop, feigning his child's script, who mailed the card to himself before departure. Either way it played into his prior plan.

Originally, the plan was for the postcard to be a reminder whenever the State Department got onerous. Careworn after years in his jacket pocket, he could pull it out whenever he needed that extra edge. The plan was that, after flashing it around in Geneva on temporary duty, it would elicit sympathy for him after the massacre. He'd return a week prior to his youngest son's birthday, only to find that his entire family were snuffed out in a burglary gone wrong.

The timing was perfect. He delighted in the detail and congratulated himself on his cleverness. State would grant his bid request. Sending a widower to a faraway post to heal and granting him a promotion on the next round of bidding was what he anticipated. He could unobtrusively milk the family annihilation by asides to coworkers. He would say that it would have been Geoffrey's fifth birthday. After a dramatic pause, he could add that had he been there he would have heroically defended them.

It all played into Foreign Service myths. A brave and unshakable officer recovering while selflessly serving abroad, his story would be murmured throughout the corridors of State. He'd be the one who survived. He would enter into Foreign Service legend.

He anticipated that State would send a delegation to meet him at Dulles airport. They would have to break the news, then usher him to a hotel room nearby. He'd put on a show of course. He'd practiced how he'd react. Then, when he landed, nothing.

No one was there! Further, when he went home his family was

still alive. He'd have to attend the birthday party. The postcard went into the trash.

He formulated a new plan quickly. This time the storyline would be that unknown thugs wiped the Bishops out. He would be the man who was killed along with his family. Perhaps his fellow officers would eulogize him as the FSO who was courageously struck down while defending his family.

It was all going, more or less, as planned thus far, he told himself. Yet his anger flared up as he looked in the rear-view mirror and saw the blanket covering his dead and bleeding family. Enraged once again, he tore the mirror out of its socket and tossed it on the car's floor mat.

His father's pistol and the nearby shotgun were comforting. If his flight really got bad, he could ditch the car and make for Creswell. Any local who would hide him in the backcountry could keep the shotgun, and the car. That was if everything went wrong. Still the night and the miles passed on, to the silent rhythm of highway lights, and the occasional red taillights of wandering lost souls.[28]

It was still dark when the 1974 Station Wagon pulled into the remote, sandy area Bishop had chosen as the burial site. The site featured bush and pine plantings and was about 40 feet off a logging road. There he could dig quickly and put the family into the shallow grave.

He dug a three-foot-deep-pit. The FSO then put Breton in first. Then he put Annette in. Then he put William Bradford III on top of Annette, and then five-year-old Geoffrey and Lobelia, still wearing her fur-collared Sachs coat, on top.

Leo laid by the car, patiently waiting with a few dog biscuits, while his master did this. Bishop lit a cigarette and tossed it. Then he emptied the contents of the gasoline can onto the bodies. He lit up another match from the box he had pocketed earlier that night. It was then that things started to go wrong.

---

[28] The chosen burial site was not far from the Harvey Point Defense Testing Activity facility, owned by the Department of Defense. Harvey Point is located on a peninsula in Perquimans County, North Carolina along the Albemarle Sound. At the time, the area was a 'haven for Federal Government covert activities.' (North Carolina Attorney General - Rufus Edmisten)

The gas can at the burial site in Tyrell County, North Carolina

A sudden burst of flame caught the 5-gallon can. That would not have mattered if it had not singed Bishop's hand. It also caught some of the dead leaves that littered North Carolina's late-winter ground.[29] It was, quite literally, wildfire.

Bishop may have waited longer. If his plan was to burn the bodies enough so that wild animals might not root them up out of the shallow grave, it was sound. That, however, required time. Weary as he was at that point, he had to see that he was running out of time. Daylight was breaking. Sunrise would be at 6:35 AM.

By the time he pulled out of the sandy area, there was enough light to identify the car. A passerby spotted a Rust Colored Station Wagon pulling out of the dirt road, and onto the paved country road. It was about six thirty, and the piney wood forest was burning.[30]

---

[29] It is also likely that torching his family was his final act of disdain.
[30] Three Tyrrell County residents saw a similar car near the gravesite hours before the fire alert. The above refers to the sighting, at or around 6:30 AM, of a similar car driving away from the site. As there was daylight and a fire the sighting can be considered credible, and a data point on the timeline. (There was another report of a car matching the Bishop family's car's description by the fire site at 10:00 AM, which appears less likely and yet does not affect the timeline.)

Wilma Swain spotted a wisp of smoke while scanning the Forest. The US Department of the Interior, Fish and Wildlife Service keeps a watch for brush fires. This wisp was some miles away, and so she got on the radio and called Ranger Ronald Brickhouse to check out the fire. Ranger Brickhouse was driving in the area. A good ranger will investigate any fire to see if he can stop it before it gets out of hand. He pulled into the site at or around 12:40 PM.

When he arrived on the scene, about three acres were ablaze. A wildfire of that size is manageable. Last year's dead wood and leaves were burning. He diligently went to work.

He put out most of the fire when he noticed a little pile of dirt. It was a casual glance. Had there been no pile of dirt and no fire, the mass grave could have gone unnoticed for some time. With the advent of new plantings, it may have gone unnoticed for years.[31]

Ranger Brickhouse's first thought was that the fire started with a hog burning. There were plenty of hog farmers in the area. When a diseased hog dies, it is legally not fit for sale. Usually a hog farmer writes the sow off, digs a shallow pit, and sets it on fire. A pit of that size could accommodate an eight-hundred-pound hog or a few smaller hogs together.

When Ranger Brickhouse got closer, he stopped short. A gas container was smoldering. Then his stomach turned. This was no hog. This was human. Worse. It was not one person. It was people.

This was at a time prior to the introduction of cellular phones. Fish and Wildlife rangers had communication devises in their cars. So, Ranger Brickhouse radioed Wilma Swain.

The police too were sickened. Exhuming the bodies was grisly work. Ranger Brickhouse, a rank and file employee, more familiar with animal decay than human decay, grew even sicker.[32]

As the police recovered the gas can, the shovel, and the pitchfork, the police caged for clues. Had Bishop not left in such haste, had he not scorched his hand, he might have taken the implements of concealment with him.

He could have tossed them in a lake. He could have abandoned

---

[31] The choice of the sandy ground off an old logging trail near a CIA training site was as well conceived, as the use of gasoline was disastrous for Bishop. No one is supposed to come within a mile of a CIA installation's fence.
[32] Bishop did not have to use the hatchet. All five bodies fit into the trench.

them somewhere along the way. In farm country or in the depths of a forest, some woodsman or poor farmer happy to acquire another tool could have picked them up. This error was compounded when, upon examination weeks later, the authorities found one of his fingerprints on the gas can.

As it was, the bodies were initially unidentified. There were no reports of five missing persons either. The corpses could only be listed as three children and two women. It would take eight days before anyone was able to identify them. In the meanwhile, Bradford Bishop was on his way to the next phase of his plan. He had to meet his accomplice.

* * *

Plans go wrong. This is particularly true of plans modified and executed in haste. The lack of sleep and physical exertion it took to dig a bathtub-sized pit and lower five bodies into it had to take a toll. It was below 50 degrees Fahrenheit (10 degrees Celsius) yet Bishop had to have worked up a sweat.

On he drove, south to the Jacksonville area of North Carolina. This rural location is known for the nearby Marine training facility, Camp Lejeune. As Bishop needed an accomplice, and the drive from Tyrell County takes about two and a half hours. It is likely that the accomplice met him somewhere in the Jacksonville area.

This was in an age of public telephone booths, so Bishop must have made contact via a landline telephone. He could have stopped along the way, or upon arrival, and used a pay phone to make sure the accomplice was there to meet him. It is also likely that he made the call from a gas station to replenish the Chevy Malibu Station Wagon's tank.[33] It is reasonable to assume that Bishop arrived in Jacksonville before noon on March 2, before Ranger Brickhouse arrived at the scene of the burial.

The next point on the timeline was when Bishop stopped into the Outside Sports Store between Five and Seven PM. There he

---

[33] The 1974 Chevrolet Malibu Station wagon averaged between 7 to 15 miles per gallon. The estimated cost of gas to make the journey would be about $300 or more. He could have been running low on cash at this point.

made another mistake. He used his Bank Americard to purchase $15.60 of Sporting Goods.[34] The Cashier recalled that the item was a pair of tennis shoes. (With the spare tire well in the trunk filled with blood, it has been speculated that, a change of shoes might have been what he had in mind.)[35]

One notable part of the description of the purchaser was that he was wearing a suit. He was shaved and noticeably neat. This was the late afternoon/early evening of the day he dug the grave and buried his family. He had not slept that night. So, he must have had a place to wash up and, possibly, take a nap. Staying at a motel and reporting his Maryland license plates at the front desk would not have been a good idea.[36]

It was also recalled that a "Caribbean-looking" woman of about his age who had a dog, matching Leo's description, on a leash, accompanied Bishop.[37] Later the description used for the woman was 'dark-skinned.'

Both are significant in that Caribbean-looking veers away from what is now termed "African-American" or 'Black,' as the America of 1976 used the term. Dark-skinned is also significant. In the polite Southern world of the early 1970's, 'Dark-Skinned' was a polite term white people often used for African-born immigrants. (This was not common in Northern cities.)

Bankston's letter, recovered later, answered what was likely Bishop's most urgent question prior to killing his family, where was the accomplice he could rely on? Bankston's reply in his final letter to Bishop at State was… "Now in answer to your question… Yes, I am most sure she is in the North Carolina State penitentiary."

---

[34] The question of why use a credit card for a minor purchase? The author posits that it was habit. The plan was, more or less, working and Bishop was, at that moment, nearly carefree. The author believes that the sale of classified documents was finalized prior to his purchase at Outdoor Sports, at or around 7:00 PM. He had consummated the deal and pocketed the cash he needed for his escape to Europe.

[35] The author postulates that the alleged perpetrator was planning to get any leftover aggression out by playing tennis later. Borrowing a tennis racquet is not unusual. Borrowing a pair of tennis shoes is.

[36] Camp Lejeune is one of North Carolina's military bases. The Nuclear, Biological, and Chemical Defense School, known as the NBC School, teaches Marines on how to survive nuclear, biological, and chemical attacks. The nearby microelectronics industry and two ports were targets of interest for foreign spies as well. Agents from Communist Countries worked the area at that time seeking classified information. Pair this with the obvious question: why was Bishop wearing a good suit in Jacksonville *before* dumping the station wagon in the Great Smoky Mountain National Park? (*And* why was he clean-shaven?)

[37] Leo was on a leash and waiting for Bishop outside the store. This indicates that Leo was either in a car or indoors for some time prior to this.

Years later, when the Bankston letter was recovered, the authorities checked the North Carolina State penitentiary system. Nothing turned up. That does not mean that the information Bankston picked up through one of the contract killers, or while in prison in Marion, was false.

The Federal system picks up illegal immigrants, people without documentation. The authorities sometimes release them into halfway houses. Some of those are in the Jacksonville area. Once released, the detainee or felon is no longer traceable within the Federal system.

Bishop could not have written and posted his final letter to Bankston until Thursday, February 26th at the earliest.[38] It could not have been delivered to Bankston in the Federal Penitentiary before the day of the Murders, March 1st. If Bishop could not try to enlist the help of those who failed to kill his family in January, he must have found the accomplice on his own. He had to find her after February 26th and prior to March 1st.

Putting this scenario against the background of State's promotion list, Bishop probably turned to Bankston, while in a bereft state of mind, for answers.[39] It had to be early in the planning of his second attempt at family annihilation. Bankston answered his question writing "I don't see what that has to do with me Mr. Bishop. I was only interested in Mexico and/or Central America as you know."

Bishop was grasping at straws at that time. Of course, he had to have someone who would not talk. Insofar as anyone knows, Bishop only had $400 or so in cash on him when he fled. This brings us back to the basic question, what is the most valuable thing on Earth? What thing has more value than gold, more value than platinum? The answer is a valid US passport.

For refugees around the world, a valid US passport is more than freedom to travel. It is more than US citizenship and a better life. For some it is life itself. Family members and loved ones could

---

[38] 1976 was a leap year
[39] He had written at least one letter to Bankston after the first plan failed. He probably wrote two letters to Bankston in Marion prison before his last communication seeking a specific woman to be his accomplice.

be reprieved from a wretched end under a murderous regime. Under these conditions, Bishop could threaten all of them with disclosure if caught. Deported, or left to rot under a violent dictatorship, they would be banned from the United States forever. Anyone granted this bonanza would rather die under torture than cross Bishop.

It is likely that Bishop took some rest, perhaps for a day or two. There are tennis courts in the area. Later, he took off under the cover of darkness from the Jacksonville area. It is also likely that his accomplice followed him to the Great Smoky Mountains National Park some few hours after. It is a five and a half to six-hour drive to the Elkmont entrance of the Great Smoky National Park.[40]

It is also likely that Leo was taken for a walk before the drive, so as not to slow the escape plan down. Sunset was at 6:04 PM that day and 6:05 PM the next. The deserted Great Smoky Mountain National Park is black as pitch at night. There are no house lights. Bishop had to time his arrival at the Elkmont camping area entrance with enough light to set up the false trail he planned on planting.

The Great Smoky Mountains Park is the busiest national park in the United States. With the first flush of spring near, campers and hikers were about to arrive. The unseasonably warm weather had brought a few hardy hikers out already. Elkmont is the only public entrance to the Great Smoky Mountains National Park open to the public year-round. Its ample parking lot is largely deserted during the winter months. It is an easy place to drive into.

Some vagabonds roam the vast park. The comings and goings of any one person is not noticeable. It would be unusual if someone living off the land did *not* show up somewhere at any given month. Vehicles parked for up to 14 days were common. Two cars entering Elkmont together during the winter off-season, however, might

---

[40] For the purposes of this book, the author assumes Bishop drove from Jacksonville to the Elkmont park entrance shortly after his purchase at Outside Sports. Although logically, he wouldn't purchase tennis shoes until after the bloody car was dumped. It is possible that he may have wanted to get a game of tennis in before his departure.

attract attention.

Accordingly, Bradford Bishop first pulled into the deserted Elkmont campground, probably as dawn broke at 6:34 AM. (Car lights in the impenetrable ink-like ebony of the vast forest night attract attention.) He parked in front of the boarded-up summer cabin of F.B. Kuhlman, a Knoxville beer distributer. There was space in the nearby lot for a dozen cars. It was established as a parking area for those intent on penetrating the deep forest.

A barely discernable path, Jake's Creek Trail, starts by the Kuhlman cabin. It runs off Tennessee highway 73, which runs from Gatlinburg to Maryland. Further, Elkmont was an old lumbering town. There was a network of trails from that point on, running in all directions.

Brad got out of the car and laid the false trail for about a mile up the main track. He walked along the trail by dense Pine and Hemlock trees, with their thick underbrush of Laurel and Rhododendron. Then he returned. He sat on the porch of the nearby summer home. Insomniac though he was, he must have been even wearier than he had been the night before. It may have been that he had not slept for more than a few hours for over the past two days. Perhaps he was running on adrenalin.[41]

It is also likely that he took Leo with him as he fled the Park. Dogs are loyal to their masters. Were Bishop to unleash Leo and set him free in the Park, the dog might hang about the parked Station Wagon, attracting undue attention. "His sports jacket was draped over the back of the front seat of the passenger side. There was a suitcase on the seat and his shaving kit on top of that. Then there was a heavy car coat folded on top of that. A box of dog biscuits, standing upright, was on the front floorboard on the passenger side.[42]"

His accomplice parked her car by the central "You are Here" sign and waited. He saw her from where he sat on the Kuhlman

---

[41] The author posits that, without the steep hierarchy of the State Department to deal with, Bishop no longer needed serax and ultimately got the deep and reposing sleep he craved. This would explain the serax pills he left in the Station Wagon. For the purposes of this narrative, the author assumes that at this point the murderer had a good night's sleep without medication.
[42] Harold Swanson, Special Agent FBI, UPI Vines

cabin porch. He walked up to the sign. He got into his accomplice's vehicle and was whisked away.

This would be the last anyone could be certain of what became of him. He wasn't the only one the public (and law enforcement) would wonder about. Leo, his golden retriever, disappeared as well, and dog-lovers throughout the region wanted to know what became of him.

The last bit of evidence of what became of Leo was found in the Bishop's 1974 Station wagon. Dog biscuit crumbs were found on the car carpet at the front passenger's seat. Days later there was a report from some hikers. They had seen a dog matching Leo's description wandering loose in the forest. Law enforcement assumed that a local family found Leo, fed him, and kept him.

The Chevy Malibu was passed over by the few full-time residents of the Park, and at least one ranger on his rounds. All took a cursory look, and then went on their way.[43] There were four or five other cars parked nearby, so one more was not eventful. One of the full-time residents, who passed by later, said that he saw the parked car, but let it slip his mind. Later he called the rangers. The Park ranger who was called noticed the car parked either on March 5th or 6th. By the 10th he alerted the police.

On closer inspection, the Ranger spotted blood. He reported the bloody blanket. The hatchet and the shotgun lay in the car unused.[44] The ranger reported the Maryland license plate: DGL-896. The plate number turned up. It was the Bishop's car. By the 12th of March the police had a warrant out on Bishop. The search up until then had concentrated on Eastern North Carolina.[45]

The authority's first reaction was that Bishop had enough time to hike out of the Park. If he had a hiking plan, and knew his way about, he had a solid head start. He could have picked up a ride, and/or gotten on a bus, and headed for Chicago or points north. In 1976 it was easy to slip across the Canadian border.[46] Leaving his

---

[43] As with the toll collectors on the night of the murders, the front seat looked fine. It was the back seat where the blood was.
[44] The presumed murder weapon, the short sledge hammer, was never found.
[45] Bench Warrant 17511
[46] Plenty of men from Appalachia went to Chicago to find work. A man with several days' growth on his face would go unnoticed among the migrants on a bus north. A plane out of a Canadian airport could be inexpensively booked or taken on standby to Shannon airport in Ireland. From there he could be back on

shaving kit behind may have been an oversight, or it may have been part of a plan to grow a beard. Just as Bishop planned, they started to search on the Tennessee side of the Park in pursuit.

What Bishop could not know was that the bodies of his family were already exhumed. He had not considered that more than ashes remained. A gust of wind, and the hasty and unprofessional use of gasoline, pointed to an amateur as the culprit. Bishop's plan was originally to fake the disappearance of his entire family (including himself). They would be lost among the legendary missing of the Great Smoky Mountains National Park.[47]

As it was, the missing keys to the murder lay much deeper than that. The Montgomery County Police did what they do best. The North Carolina State troopers did what they do best. The FBI did what it does best. Each knew how to investigate and police its own jurisdiction, which each did.

What they did not know was what came instinctively to the CIA and the NSA. Their span of knowledge and experience covered black operations, dirty tricks, and torture. Annette's brother, deeply disturbed by these events, called the investigation at 8103 Lilly Stone Drive 'a circus.' Different groups with no reference to each other were trampling over the evidence. It was as if "the Chinese Army" was conducting the investigation, he added. This was true.

Each entity with an interest went to 8103 Lilly Stone Drive, and each was not talking with the other. But what was plain to the CIA was beyond the others. It was beyond their collective police experience, and very likely even beyond their comprehension. It is likely, if the blood and human carnage did not shock the CIA investigators into silence, that they walked away muttering, "Only the UDBA kills like that."

---

the road again.
[47] Free maps of the Park, available at the welcome center, were found in his car.

Balkan Revenge

Sunday morning in Carcaixent was quiet. Carcaixent is always quiet on Sunday mornings. Carcaixent is a town and municipality in the province of Valencia, Eastern Spain. The town has about 20,000 inhabitants. It was on just such a Sunday, the 20th of April, 1969, when Vjekoslav Luburić settled into his favorite chair. His son went out on an errand prior to church services. His trusted assistant made coffee for him, as usual. The two were alone.

Vjekoslav Luburić was known locally as 'the Polish General.' Although he scoffed at the locals who called him that, it was a useful cover story. Poland was a nation of Roman Catholics under Communist rule in 1969. General Francisco Franco, victor of the Spanish Civil War, ruled Spain at that time. Franco was an anti-communist and granted refuge to those who opposed communism in Eastern Europe. He was particularly fond of "Maks" and the Blue Division (División Española de Voluntarios.)[48]

"Maks" was Luburić's nickname. And Maks Luburić was indeed a General; but not a Pole. He was a Yugoslav national and a Croat. After a boyhood of petty crime, he left for Hungary. He returned to Yugoslavia when the new state of Croatia was established. The new state was set up by the Nazi's in 1941 after the German Wehrmacht crushed the Yugoslav forces in six weeks. The new state's leader was Ante Pavelić. Pavelić was the leader of a group the West knew little about, the Ustaše.

The Ustaše were close allies with Hitler's National Socialists and Workers Party. Maks, upon the ascent to power, served them loyally. Indeed, he became the youngest general in the Ustaše regime. He didn't fight on the Eastern Front as did the Blue

---

[48] Although Spanish dictator Francisco Franco did not bring Spain into World War II on the side of Nazi Germany, he permitted volunteers to join the German Army (Wehrmacht) on the clear and guaranteed condition that they would fight against Bolshevism (Soviet Communism) on the Eastern Front, and not against the Western Allies or any Western European occupied populations. Initially, the Spanish government was prepared to send about 4,000 men, but soon realized that there were more than enough volunteers to fill an entire division: 18,104 men in all, with 2,612 officers and 15,492 soldiers.

Division. He commanded concentration camps.[49]

The Pavelić regime, the *Nezavisna Država Hrvatska* or NDH, has been called the most murderous regime in Europe. Even Heinrich Himmler's (Then Head of Hitler's SS) adjutant was appalled at the brutal methods used to execute the Untermensch.[50] This is what the 'Polish General' did throughout the War.

At the close of the War Ante Pavelić fled to the American Occupied Zone of Austria. He handed command of the Ustaše over to Maks and instructed him to keep on fighting, even though the Germans had surrendered. Maks carried on the War inside the reconstituted Yugoslavia, but only after he eradicated the concentration camps he ran.

The disposal of bodies was a huge task. So many bodies were buried that an aerial photo picked up a massive stain over 40 years later. Some of the dead were tossed into the river. Some were incinerated; but nearly all of them were bludgeoned or hacked to death. (The sledgehammer was a favorite tool used, though knives were used as an after-thought.) Maks then had the small hamlet next to the camp razed to the ground. There would be no evidence; and indeed, the concentration camp he ran became a side note to the European Holocaust.

Afterward the struggle continued against the victor, Marshall Tito, and his communists. Maks and the remaining Ustaše were called the 'Crusaders.' They were largely militia. The regular troops fled into what is now Austria to surrender to the British. The crusader operation sputtered out in just over a year after the German surrender. Maks fled to Spain where Franco took him in and gave him asylum.

Pavelić's choice of Maks to carry on the struggle was sound.

---

[49] Ante Pavelić was ordered by Hitler to put a "river of blood" between the Serbian and Croatian nations, this is what Vjekoslav Maks Luburić did. The Serbian guerrilla organization led by General Draja Mikhailovitch at one time issued a list of people destined for death by assassination. (Pursued after the War by the UDBA) First on their list was Ante Pavelić. The UDBA had a keen interest in Vjekoslav Luburić as well.

[50] *Untermensch* (German pronunciation: [ˈʔʊntɐˌmɛnʃ], underman, sub-man, subhuman; plural: *Untermenschen*) is a term that became infamous when the Nazis used it to describe "inferior people" often referred to as "the masses from the East," that is Jews, Roma, and Slavs (mainly ethnic Poles, Serbs, and later also Russians).

Maks had personally executed two ministers of the Pavelić Regime, who wanted a negotiated peace with the British. That was the kind of dedication the Pavelić Regime expected and secured.

While in Croatia Maks went to a Jewish Cemetery during a burial. Suspecting that valuables were hidden in the coffin, he drew his pistol and ordered the coffin opened. He was right.

There was a collection of gold and jewels in the coffin. He then killed a mourner at random. He then ordered that the dead man be buried in that same coffin. It was a wartime incident he was proud of.

After he settled in Spain he drank a great deal of red wine. He was over 220 pounds (100 Kilos.) He carried it well for a man not more than five feet seven inches (152 Centimeters). He was often gruff and never shed the military manner of a man involved in hit and run tactics and merciless killing.

While in Spain, he regularly frequented Blue Division gatherings. There he loudly berated communists. He didn't understand how some of his former Ustaše associates in exile would favor a democratic Croatian State. There were also those who favored taking advantage of the Soviet Union's fears of Tito. They would even accept an independent *communist* Croatia, so long as it was an independent state. Nothing could get him angrier than Bolshevism.

From the municipality of Carcaixent he plotted. He published a newsletter that went out to sympathizers around the world. There was an attempt to overthrow the Yugoslav government six years earlier. That insurgency came to nothing.

Nevertheless, the old 'crusader' was undaunted. He planned another insurgency. This one, he said to those close to him, would be in three or fewer years. He would return to a new state of Croatia and resume where he left off in 1946. One glimpse of his Carcaixent residence made his intentions plain. It was a place of operations, not a home.

There, on Sunday April 20th, 1969,[51] his trusted assistant went into the kitchen to brew coffee. He had a sledgehammer and a knife

---

[51] While it is true that Adolf Hitler was born on April 20, 1889, the Author sees opportunity as the key element in choosing this date, and not the anniversary.

close at hand. He unbuckled his belt and slid it off. There was a zipper sewed into the inside. He unzipped it. There he had secreted a white powder in plastic. He poured the powder into the cup. He filled the cup with fresh coffee and stirred it well. He took the cup out to Maks.

He waited. He waited while Maks finished the coffee. He waited until the poison took effect. Maks started to get drowsy. Then Maks jerked upward. He was going to vomit.

The assistant grabbed the 'Polish General' and pulled him to the kitchen sink. He pushed the General's head down into the sink. As Maks vomited, the assistant reached for the sledgehammer.[52]

The ghosts of two awful world wars still haunted the landscape of 1976. The new world of the twenty-first century had not yet been born. Bishop knew the landscape well. All indicators point to a new career for Bradford Bishop in this wild world. This time it was not beyond Shady Grove, but beyond lawful society. It was a world still reverberating from those catastrophic events.

Many would say that Luburić's assassination was an appropriate end to a violent chapter in Holocaust history. Yet, like the concentration camps Maks ran, there was more to it than closing a chapter of European history. The trusted assistant wasn't Jewish, nor was he a Serb. He was a Croat. This wasn't about the Holocaust. Nor was it about the people Maks murdered. To those who lived in 'the other world,' the twilight world of espionage, it looked like 'wetwork.'

Wetwork wasn't what Soviet agents (KGB) did anymore. Further, this was wetwork with needless and excessive force. That was the UDBA's trademark. They were a secret service that truly frightened the Soviet Union's KGB. Indeed, the UDBA worried Stalin

---

[52] The official statement held in the former Yugoslavia has it that Vjekoslav Maks Luburić started to vomit as he sat in the chair. Then his assistant rushed him to the sink where the hammer was at the ready. His assistant claims to have smashed his head while it was over the sink. He stated that he hit Luburić hard enough to bring him down. In his account he stated that Luburić, growled, started to get up and was still dangerous. The assistant followed up with immediate and continuous blows to the head. Luburić was knocked down again. Luburić was finally dispatched with the knife. The body was unidentifiable when it was later found under a bed on the second floor of the residence.

more than American Intelligence.[53]

The UDBA (Uprava državne sigurnosti or the Yugoslavian State Security Service) had recruited Croats. The UDBA served Marshall Tito and his communists well. Yet there was a flaw, even for those who meted out 'sledgehammer justice.' Croats of *all* political persuasions wanted an independent Croatia.

Thus, many of the UDBA's own agents wanted an independent Croatia. When Yugoslavia unraveled, these self-same agents would turn their wetwork on their former political masters. It was all very Balkan. It was all very UDBA.

The comfortable world of Federal Civil Servants in Montgomery County and the county police were at a loss. The blood and carnage at 8103 Lilly Stone Drive was beyond their collective post-World War II experiences. The term 'wetwork' was not in their vocabulary. Only experienced CIA agents could comprehend it. It appears that only they could read the signs. And they weren't saying anything. Except to mutter...

Only the UDBA kills like that.

---

[53] It is said that the two things that kept Stalin awake at night was the UDBA and Carl Gustaf Emil Mannerheim. A colorful figure with an impressive resume. Mannerheim served as the military leader of the Whites (versus the Reds) in the Finnish Civil War. Regent of Finland (1918–1919), commander-in-chief of Finland's defense forces during World War II, Marshal of Finland, and the sixth president of Finland (1944–1946), he defeated the Bolsheviks during the Russian Civil War and fought Stalin to a standstill in what is now called the "Winter War."

The Great Smoky Mountains Search

After the shock of discovery and grisly unearthing of the five bodies in Tyrell County, the hard slog of identifying them began. None of the bodies had any identification on them. The older woman was wearing a jump suit and a coat.

The coat was from Saks Fifth Avenue; and there was a Saks store in Chevy Chase, Maryland. The younger woman's shoes were from Hahn's Shoe Store. Both had hair styles that indicated that the victims were 'city women.'

The three boys were wrapped in sheets. The younger woman had a denim jacket, jeans, and tennis shoes on. With little else to go on, the coroner placed her age at 25.

Funeral hearses took the bodies to North Carolina Memorial Hospital in Chapel Hill for identification. The North Carolina State Bureau of Investigation (SBI) sent 15 investigators and a US $90,000 mobile command post to Columbia. It was a notoriety Columbia did not want.

All police personnel were puzzled. There were no missing-persons reports in Tyrell County. Dr. Page Hudson, the State's chief medical examiner and an assistant came to do an autopsy on the remains the next day. He was impressed by the ferocity of the multiple blows the three boys suffered. It wasn't just about killing them. He reckoned all but the older woman were killed with the first blow.

He estimated the older woman to be 60 years old and in good health when she was murdered. Some people could have survived the blows that he initially thought killed her. He concluded that whoever killed the older woman created a severe emotional reaction. In his opinion the woman had died of fright.

The finger prints taken off the corpses turned up nothing. The investigation grew from checking absentee children in schools in a three-county area, to covering the Eastern Seaboard. After four days nothing from Maine to Florida had turned up. The SBI went to the Tyrell Hardware Company in Columbia to see what could be gleaned from the burnt shovel. The store gave the police the manufacturer's phone number, but that was a dead end.

As the grisly reports flowed out, the citizens of Tyrell County were deeply disturbed. They locked their doors. Something evil was afoot. One local reported that his dog was behaving so strangely that he almost had to put it down.

Photos were taken and posters were made up. The shovel and the old pitchfork were burnt, yet OC[54] Hardware was still clearly legible on the shovel's handle.[55] An exhaustive area search came up with a possibility, Poch's Hardware at Montgomery Mall west of Bethesda, Maryland. An agent of the FBI brought pictures of the victims with them and circulated them at the store. On March 8th some startled residents said, "That's the Bishops."

A startled neighbor with Bradford's office number at the State Department called Foggy Bottom. She was told that the Foreign Service Officer had been gone since Monday, the first. No one else had bothered to contact him. He was a 'short-timer' now. Fellow FSOs had shut him out. It was better for those still at Main State not to see him again.

At this point it might be helpful to review what was missed. Foreign Service Officers do not readily present helpful information. They are trained to remain silent until they can repeat the official line they have been given. In any police investigation active-duty FSOs have to be coaxed.

The police were at a loss. They paid a routine visit to the Division of International Trade Activities and Commercial Treaties, Office of International Trade Bureau of Economic and Business Affairs, Bishop's office. Bishop had been so secretive all his life that no one really knew him. It should come as no surprise, that no one at State thought he was capable of family annihilation. Foreign Service Officers' first loyalty is to their career. 'Burning one's bridges' behind one is unthinkable in a world of sycophants.[56]

Nor did a search of 8103 Lilly Stone Drive produce many clues. Indeed, when the various teams left the crime scene some evidence, such as a letter to Lobelia postmarked in late February, was overlooked. The letter would have brought another lead into

---

[54] There is also a report that the letters OCH HDW were still legible.
[55] Bishop, either through laxity or haste, did not remove the sales-tag from the newly purchased shovel.
[56] There are two ways to the top: Sycophancy or Rebellion. It has been said that the art of Sycophancy has been developed to its highest degree of proficiency at the US Department of State.

the investigation.[57] Neither was Bradford Bishop's diary retained. It would turn up at a garage sale years later.[58]

* * *

The Bishop family annihilation was deeply disturbing for the ten-year-old community of Caderock Springs. They were peaceful and prosperous. Houses selling at $36,500 ten years before had risen to over $100,000. Prosperous Washingtonians had moved in. Although Bradford Bishop blended in, he had no intimate friends in the community, yet he was not regarded as a recluse.

It was even more difficult for the children of the community. Their safe pocket of suburbia near turbulent Washington - far away from its slums - was shaken. The police were now frequent visitors. They chipped away pieces of brick from the Bishop home's exterior to obtain blood samples.

The children of Caderock Springs had bad dreams. Their parents locked doors and bolted their windows shut. Shortly after the killings at least three of the neighborhood homes were burglarized. Outsiders would drive past their modernist homes slowly, asking which home the Bishop's was. The killing of two Montgomery County police on the 28th of March by a teenage neighbor, while fleeing a bank robbery, accentuated the fear.

The stress intensified. There was an execution style murder of five people at a Roy Rogers restaurant in nearby Fairfax County, Virginia days later. A badly wounded survivor provided the FBI with a sketch of the murderer. The cartridges from a 32-caliber pistol were recovered, but nothing more. All the police had to go on was the prominent chin in the sketch, which could have been that of Bradford Bishop Jr.

The Roy Rogers restaurant was near a highway interchange. Could Bishop have struck again? A Georgetown psychic was eager

---

[57] Jacques D'Amboise, a celebrated dancer and a long-time friend of the family, wrote to Lobelia that he was in Washington. He was planning on staying with the Bishop family on the night of the murders. When he injured his foot in a rehearsal, he telephoned to say that he could not come. Otherwise, he would have been at the Bishop house on March 1st. No one thought to contact Mr. D'Amboise about this until the 21st century.

[58] It is possible that Bishop made up the diary and slipped it into the auction long after the murders, to mislead investigators. After careful inspection, the author believes the diary to be authentic.

to take up the task of tying the two mass murders together. Reluctantly investigators took up the offer, but nothing came of it.

The psychic only illustrated the deep concern among the adult community in and around Caderock Springs. The local River Road Unitarian Church gave a sermon on emotional investment in the family. Both the local Catholic Church and the Swim and Tennis club held memorial services. The body of Lobelia Bishop was flown to California to be laid to rest by her husband in North Hollywood. The bodies of Annette and her sons were cremated. The Swim and Tennis club planted and dedicated a Japanese Cherry Tree to the victims outside of its clubhouse.

* * *

By the time Bradford Bishop and his accomplice cleared the Great Smoky National Park and took to the Highway, the sun had set and darkness covered Jake's Creek Trail. Bishop had good reason to pick the spot. Not only was it a place where he could ditch the Chevy Station Wagon without creating suspicion, it was a place he knew. He also knew that people had disappeared in the Park over the years.

The rough terrain of the Great Smoky Mountains Park covers over 816,000 square miles. Wild hogs roam the Park and can be dangerous. The rangers try to cull them every year. There are black bear and other dangerous animals in the Park as well. Bad weather can come on quickly. Further, people have disappeared there over the years.

Notably, a 16-year-old girl, Trenny Lynn Gibson, disappeared there in October of that year. She was on a high school horticultural field trip. She left with 40 students on a school bus, arriving at 12:30 PM. They were not to leave the path and only to go to "Andrews Bald," a well-known spot and to return by 3:30 PM. The temperature dropped. Many of the students did not have warm clothes. They started to jump up and down to get warm. It started to rain. So, the students moved quickly to get back to the bus.

When a group of students stopped to rest she pressed on. She was breathing deeply as she pressed forward. To some eyewitnesses it looked like she took a right turn off the trail. She was never seen again.

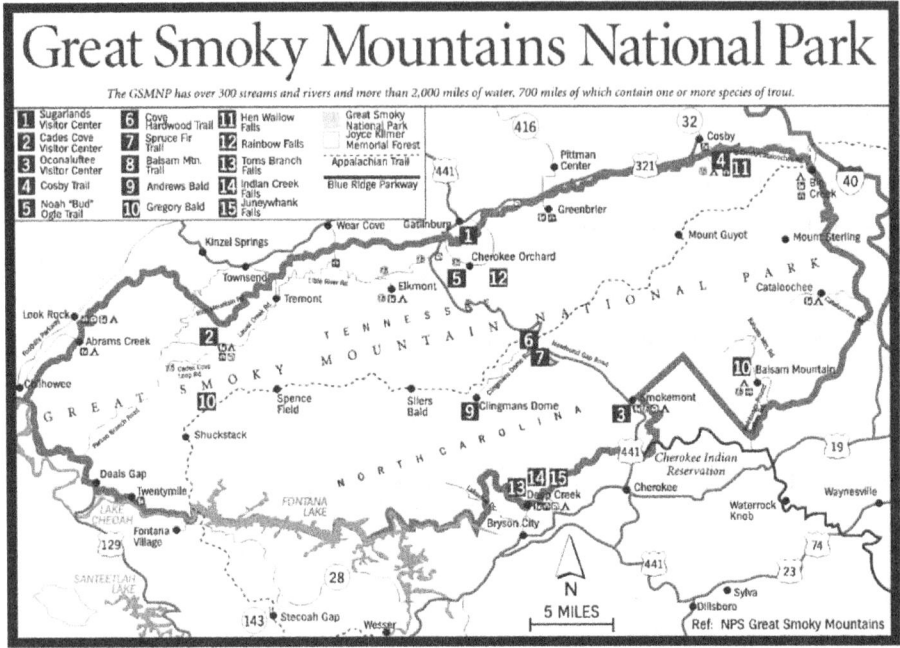

By the time the search for her started strong winds and heavy rain raked the area. The temperature dropped to the low 30's. The full-scale search included bloodhounds and German shepherds. Three wet cigarette butts and a can of beer, with some beer fresh enough to smell in it, were found near the spot she disappeared. National Guard helicopters were deployed, but only after the fog lifted the next day. The thick foliage and humidity hampered search parties. Trenny was never found.

This incident, seven months after the Bishop's station wagon was abandoned, supported the theory that Bradford Bishop, out of his mind, had wandered off into the Great Smoky National Park and died. Perhaps his remains would be found one day.

This is one of two enduring theories of what became of Bradford Bishop. He was an avid outdoorsman and had been to these places before.[59] The car was circumstantial evidence that he

---

[59] It must be assumed that he knew the area of Tyrell county around Albemarle Sound.

took to the deep forest and tried to hitchhike out of the Park. He had plenty of time to do this. It was not until midmorning, March 9th, that the bodies of the Bishop family were identified.

Whenever police authorities worldwide ran out of leads, clues, or guesswork, this theory was their 'out.' Just as Bishop planned it, the theory allowed the trail to go cold. It would be the precarious end to many fruitless investigations. Yet there was more.

For anyone who knew Bradford Bishop Jr. there was always something more. Bishop, like so many Foreign Service Officers, wanted fame. Amongst US Government employees, FSOs are noteworthy for their astonishing illusions of grandeur. If Bishop could not be an ambassador by age 50, he would be something else. He would be something beyond what those who *'should be put in their places'* could ever achieve. In this context, any analysis of Bishop's motives and planning should not be opaque.

Foreign Service culture is an honor and shame-based subculture. FSOs are honored when they meet group expectations. They often feel shamed for being inadequate. Shame is a negative, public rating. (This is why so many certificates of appreciation are issued by Main State.)

When Bishop was stripped of his perceived glory, he felt that the community rejected him as worthless. (It had.) Avoiding shame and acquiring honor is the operating system behind day-to-day life in Foreign Service Culture.

He was a Foreign Service Officer spurned. He lost his social credit rating. He wanted to do what he always wanted to do without hindrance. He wanted to travel the open road. Most important of all, he wanted to be a legend. It was all very careerist.

* * *

William Bradford Bishop Jr. was indicted by a Grand Jury in Montgomery County the day after the rust-colored Chevrolet Station Wagon[60] was discovered. The police picked up a warrant for the Foreign Service Officer's arrest late in the day on March

---

[60] A Chevrolet spokesperson later stated that the color on the 1974 model was "Bronze 66," which is 'quite different,' he said, from "Bronze 76" which was featured on the current model.

12th. The local authorities, aided by the FBI set out for the Great Smoky Mountain National Park.

The FBI agents arrived about 9:30 AM in a convoy of vehicles. They came wearing white shirts, jackets, ties, and hiking boots. The two bloodhounds, named J. Edgar and Miss Randy took up the scent by the abandoned station wagon. They went right to the porch of the boarded-up summerhouse. Then they took to the trail.

They went up the trail. They followed the scent for about a mile into the deep woods and doubled back. They kept to the trail until they got to the parking lot. Then they went directly to the "You are Here" sign and stopped. There the trail went cold.

After that, the dogs were useful only to the television crews. The crews relayed video of the bloodhounds to television audiences in six states.[61] It became a dawn to dusk search into the deep forest and beyond.

The FBI agents set up six teams of two to three each and fanned out to a mile radius from the parked car. In the presence of a Park Ranger, the police opened the car with a coat hanger. They surveyed the insides before towing it to the Park's maintenance yard, an old service station. There they noted that the gas tank was three-quarters full and the odometer was at 17, 711 miles.[62] They noted that the hatchet was beneath the bloodstained blanket. They also observed that the shotgun was a 12 gage Mossberg and was still in its case. The shotgun was found, along with a box of ammunition, in the rear of the vehicle.

The police put out an all-points-bulletin and questioned whomever they could hiking in the Park. More than one hiker reported to the headquarters set up in Gatlinburg, that a man in street clothes and a duffle bag and tent was seen hiking the Park. They sought out any sightings of vagabonds anywhere.

The resident, who first spotted the parked car as suspicious, reported that he saw a 'sandy-haired man' stumbling past the house two days after he spotted the abandoned car. The man wore a blue parka and had a jersey on underneath. He had a beard as

---

[61] The bloodhounds were brought to Outdoor Sports over a week later. The dogs did not react. There was no scent.
[62] Bishop purchased 15 gallons at the Texaco Station prior to the murders.

well. The witness estimated the beard at about a week's growth. The man was also described as 'awfully dirty.'

Further, a police officer from nearby Gatlinburg had spotted a suspicious man a few hours before the parked car's discovery. It was nine in the morning. The local police authorities complained that they should have been alerted to the car's discovery more promptly.

Bishop could have been anywhere. The Appalachian Trail ran a few miles from where he parked his car. He could easily have made his way to the trail and been on his way to Georgia by the time his car was searched.

The search produced maps as well. There was a map of the Tennessee/North Carolina border area. There were maps of Miami and Georgia, as well as a map of the Park. Perhaps the fugitive was heading south. Perhaps he was hiking the trail.

Twelve Explorer Scouts who said that they camped with a couple who saw a man in street clothes bolstered this. They all camped on Derrick Knob. The couple, identified as 'Mike and Betty,' were from Cleveland and on their way to Florida. They reported that the man said he was hiking to Newfound Gap. The FBI sent agents to the trail.

Ultimately, the man in street clothes with the duffel bag was located. He was a frequent hiker of the trail and lived in North Carolina. His story checked out.

And then… nothing.

Great Smoky National Park, Historic District:
Kuhlman Cabin and Jake's Creek Trail.

Part Two

The Best and the Brightest

Peace Corps Ethiopia by Norman Rockwell

The Golden Life

The members of the Kappa Sigma fraternity held their dance party in the ballroom of the Plaza Hotel. The hall was decorated with their fraternity colors: red, green and white. The walls were adorned with the Colorado College banners and pennants. It was Saturday, October 20, 1917 and Bradford Bishop Sr. was a fraternity pledge.

Colorado College is located in Colorado Springs, Colorado. To this day it offers a degree in geology. This was what the senior Bradford Bishop was there for. His mother, Lucy N. Bishop lived nearby in Manitou Springs, Colorado.

College was enjoyable for the senior Brad Bishop. There were picnics and house parties. There was an upcoming Sophomore barbeque for Halloween, October the 31st. The entire college was enthusiastic. The barbeque would feature a huge bonfire, which was to last all night. It was all very innocent. It was all very much part of a bygone age.

America's involvement in the First World War was winding down. Young Bradford Bishop Sr. registered for the military on September 12, 1918 but was not called up. America was preparing for the 1919 offensive. Few in America would have guessed that the Great War had only two more months to run.

The War Relief League was active in Colorado Springs. That same weekend it sent 3200 dressings, four sheets, a rubber sheet and woolen articles (sweaters, socks, mufflers, etc.) for use on hospital trains. Such was war work on the home front. Then the Great War ended.

For many it was a generational divide. Charles Corder Bishop, Bradford Senior's elder brother by five years, had already served as a national guardsman in the 4th Illinois infantry. He was promoted from a private to a non-commissioned officer. Although he was 'mustered out,' he reported to his draft board to re-enlist. As he awaited the anticipated call up, he worked as a bookkeeper at the Colorado Springs National Bank.

About 24 million Americans registered for the draft between 1917 and 1918. Although American literature is noted for the 'lost generation' of writers deeply affected by the War, most Americans were pleased to go along with the 'return to normalcy,' heralded by the new American president, Warren G. Harding. Harding wanted the world to return to the prewar period. It was perceived as an age of innocence. In reality it was an age filled with entrepreneurial energy, as was Bradford Bishop Sr.

The Bishop family was in this mainstream. They were solid Midwesterners who were happy to get on with business. Both Bradford Bishop Senior and his brother Charles moved to California. Bradford found lodging in Long Beach Township, County of Los Angeles. He took up rooms at 149 Broadway. He was already an independent contractor (working as a petroleum engineer) by 1930. By then, at age 31, he had his eyes firmly fixed on his future.

The Mount Poso oil field, in California's Central Valley, was discovered in 1926. It was a complex agglomeration of petroleum pools in structural and stratigraphic traps. It divided into six general areas, all of which cut by faults and many of which are discontinuous, even within named areas. The geography was tailor made for an independent geologist.

Ever the self-starter, the senior Bishop was just the kind of geologist the petroleum industry needed. The Mount Poso oil field was shallow in comparison to other central valley fields. An independent 'wildcatter' could prospect and then put together a deal and drill. Such a well in a small field, like those found in the Mount Poso area, could turn up dry. On the other hand, it could make the entrepreneur a fortune. This would-be Brad Senior's life and he was pleased to take up the challenge. Like so many before and after him, he was pleased to make then sparsely populated Southern California his home.

Brother Charles established his own auditing firm. He had married at 24 and moved to Glendale, in Los Angeles County. He already had two daughters, Dorothy and Helen, by the time his brother Brad married.

Brad was the risk taker. Charles stepped in to help him when help was needed. Both brothers were self-employed, and from a background of self-employment. This was the American way in the nineteen-twenties. It was the family culture of the time. Charles branched out to become the co-owner of a pharmacy. Bradford Senior remained an independent oilman, riding an economic roller coaster through good times and bad.

Both Bishop families dodged the brunt of the Great Depression and the Second World War. Bradford Bishop Jr. was born on August 1, 1936 in Pasadena, California. He was part of the "Quiet Generation," those born between 1930 and 1944. That generation had a low birthrate due to economic depression and war. Resources were sparse and, as a group, quiet generation members were far more reserved than their children were.

William Bradford Bishop Jr. himself did not suffer as a child. The family had a live-in maid. They owned their own home. The Bishop family fortunes rested on oil contracts and discovery. Given that, by 1933, some 13 to 15 million Americans were unemployed, and nearly half of the country's banks had failed, the Bishops hardly felt the Great Depression.

Bradford Junior's mother, Lobelia Amaryllis Saint Germain was born in French-speaking, Canada. She was raised in Duluth, Minnesota and went to high school there. She was the youngest of three sisters.[63] She came from humble origins. Her father was a retail salesman for a glass and paint company. He worked on commission. Her sister Violet, the oldest of the three, was a bookkeeper in the same company.

Their mother was born in Germany. She died in Duluth at age 33, when Lobelia was only three. Lobelia moved west when Los Angeles was undergoing a boom thanks to Hollywood's major studios. It was coupled with the oil boom in the Central Valley.

Lobelia Amaryllis Saint Germain lived a modest life in California. She wanted to be an actress and a singer. She loved the arts with a notable preference for ballet and opera. She aspired to greater things as well. California Society was mobile. In other places, such as New England, she could not have been as successful. There she would have been regarded as a social climber.[64]

The senior Bradford Bishop had been raised in Illinois with his parents and his older brother, Charles. The 1901 oil discovery in

---

[63] Violet, Lilly, and Lobelia
[64] Both Lobelia and Amaryllis are names of flowers. It is notable that in societies throughout the ages, children of people of humble origin are often christened with floral names.

Texas was still making millionaires. California, he thought, could be another Texas. The Mount Poso oil field area, in the foothills of the Sierra Nevada in Kern County, had that kind of potential.

An added bonus, Bakersfield and the Central Valley were as Midwestern as the Pacific Coast was varied. The nearby coast had Chinese and Japanese communities. It was also stucco-clad with Spanish Colonial influence. The package excited Bradford Bishop Senior.

South Pasadena had easy access to Kern County and the Mount Poso fields. Brad Sr. could whisk away in a Model 'A' Ford on Route 66. The town's streets were lined with Redwood, Ash, Sequoia, and Sycamore trees. No Palm trees grew along the streets then. South Pasadena was close to Hollywood as well. It became a stand-in for Midwestern towns in film and television. South Pasadena had an 'anywhere in America' feel to it. There the two Southern California booms, the Film Industry and Oil Industry, met.

Bradford Senior thrived. Ever an independent, he worked with firms like R.R. Bush Oil, a California outfit, first with exploration and then by leasing the driller's mineral rights. Sometimes he did well and sometimes he did not. He enjoyed the business, the roller coaster ride, the freedom, and the thrilling potential.[65]

He took a chance on Murdoch Number 1-1, near the edge of the Mt. Poso field. It came up dry. After drilling and bottoming out at 1,827 feet, it had to be written off. Abandoning the well could have been depressing. Although he wasn't happy about it; Bradford Senior always kept a cheerful outlook. He was easy going; and understood that for wildcatters hope springs eternal.

It was a good thing that young Bradford Jr. was in public high school at South Pasadena High at the time. Young Brad Jr. had been going to polytechnic Elementary school (nowadays simply known as 'Poly') in Pasadena. It was a private school with a rigorous academic curriculum. Poly was one of the best elementary schools in the nation. It even had a 15-acre campus.

It would later be notable as a 'feeder school' for elite American Universities. It was also notable for its Pet and Hobby show,

---

[65] This was a notable aspect that later investigators missed. As the old saying goes, "The apple does not fall far from the tree."

featuring a plethora of dogs. Bradford took a liking to canines, and he kept an appreciation of dogs for the rest of his life.

After Poly, his mother would drive him and his friends to the beach. It was a rare treat for his school friends, who happily took Lobelia up on her offer of a ride. Being chauffeured to the beach, and the sunshine over a limitless ocean, was sublime. It was a Pacific coast version of the Midwest without the snow.

Lobelia was always energetic. With characteristic vivaciousness, she threw herself into the world of socialites in the Los Angeles area. She was the hospitality chair of the Pasadena Guild of Children's Hospital. The Bishops were not churchgoers. Yet Lobelia set up a festive wassail bowl, an old English tradition for Christmas. For the young Lobelia, nothing was too good for her Brad; and she could now be a mother and have a life in the arts as well.

Prior to this Brad Senior's tastes were characterized by the Annual Oilmen's Barbeque and Gold Tournament of the San Joachim Valley. Notably, the function was followed by Vaudeville. Lobelia brought sophistication to the Bishop family and brought Bradford Senior himself out and beyond the wildcatter's world.

Like many wealthy patrons, Brad senior now sat on a Board, the Board of the Children's Hospital Guild. He became a member of the Pasadena Philharmonic Committee. He raised money for the Children's Hospital Doll Fair. He hosted a table and raised funds for the supper dance for the Tennis Finals. (Brad Senior was fond of tennis.)

He and Lobelia continued their socialite activities. She went to the "Honker," a successful and highly rated restaurant in Pasadena. They took a vacation at the Inn at Rancho Santa Fe. They were such influential socialites by then, that the Los Angeles social column reported on it. The oil flowed and they basked in the limelight. It was at the ballet, however, that Brad Senior found a lasting love and appreciation of an art form. So much so that he became the president of the Pasadena Civic Ballet.

* * *

In June of 1951 the New York City Ballet's first American performances outside of New York started in Chicago and came to the Greek Theatre at Griffith Park. Ruthanna Boris, Nora Kaye, and André Eglevsky had joined the Company as Principal Dancers. Jerome Robbins choreographed *The Cage*, and Ruthanna Boris's *The Cakewalk* premiered. Lobelia wanted to see it; and she persuaded Brad to come.

There Brad Sr. was captivated. He had never seen such graceful leaps and pirouettes. The athleticism and grace won him over that night. He became a balletomane and remained so for the rest of his life.

The Bishops threw a party for the ballet company. At one point, when speaking with André Eglevsky, the new head of the company and an international superstar Eglevsky introduced them to a promising, young dancer, Jacques d'Amboise. He was not yet 17 and Lobelia took an immediate liking to him. On impulse, she invited him to stay with them. "Why pay for a hotel? Come stay with us. We would love to have you," she said.

And so, a long relationship with the Bishops began. Jacques moved into the guest bedroom of the Bishop home in South Pasadena and entered into the Bishop's family life. Their home was spacious; their outdoor pool was an impressive feature for the young dancer from New York, and fun. In the course of his tours of California Jacques bonded with the Bishops.

Bradford Bishop Junior was about two and a half years younger than Jacques. They played Robin Hood together. (The movie, the New Tales of Robin Hood came out in 1951.) They played Daniel Boone and Jim Bowie, as well. Together they would screech, pretending to be wild Indians amid the orange groves.

They also played chess, during which Bradford would concentrate intensely.

Tellingly he would clench his jaw while contemplating a move. In all things, Brad Junior was easy-going, but with a determination to win when it came to competition. He was always the center of attention in Lobelia's home movies. Home movies were a notable sign of affluence at a time when affordable Kodak Box "Brownie" Cameras, were widely used instead.

Brad Jr. was gangly, athletic and strong. He had his mother's broad cheekbones and large frame. He had his father's hair and quiet reserve. A highly intelligent child, he was a quick study. He was analytical and remote yet appeared unspoiled in an environment of sudden affluence.

He had a dozen close friends throughout high school. Brad was a member of the 'Bengals,' a service organization. He played football for South Pasadena High School, which at the time was districted to include San Marino, a wealthier community. He played 'End,' and, by his senior year became a letterman, a varsity athlete.

There were both male and female cheerleaders at that time. The girls were called 'song leaders,' and the boys were called 'yell leaders.' Young Brad got to play first string by his senior year, with all of them cheering him on.[66]

Lobelia fussed over her husband. At a time when women were professional homemakers, she made a beautiful home for her family. She habitually rose before everyone in the household, prepared breakfast, and set the table. She channeled some of her tremendous energy into volunteering. She took courses as well: Italian language, Opera, Renaissance Art, Cooking, and Floral Arrangement. All of this went into her homemaking and influenced her son as he grew up. Without a great deal of education herself, she wanted her outdoorsman son to become an intellectual.

She felt that because she had not become a singer or an actress, that she had not accomplished enough in her life. Yet if she became a good mother to Brad Jr., it would give her meaning. She put a family together, which included friends like Jacques.

---

[66] He was not a star on the team. In retrospect, some accounts describe him as a 'second string' player. He was elected to vice president of his class, but not class president. This may have disappointed Lobelia.

During Brad's high school years Jacques was on his way to becoming an international star. Bradford Sr. was so impressed that he wanted his son to enroll as a ballet dancer. Brad Junior preferred football.

Jacques became an American celebrity before Brad Jr. graduated High School. Jacques danced in *Seven Brides for Seven Brothers*. The musical became a film, and Jacques was on the big screen. The film came to South Pasadena and, indeed, played all over California.

In his senior year, Brad Jr. was elected class vice president. His friend, Jim Roodhouse, was elected class president. A convivial person, Jim remained active in Class of 1954 affairs all his life.

It was on the football field and on the tennis court, that Brad Jr. felt most comfortable. His parents continued to press him to become a dancer like Jacques, but this was not for Brad. Football and tennis were his sports, and he hoped to distinguish himself as he played. His mother pressed him on, and he wanted to win whenever he was on the field or the courts. This determination was particularly appreciated by one of the cheerleaders.

Annette Weis was a pretty, healthy cheerleader with brown hair. She had broad cheekbones, notably large eyes, and a vitality and laugh that were similar to Brad's mother Lobelia's. When she visited Brad's home, Lobelia took an instant liking to her.

The nineteen-fifties in Southern California were good times for the Quiet Generation. The high school couple double dated with Brad's friend Barney Mills. Barney had a 1953 Green Chevrolet Coup. Barney and his future wife would drive Brad and his future wife, Annette, to the beaches north and south of Laguna Beach.

Life was going smoothly, indeed quite well. Brad was part of a prominent family. They were capable people without pretensions. His father was a patron of the arts, and an oilman. His mother was frequently mentioned in the Society Columns of the Los Angeles Times. He had his friends, a Mediterranean climate, popularity, and social standing. The weather in Southern California was indeed delightful, but underneath there was far more pressure to succeed that many would care to admit. The state of California had yet to project an image of itself as easy-going.

Brad Jr. had his place in the prosperous, cozy, and still small-town world of Southern California. It was then a town of 'Mom and Pop' stores. Yet he got away to the Great Outdoors, with his close friend Ron Currie, whenever he could. With his father away at the Mount Poso Field, such trips were a release from his mother's expectations.

Annette had an interest in art. As a woman of the day, she was as helpful and hard working around the house as Lobelia. Like Lobelia she would prepare meals, and clean. Further, she loved the outdoors and was a good tennis player, like her boyfriend Brad Junior. At a time when it was common for young women to marry immediately after high school, Annette was following a traditional path.

Typical of Brad Junior's life during that senior year was when Jacques stopped by. On one of those visits, he asked Lobelia where Brad and Annette were. "They are out bushwhacking in the woods somewhere," Lobelia replied and then added, "She's such a darling." (This was something Lobelia would habitually add concerning Annette.)

The Bishop family was small, but still a family. Uncle Charles went on to develop an accounting business and became a part owner of a pharmacy. He raised his two daughters, Helen and Dorothy in Southern California. As with most members of the Quiet Generation, they too followed a well-worn, traditional path.

For those women who went to college in the nineteen-fifties, marriage upon graduation was commonplace. (Some would say nearly universal.) Helen Louise Bishop, Charles Bishop's daughter and Bradford Junior's cousin, was no exception. She attended Stanford and was a member of Alpha Omicron Pi, a sorority. She married on August 17, 1946 to Guy Combes Jr., who went to University of California at Berkley. (UC Berkley)

Brad Senior's father and mother, as well as his brother and wife, Mr. and Mrs. Charles Bishop presided. As a well-known benefactor of Southern California Charities, Brad Senior was celebrated in the press as he cheerfully oversaw the festivities. He was pleased to do something for the brother who had done so much for him. The marriage took place at Saint James Episcopal Church, and Lobelia took care to insert the details into the social column.

This was the world William Bradford Bishop Junior grew up in. His family was small, and Uncle Charles was always there to help his younger brother through the difficult times. His mother was always there to urge young Bradford on to greater and greater success. It was a time when couples married after school and settled down, perhaps to purchase a house they could boast about.

He, like his friends, had a high-school girlfriend with whom his mother was pleased. So pleased was she, that she regarded Annette as the daughter she never had. This was all part of the Southern California ethos in the early 1950's. Then the letter arrived.

As a high school senior Brad had considered the University of Southern California in the University Park District of Los Angeles. UCLA was where the best students went. It produced businessmen and professionals. His high school grades were good. If matters were allowed to take their natural course, that was how things would have turned out. He'd go to college near home. He'd keep up with his friends, go to the beach, and play football. And so, like all high school seniors, he waited for what acceptance letters the mail would bring.

Acceptance to a California school was what was expected. (Yet his mother wanted more) The letter he received, however, was from an Ivy League School. To the delight of his mother, William Bradford Bishop Jr. was accepted into Yale University.

The Bitch Goddess Success

"In the confusion of all ranks, one attempts to appear what he is not."
—Alexis De Tocqueville…

I've seen the Dean. He thinks I'm keen,
Cause I wear a pair of white shoes
—*Edwin Lynn Wolff* – 1950 Yale Class book

On an autumn day in 1954 Bradford Bishop Jr. reported to Payne Whitney Gym. There he ascended to a windowless room above the gym itself and was told to remove all his clothing. The men in charge were dressed in white. They affixed four metal pins to his vertebrae with adhesive. They had him stand against a wall illuminated by a floodlight. Then they photographed him.

He was told that this was a 'posture photo.' It was a routine feature of Freshman Orientation week. Had his posture been deemed erratic, he would have been sent to remedial posture classes. This was a long-established procedure at most Ivy League and Seven Sisters schools.[67]

This was only the beginning of his Yale experience. Yale's student body was all male at the time. One of the many jokes that went about concerning the photos was that it was 'the measure of the man.' It was one of the first curios he experienced when he plunged into the cold, monastic life of a Yale undergraduate.

He got into Calhoun Hall (named after Senator John C. Calhoun.) Today's students might call it a dormitory. It was then, and still being called a 'College.' It was then more akin to an expensive American prep school, or an English 'public' school. It featured a welcoming fireplace in the expansive Whitridge room. Calhoun had its own coat of arms, designed with the University Coat of Arms and the Cross of Saint Andrew above. Each student had his own rooms and a shared room with his roommates. There was even the new IBM machine, tended to by Lydia Rammlein at

---

[67] Among the cultural elite who underwent this over the years were: George Bush, George Pataki, Brandon Tartikoff and Bob Woodward who were required to do it at Yale. At Vassar, Meryl Streep; at Mount Holyoke, Wendy Wasserstein; at Wellesley, Hillary Rodham and Diane Sawyer.

the Master's Office.

The Master was the housefather. There was a new housefather that semester. His name was Archibald S. Foord (spelled with two o's). His son lightened the somber, old hall by squirting the resident students with a water pistol. The dining room manager, Edna, had the dining room table numbers memorized by the second meal. Jacket and tie were the preferred dress at the dining area, and all meals were served at tables. Maxie, who served the boys, would obligingly serve a second piece of pie when asked. It was, at that time, arguably the most desirable College at Yale in 1954. The residents simply called it the 'Houn.'

There was no shortage of pledges.[68] Under the old allocation system, Calhoun was a magnet for any who sought success. Men who became chairmen of various organizations, class secretaries, and fraternity presidents, descended on the 'Houn in droves. Notably the 'Houn attracted athletes.

The prior class had the Class Secretary, the Class Treasurer, the Chairman of WYBC (Yale Radio) the IFC (Inter-Fraternity Council) President, the basketball and football captains, Olympic crewmen, and five starting football players. Using the yardstick of names and titles, it could be said - and was indeed said by many - that Calhoun was "the Best College at Yale."

The 18-year old, Bradford Bishop Jr. was now in the 'Big Leagues.' As a matter of course, he tried out for the Yale University football team. It was then that he received another splash of cold water. The tryouts were a sham.

The players were already chosen. Only a superlative player, overlooked by Yale's scouts, could have made the team by the time of the tryouts. He went on to play football for Calhoun College, but that was intramural football. (It was then called 'club ball.') It was a poor substitute for being on the University team. Brad saw it all as 'fixed.'

He was a typical high school boy, not a prep school boy. It was common then, for high school boys, to find Yale a more alien world

---

[68] Pledging is a process with multiple stages that can take up to a year and a half. In some fraternities, pledging takes place over a matter of weeks. The other big part of pledging is proving oneself worthy of being made a brother.

than their prep school colleagues. Usually the high school boy either became a recluse or turned to extra-curricular activity, as a means of more rapid assimilation into the group. Brad did not make the cut. He did, however, see something in the *Yale Record*, a college humor magazine. He twice submitted jokes during his years at Yale. They ran like this: 'Once a girl was so thin, that when she swallowed an olive three guys left town.'

Although he told his mother that he served on the magazine's board, there is little evidence of his involvement other than the submission of a few jokes in two issues. It is possible that he carried a few bundles of issues to buildings for distribution. He appears in a group picture of the *Record* staff; yet he was only listed as a contributor, over his five years at Yale, in two issues.

Humor was his vehicle. With it Brad limped along at Yale, socializing and trying to assimilate among his new, and more acclimatized, college friends. Acclimatizing to the East Coast included getting used to the humidity. That and the realization that he had an accent were only two of the more unwelcome surprises.

It is common for freshmen, who were accomplished in high school, to become suddenly mediocre and depressed in college. This is because, by definition, the competition intensifies. An all-male environment adds to this.

The Ivy League was still an East Coast phenomenon at that time. Alaska and Hawaii were not yet states in the union. It should come as no surprise that Bradford Bishop's sleeping disorder first manifested itself at this time.

He was no longer the son of a prominent patron of the arts. His mother was frequently mentioned in the *Los Angeles Times*, not in the *Boston Globe*. He was no longer the vice president of his senior class. He was no longer a player on the South Pasadena High School Team. Song Leaders and Yell Leaders were no longer cheering him on. He wasn't an easy drive away from the blue Pacific. The nearby Connecticut River held no such charms. Even the green Atlantic wasn't a convenient ride away. Besides, Connecticut was cold. (Not a palm tree in sight)

The Connecticut River was, however, the site of the Freshman picnic. Yale's traditional picnics were for freshman and seniors. Bishop's class consumed 2,500 weenies in two hours.

When A. Whitney Griswold, the 16th President of Yale, came to address the freshmen at the picnic, he wore a cloak of Ermine and carried the Mace. He told young Bradford, and those gathered by the river, that they were in a 'select group.' For every one accepted into the freshman class, four applicants were rejected.

Griswold came with more than a cloak and mace. He was accompanied by Yale graduates Dean Acheson and Robert Taft. There were also eminent guest lecturers and a host of visiting celebrities throughout the term. These included Broadway star, Jayne Mansfield,[69] as well as Frank Lloyd Wright and Phillip Johnson on Architecture. But for the 'Houn and Bishop the burgeoning 1950's cinema was the notable draw.

There was Christopher Lee in "The Mummy." But there were also a great many films viewed apart from academic supervision. Perhaps the most notable film of 1957 was "Attack of the Crab Monsters." It, and other monster movies, became icons of the nineteen fifties.[70]

Ice Cream defined Yale in the 1950's as well. Well into the 21st century the 'Ice Cream Riots' were part of Yale's reputation. New Haven had several ice cream vendors. At the time New Haven was known for Hood's Ice Cream and Sealtest Ice Cream, among others. Yet it was the Humpty Dumpty Ice Cream Vendor who gave Yale - what some freshman came to call - *our finest hour.*

It all started with the usual late afternoon ice cream sales. The high school students of New Haven preferred Good Humor ice cream. The Yale underclassmen preferred Humpty Dumpty ice cream. In the 1950's New Haven's high school was located in a building which was later purchased by, and incorporated into, Yale. There was a parking lot across the street from the building. Yet there was only one available parking spot on that fateful day.

---

[69] She posed nude for *Playboy* in 1955. This improved the magazine's circulation and drew Yale student attention.

[70] A sign of the times was when the freshman class behind Bishop's sophomore class adopted a wayward duck. The school ordered the duck removed and suddenly the freshman class had a cause celeb. They dubbed the duck 'Igor,' a common name given to minor characters in nineteen fifties horror movies. The Class representatives argued that caged birds were allowed. The duck therefore was covered, though hardly caged. Ultimately the freshmen won this battle, although there would be many more to come where Yale underclassmen were not as successful.

Both Humpty Dumpty and Good Humor vendors claimed the spot. Yale students gathered and took the Humpty Dumpty vendor's side. It is truly unfortunate that, at that moment, New Haven's high schools let out for the day.

They streamed out of the Hill House and Wilbur Cross High Schools into the parking lot. They joined the increasingly heated discussion. Someone took a swing. Another punch was landed, and the fight was on.

Students from both schools rallied to support their comrades. Knives and lead pipes came out of nowhere; and the police were called in. The police of the nineteen fifties did not work under the restraints that police operate under today. The New Haven police pulled out their Billy Clubs and started to clear the crowd.

This did not succeed. Back up was called in. Eight Yale undergraduates wound up in the hospital; and the Humpty Dumpty Vendor slipped away just in time.

This is what is historically categorized as 'Town and Gown' riots. Such disputes have gone on for hundreds of years amongst Europe's finest Universities and the communities they are located in. In the case of Yale and New Haven, these differences too often resulted in assault and injury.

A cursory look at New Haven and Yale of the day tells the tale. Yale was very 'shoe.' 'Shoe' is a traditional, Yale term. It comes from 'white shoe,' a pair of which expresses the Yale ethos. That and York Street clothing, a top-of-the-line outfitter in the nineteen fifties, were what 'Yalies' wore. If you were doing things the Yale way you were 'very shoe.'

Indeed, when anyone in the Houn was studying on a Sunday night, fellow students would say that studying on Sunday night was not 'very shoe.' Considering that New Haven was a working-class town, with many New England ethnics, friction should not have come as a surprise to anyone.

Another notable display of Town vs. Gown friction was a massive snowball fight. It happened on a late Friday afternoon. Fridays should have been quiet, but this was Yale.

This wasn't just any snow ball fight. An estimated 1,500 students from the schools went at it. A New Haven policeman was injured and a truck driver was sent to the hospital.

It started on the site of the earlier Ice Cream Riot. Someone had thrown a snowball that broke the ventilator on a fish truck. The 20-year-old driver was up at arms. One thing led to another. The high school students joined in. So, did the Yale Undergraduates. The number of students throwing snowballs swelled, and the fight was on.

About 100 students were throwing snowballs when the first police officer arrived. It rapidly escalated from there. More police arrived. Now there were hundreds of students on both sides of the parking area. The police had to bar traffic for two blocks while they quelled the melee.

The traffic jam, comprised of nearly all of the adult population of New Haven, was trying to get home for the weekend. By the time the New Haven police started arresting students, and professors came running out of their offices to plead with them to cease and desist, the snowball fight had swollen to the estimated 1,500 boys. At that point the Yalies wisely melted away.

Only ten Yale boys were actually subdued. One, who was tossed into a police car, simply slid over to the other side of the back seat, opened the door, and made good his escape. New Haven was beside itself. The University put all its 4,000 students on Social Probation. Not to be outdone the student paper, the *Yale Daily News*, put out a special edition telling the administration that such probation was "inexcusable.'

Bradford Bishop Jr. was not one of those caught. Nor does he surface in the conflicts of Town and Gown but twice. He was arrested for Jay Walking, in his sophomore year.[71] This was the Saturday of the Brown vs. Yale football game.

The police used Jay Walking as a way of putting suspicious characters under arrest; and thereby giving them a record, the local police precinct could refer to during the next student riot. Jay walking is violating civilian pedestrian laws. For New Haven that meant keeping young men off the streets. Yale won game, the weather was good, and the police were braced for another student riot. Brad was one of the unlucky few that day. He wasn't on the

---

[71] October 1, 1955, noll, Rec. 131-301

sidewalk.

The second incident was when his college roommate was assaulted near a local bar. He was not in the fight this time. Yet it is a telling encounter.

His roommate was in a scuffle with townies and attacked with a knife. The young man was pinned to a wall and suffered a wound to the leg close to the groin. He was lucky to come out of it with a superficial wound.

Brad's student colleagues celebrated this exploit for about two weeks. It was with an unmistakable eagerness that young Brad listened to him recounting the tale. As the Yale student with the knife wound recalled the incident for small groups of undergraduates, Brad lit up. The enviousness he quietly displayed was unmistakable.

Bradford took risks. He was a thrill seeker. His risk-taking behavior would get him into trouble in the future. This was the first real look we have at the young Bishop's underlying nature. He was not a notable risk-taker in high school. These are clues as to what would bring trouble and strife down on his head. It wasn't the only life-long theme that drove him.

What drove him into mischief was the single overarching theme of his life. He suffered more from it than any other thing. There were times when he felt taunted by it. It was part of what kept him from falling off to sleep at night. To his mind, it was the most desirable, yet elusive thing in the world. Bradford Bishop had to win; and was haunted by his perceived lack of success. He wasn't 'a comer.[72]'

When he returned to California during intercession or academic breaks, he attended parties and receptions, Lobelia saw to it that he was written into the social column. After all, her Brad was from Yale. Yet, young Brad knew he did not stand out there. He had not lived up to Yale as he had shined in South Pasadena High School or 'Poly.' This weighed on him.

This was most likely the root cause of Bradford's insomnia. That he had no real problem sleeping prior to his entry into Yale was a red flag. Once at Yale, he could not understand why he didn't

---

[72] (Nineteen fifties slang) Someone likely to succeed

get a solid night's sleep. He wrote home about it.

His mother did not understand it either. Ultimately, he took serax, a prescription drug used to treat anxiety. It is a medication, which belongs to a class of drugs called 'benzodiazepines.' Over the years, it has been sometimes described as a 'sleeping pill.' Bradford's condition was more one of anxiety and depression than sleep deprivation.

Things were not going according to plan. Brad was a Californian in a monastic, male, Ivy League school. There were no girls for him to flirt with. His classmates were not like the friends he had in South Pasadena. Many of his new colleagues were from prosperous New England families. (Old money, New England Socialites)

A cursory look at the Yale roster is telling. One 'Houn joke Brad's classmates, with whom he shared rooms, would tell was to refer to their rooms the 'Presidential Suite.' This was because, among them, there were those with the surnames of past presidents, Pierce, Lincoln, Polk, etc.

Californians were different and, in the 1950's, marginalized. Then the West Coast stood on the fringes of major debates and artistic events. There were no major league baseball teams in California in 1954.[73]

California was a vacant space to many in the East Coast establishment. In retrospect, the counterculture, which would bloom in the 1960,'s, largely had its origins along the California Coast. The "laid-back" California culture had yet to be exported, or even properly defined. It is often forgotten how driven a young man growing up in that region during the 1950's could be. (Even more so if driven on by his mother.)

This further fed into his alienation. The touch and feel of the West Coast was absent. Except for seasonable apples and pears, the fruit in New England wasn't fresh. In California, one never had to wait for fruit or vegetables to ripen. The pineapple was canned and there wasn't an avocado in sight. No one had ever heard of Jicama,

---

[73] At the time California had its own Pacific Coast League. The San Francisco Giants were established in 1958, and the Brooklyn Dodgers moved to Los Angeles in 1958.

let alone consumed it.⁷⁴

Brad came up with a strategy to cope with Yale. He simply purported to be a descendant of William Bradford, of Plymouth Colony. William Bradford was one of the original pilgrims, the Governor of Plymouth Plantation, and the only Pilgrim forefather to write an account of the founding. A chip off Plymouth Rock is a hard card to trump; and difficult to disprove in the nineteen-fifties. It also titillated the girls.

Bradford could charm the women during mixers. Part of this was the stimulus of competition with others, but a great deal of it was his natural inclination to flirt and conquer. He kept his escapades secret, another lifelong trait. He also kept his colleagues at the 'Houn guessing.

Extra-curricular activities such as these were a way of letting off steam. Yet the insomnia remained. It would remain so long as Brad tried to fit into Yale. He wasn't keeping up with anything except social activities. He wasn't very 'shoe' and he wasn't succeeding in academics either. His stated medical future as a doctor was another sham. He was a C student.

To the young Bishop this was an uncomfortable situation. He wanted to be the master of his own fate. The frustration came when 'Houn undergraduate after 'Houn undergraduate succeeded in something or other. Everyone appeared to be excelling except himself.

The ball players were succeeding on the field. The more studious ones were excelling at academics. Indeed, the glittering stars of American life, swanning about Yale and out again, gave Bradford the impression of continual movement. This intensified as he took comfort in the *Yale Record*, America's oldest college humor magazine.⁷⁵

He found some relief in humor. Yet he was a billiard ball in the great scheme of things. Everything seemed to be determined by

---

⁷⁴ It was here that the young Bradford's philosophy lessons dovetailed into his Yale experience. Jicama or some fresh fruit could trigger off a Proustian moment. The philosopher Marcel Proust deduced: involuntary autobiographical memory is a subcomponent of memory. This occurs when cues encountered in everyday life evoke recollections of the past without conscious effort. (As opposed to voluntary memory, its binary opposite. That is a deliberate effort to recall the past.)

⁷⁵ The Yale record is credited with coining the term "Hot Dog" in its October 19, 1895 issue.

chance. He was an American Studies major and had no outstanding talents to propel him in any direction. He could not sleep.

The drug serax (15 MG) was prescribed. Today serax is an over-the-counter medicine. It was intended to treat anxiety. His family doctor in California prescribed it, and ever-energetic mother mailed it to him as needed.

Serax kept him groggy. He'd try to sleep in his room at the 'Houn and could not. He was up at all hours, often passing his sleepless nights by writing his mother and Annette. He thought that he, himself, was 'all doped up' during the day. His mind wandered in class. His grades suffered even more. He was striving to get somewhere. Then it got worse.

Yale at the time lectured its attendees on "the Bitch Goddess Success." This was purported by no less a personage than William James (1842 to 1910) philosopher and psychologist. He was oft quoted at Yale: "The exclusive worship of the Bitch-goddess Success is our national disease."

Brad was now under attack. He had risen to the Ivy League and intended to succeed in life after University. He now found Yale lecturing the elite of American Society, the 'Best and the Brightest' as they would come to be called, on the dangers of Bitch Goddess worship. It was inconceivable, to the son of a petroleum entrepreneur imbued with a pioneering and 'can do' spirit, that when faced with daunting odds, success was not encouraged. Yale graduates had privilege and opportunity in the expanding US economy of the nineteen fifties. Not to pursue financial success, after the sometimes-hardscrabble life of boom and bust his father knew, just didn't prove out. Was all of it for nothing?

Many students agreed with young Brad but related to it as those with connections and easily attainable wealth might. It was a studied unconcern for money. They came from privilege on a far greater scale than the insomniac undergrad. Many prep school boys could see the reasoning behind 'stop and smell the roses,' or not to 'work oneself into the ground.' (That part of it was very shoe indeed.) And so, William Bradford Bishop Jr., even with his manufactured Plymouth Rock credentials, endured additional stress and tried to sleep.

His room was cluttered and messy. Often, he rose from his fitful sleep at 2:30 or 4:00 in the morning. He would write home in the hours prior to the morbid dolor of first light. Even with serax he still had trouble getting a full night's sleep.

As classmate after classmate brought home athletic or academic laurels, he felt that the world was passing him by. Everything was going too fast, and he was sidelined. He wasn't making those goals he set for himself fast enough (or at all.) His mother wrote to him… "We hope that the troubles of the world are not really settling down on you to make you miserable again. I pray God that those damn nerves are not upsetting you…"

At this point it seemed that he was about as far from leading the graduates of his South Pasadena High School as he would ever get. It had to be maddening that he was no longer winning amongst competitive Californians but trailing behind smug Eastern establishment-types. At one point, as a joke, he dropped a waste paper basket from the second floor on the 'Houn sewing circle,' as the evening gathering around the fireplace called themselves. It was all taken as good fun by the sewing circle. They liked the C student who could not sleep. Yet young Brad could not have been more anxious.

His mother was proud of him, and a patient letter reader. He was her masterpiece. She wrote back with practical advice, "You have had a fine education, you seem aware of your blessings, you have a strong personality and brains, so why shouldn't you succeed – in anything you choose to do?"

Tellingly and notably he replied with his favorite analogy, "I feel rather dull and unspent… and [that] I was a great billiard ball being tossed about at the pleasure of the fates."

In a moment of weakness, at about four o'clock one caliginous and starless morning, he wrote to Annette. He asked her to be his valentine. Nothing could have pleased both she and Lobelia more.

Annette Weis

Times got tough for Brad's father. Oil exploration had its ups and downs. His business wasn't doing well. He'd been through it before. Prior to this, he could always say that the worst time he had yet was when he had to abandon that test well back in 1952; when it came up dry. It appears that this time it was worse. His older brother Charles helped where he could, but tuition at Yale was expensive.

Yale had raised undergraduate tuition by US $150, to $1,250. The University spokesman said that fees had to match educational expenses. The new salary schedule was announced for July, 1958. Yale would consider financial aid for deserving students, the spokesman added. Brad Jr. took a year off.

Yale had ways of helping undergraduates through financial difficulties. What Yale did for Bradford is not recorded, but it is known that his 'Houn brothers were supportive.[76] They wanted to see their likeable colleague get through.

Bradford had completed his junior year. He returned as a senior, after a year's absence, his friends were graduating. This further put him out of synch with his Yale cohort.

When he returned to Yale for the Fall Semester of 1958, he was asked what he had been doing. "Digging ditches," was all that he replied. Everyone who knew him at Yale left it at that. There are no other records of what he did during his hiatus, but there is

---

[76] Given his academic performance, and the tales of money and glory he bandied about, it is likely that Yale did nothing.

circumstantial evidence to fill in the gap.

Given his father's situation at the Mt. Poso Field, the young Bradford could not work for his father for pay. He had to find another way of paying for his tuition. The most lucrative short-term job during the economic dip of 1957-58 was digging trenches for the public utility.

The public utility paid well but digging was hard work. A pipe-laying outfit in Long Beach was paying US $2.81 an hour to dig ditches. Bradford Bishop Jr. did not like recalling his 1957-1958 experiences. It was humiliating to tell his Ivy League colleagues that he had to take a low-status job to pay for his tuition. Staying at home and putting the money aside for tuition is as good an explanation as any this author is likely to come up with.[77]

When he returned to Yale, existentialism was in vogue amongst the philosophical and literary faculty. Albert Camus, a French author from Algeria, had won the 1957 Nobel Peace Prize. Camus won it for *"the Outsider,"* a previous work of his that had become popular among students about to enter college. It concerns alienation and ponders the meaning of existence.

Initially this made no sense to the young Bradford. He couldn't buy into life having no meaning. If life were meaningless, what was he doing at Yale? He had dug ditches to pay for his final year of school. He had hit the books. When he played in any sport, particularly tennis, he still played to win. Was all of that for nothing?

Existentialism made sense to him when it was couched in terms of human beings struggling to find out who and what they were. Instead of listening to others, why not do something he wanted to do? Finding himself and finding meaning through asserting his own will appealed to him.

He came to understand that some things are not rational. Existentialism explains that decisions are not without stress and consequences. Personal responsibility and discipline are crucial. Yet who was deciding? Was he so cowardly that he did not seize what he wanted? Were his efforts so anemic in comparison to his

---

[77] On his security clearance forms for the State Department he lists 'Lease man' (or Leasing Agent) for his father's Oil Company as what he was doing during his year off. It sounds grander than a ditch digger and looks far more impressive on the State Department's official record.

Yale classmates, which he slavishly covered up for it by clowning?

This was his conscious, never-ending quest for identity. It became central to Bishop throughout his life. Why accept what his mother – or Annette for that matter – wanted?

He considered that the University of Southern California would have been so much easier. None of this disparagement of the purported Bitch Goddess Success. In some quarters, you weren't a man if you didn't make a lot of money.

There he'd have established relationships with his friends. He was from a prominent Californian family. There would be girls at school. He might even play football on the USC College team. He could be himself – or at least the boy he had been before he left for Yale.

* * *

The real and lasting influence Yale left Bishop with was an understanding and appreciation of Nihilism. Nietzsche on Nihilism was covered as part of a Yale education. It is a viewpoint where traditional values and beliefs (based on traditional theology) are unfounded.[78]

Nietzsche was interested in qualities that made for a superior human being. (Though, unlike Superman in American Comics, Nietzsche considered the psyche. He pondered what a psychologically superior man would be like.) Nietzsche said that evolution cannot be assumed to be finished. As humans have advanced beyond the apes in science, so the modern man would be psychologically more advanced than humans are today.

He concluded that supermen would make their own values. They would not follow the herd but be independently minded. They would make their own path.

Supermen might have to hurt people in the name of higher things. (This was permissible.) They may be selfish in strategic

---

[78] Friedrich Wilhelm Nietzsche is the founding philosopher of Nihilism. He had scorn for Christianity. In his book *The Antichrist* he postulates that Christianity makes people weak by regarding pity and similar sentiments as the highest virtues. He further professed that envy is a good thing. This is because envy informed the envious that what they envied is an indicator of what they wanted. He argued that Christianity was the religion of timid slaves who were too inept to take what they wanted.

ways. Greatness would be the reform of humanity to pagan values. The new men, among whom he was the first, would accept suffering as necessary in the context of acquiring good things. The superman would be hard for others to understand, and as a result would often be lonely.

Yet the supermen would be compassionate toward the weak as a display of the superman's great strength. Supermen would satisfy their sexual appetites however they like. They would not be humble. Instead, they would delight in their greatness. This greatness could be disturbing, but it would be the overall salvation for humanity. Significantly, Nietzsche held that salvation would be achieved through culture, art, and literature - not Christianity.

This captivated the young undergraduate during his senior year. The theories of Friedrich Nietzsche - including euthanasia for the mentally and physically unsound – made a comeback ten-years after World War Two. It was said that they were adjusted somewhat by Nietzsche's sister after his death to fit National Socialist (Nazi) theories and outlook.[79]

As it stood during Bishop's undergraduate years, the life Yale (and his mother) was preparing him for could be summed up as follows: Get a job. Go to work. Get married. Follow fashion. Act normal. Walk on the pavement. Watch TV. Obey the law. Save for your old age. Now repeat after me. "I am free."[80]

The key point that he retained started with the Ancient Greek Philosopher Heraclitus, later refined by Nietzsche. Heraclitus said that nothing in this world is constant except change and becoming. Friedrich Nietzsche agreed saying that everything, "will remain eternally right with Heraclitus' assertion that being is an empty fiction." You cannot arrive anywhere because of constant change. There is no place to arrive to. There is no there there.

We live in a chaotic world of perpetual change and becoming.[81]

---

[79] Her involvement to make it fit more neatly into National Socialist ideology is an analysis commonly put forward by Nietzsche's post-war philosopher/admirers. Christians and some philosophers think she did not have to try too hard.

[80] Author Unknown

[81] The term often used is self-overcoming (Selbstüberwindung). This is the process through which a great person can become a superman. To be the Übermensch is to rise above whatever life throws at the Great Person. This is how to *become*. If everything is in flux, so is morality. Thus, making one's own rules is more than adaptation. It is who a great man really is.

There are no fixed entities. Of course, Nietzsche might reply to Bishop, you *are* a billiard ball when substance, thing, and being are false concepts. If everything is change - and you are not directing it - the process of becoming is horrifying.

Bradford was smitten by this. For the college senior this explained why he lost sleep. If the alternative to change, reason, and being, are empty, then these cannot be eternal entities. How could anything be eternal if change is constant?

Nietzsche reasoned that, if the concept of reason and being support the concept of an after-life, then it would be what he called 'eternal recurrence.'[82] Nietzsche scorned conventional morality. He proposed that when people die they move on to relive their lives repeatedly eternally. Thus, one should do what one wants to do; thus, ensuring that one will relive a life of satisfaction again and again eternally.

Nietzsche was heralding an age *without* religion. This largely came to be in Europe as Europeans abandoned their Christian faith in the 20th century. In a sweeping statement Nietzsche famously said, "God is dead, and we have killed Him."

This had a lasting impact on the young undergraduate. Insofar as we know, he carried these beliefs with him throughout his life. They became his religion. If things passed him by and he felt like a huge billiard ball, Nihilism explained that this was in the nature of becoming. Achieving a goal was just another step toward becoming the Übermensch, the new man.

It is worth noting that the German word 'Übermensch' is translated into English as 'Superman.' American scholars impressed with Nietzsche's repudiation of morals and atheism resuscitated it, shortly after the National Socialists in Germany discredited it.[83] Few at Yale considered that there were still those in Europe who never saw the National Socialism version of Übermensch, discredited.

---

[82] The hourglass of existence is turned upside down, again and again.
[83] To summarize what is vital in understanding the murders the author offers this recap. The Übermensch lived above the 19th century world of pious burgers and the weak. He created new values of his own. He was above the others, as one alone on a mountain top would gaze down on a village of lesser people. This was the new man, mentally evolved beyond the superstitious, of which Nietzsche and his followers were the first.

All of this spoke to Bishop at Yale. The reason he perceived that things were going by too quickly was because there were no set things. Nothing was set in place, as it had been in Southern California. The only thing is the act of 'becoming.' This he adopted as his world view; yet he still could not sleep soundly.

He turned to hypnosis. At first this appeared to work. He put his forefinger in between the index and middle finger of the other hand, and he dozed off. It was what is called a 'hypnotic suggestion,' and a good way to take cat naps from time to time.

He was still perplexed when he returned to Yale. Of one thing he was certain; he wasn't going to scrape for tuition by digging ditches anymore. Telling the Yale yearbook that he was going to be a doctor was a good caption to put under his class picture.

Yet anyone who knew Brad would remember that he did not readily adjust to boredom. A medical office with a waiting room full of patients wasn't going to fulfill the adventurous part of him. A lifetime of earning certificates and the updating of his medical credentials, with the latest breakthroughs in health and prescription medicines, wasn't his style either.

He mused over what his father, ever the independent petroleum entrepreneur, did. Bradford Senior's life was the business of gambling on a calculated hunch. His was a life roaming the Mount Poso Field. It was about the freedom and the potential of living off your wits.

Bradford pondered over whether to return to California, and such pursuits as selling insurance. That life seemed so much more relaxed, and easier than climbing the stratified and seemingly pedigreed world of humid New England.

He considered returning to California. Had Yale changed him? His cohort of Yale companions had left the year before. It was as if he were 'left back' at school. It was time to gather himself up and leave. Perhaps he could pick up where he left off.

Still, for him, the 'sense of becoming' remained a guiding light. He would emerge. The adventurous outdoorsman responded to 'The Song of the Open Road,' by Walt Whitman. The Yale graduate responded to Nihilism. Now he would emerge from Yale's blustery cocoon, not quite clear on what it was to be free. But, for the moment there were other constraints.

Both his mother and Annette expected him to marry. There was the peacetime draft he had to deal with as well. For the moment, he would have to walk on the pavement whether he liked it or not.

Friedrich Nietzsche

"Egoism is the Very Essence of a Noble Soul"

Bradford Bishop Jr.

Yale Graduation Photo, circa 1959

Calhoun College Shield

Sneaky Pete

> "The CIC (The US Army's Counter Intelligence Corps) has more adventure stories buried in its secret files than a month's output of blood and thunder comic book... Unfortunately for the reading public, these bona fide cloak and dagger stories are not for publication."
>
> —William Attwood, *New York Herald Tribune* in [Paris] 1947.

Graduation was upon Bishop. Annette was in California. She and his parents would fly out to attend the Yale commencement ceremony. As if final exams were not stressful enough, he wanted to direct his future course in life. But now what?

Bradford had majored in American Studies. Even with the expanding demands for college graduates in nineteen-fifties America, a professional career requiring a further degree was an unlikely choice. That was fine with him. Bradford did not relish the thought of another monastic university environment. He wanted adventure. The risk-taking aspect of his character would not lay dormant for long. Then there was the draft. An American student at the time could seek a deferment until age 26.

He needed sound avuncular advice. The most natural thing in the world for a graduating member of the 'Houn was to talk with the House Father. Archibald Foord had been through this time and time again. Yale at this time was recruiting scholars for the Cold War.

There were four administrators on campus whom, at that time, did the recruiting. The most approachable of them was Archibald Foord himself. It is easy to picture the young Bachelor of American Studies candidate meeting with Foord, perhaps in the office.

Foord knew his boys. He knew Bradford was not a leader, nor was he highly organized. Some of his boys lacked common sense and/or sound judgment. Brad scraped along, drank beer with his cohort, and read *the Record*. The Army would set that right.

The Army was then seeking out soldiers with high scores on intelligence tests.[84] The United States Army Security Agency (ASA)

---

[84] Only a High School Diploma was required at that time.

gradually took over army signal intelligence operations. Starting in 1945 and lasting until 1976, the ASA monitored and translated broadcasts and military communications from the Soviet Union, and other communist states. What they needed were translators and analysts. William Bradford Bishop Jr. was already fluent in Italian. He was not stupid, just doped up on serax.

The ASA was specifically looking for linguists, communications, and electronics personnel for special assignments. For a young man who wanted to get out, to take to the open road, the world before him, this was an option worth looking into. There were even postings in Italy.

The recruitment flier was alluring too. "Get a chance to see the world," and "have an opportunity for sky-high adventure." ASA billed itself as a 'topflight organization." This was tailor made for the new graduate. Brad wanted to go on to something: exciting, daring, risky. During the Cold War ASA was it.

* * *

There was also a loose end. That loose end was Annette back in California. She had gone to the University of California at Berkley. She had majored in Art and she was graduating as well. She and Lobelia had grown close. The two shared a resemblance. Strangers sometimes took them to be mother and daughter.

Bradford decided to 'go with the flow.' He would marry Annette and take it from there. All of this was soon after his graduation. He married on August 2nd, took a brief honeymoon in Northern California,[85] and then enlisted into the Army in New York City on August 7th, 1959.

The wedding itself was held in California, on the terrace at Annette's parent's new home in San Clemente. It was a late afternoon ceremony on a high bluff overlooking the Pacific. Brad's high school friend, Ronald Currie, was his best man.

Ron had traveled with Brad to Mexico on outings. On one

---

[85] They honeymooned at the Riverside Alpine Hotel in Truckee, California in Squaw Valley. The hotel is known for its paranormal activity. Particularly good looking, young ladies have complained of being pinched on their bottoms while in the hotel.

such outing they were trapped all night, under a boat, during a storm. It was bracing. It was high adventure.

The wedding seemed to be a return to normalcy, the sleepless Yale years were behind him. It was all very Californian. Brad was walking on the pavement again.

He, was a Yale graduate, and a Delta Kappa Epsilon fraternity member. She graduated from the University of California Berkley and was a member of Kappa Alpha Theta (sorority). It could not have seemed more wholesome. Perhaps his four-year hitch in the Army would further 'straighten him out.'

Unusual for Yale graduates, Bishop started his military career as an enlisted man. (This would not surprise those who knew him.) Yale graduates who were interested in espionage typically entered the military as officers or CIA. Bishop did his basic training at Fort Benning, Georgia with the US 23rd infantry. He rose in rank to staff sergeant. Officially, insofar as State knew, that was all there was to it. (That and his good conduct medal.)

The Korean War record of the 23rd infantry, prior to his enlistment, was impressive. So, State's security clearance process went no further. Yet there was more to his tour in the military.

In fact, Bishop went on to serve with the Army Intelligence Agency (ASA). He and Annette moved to the married couple's quarters of Fort Holabird, Maryland. That was on the record too. What did not appear on the State Department radar, was what private William Bradford Bishop did *after* boot camp and at Fort Holabird.

He took an honorable discharge for immediate reenlistment into the Regular Army on June 15th 1960. His Military Occupational Specialty (MOS) was Military Intelligence Specialist (Investigator).[86] Yes. G-2, counterintelligence.

Fort Holabird was a spy school. The mission was to provide electronic communication security in support of US armies in the field, and the *National Defense Effort.* Central to this was Electronic Intelligence and Signals Intelligence (ELINT and SIGINT).

Fort Holabird (At that time the US Army Intelligence Training

---

[86] His Serial Number was 12-582-987, Security File Number H9-001-930, Selective Service Number 4-92-36-228, Social Security Number 12-582-987. The Army gave him a passport on July 6, 1961, Number B-441123 for official travel to Italy for two years.

Center) is located in the southeast corner of the City of Baltimore. It was established in 1918 along a marshy area near Colgate Creek. Originally 96 acres, it grew to 350 acres with 286 buildings. It was close to Washington with easy access to the capitol via road, water, and rail.

It had a long military history. This included the military's first test of a proposed vehicle for the army. The vehicle met all standards and then some. That was in 1940, and the vehicle was called the 'Jeep.'

Tanks were tested there as well. Some of the locals still called the place where they were tested, 'tank hill.' By the time Bradford Bishop and Annette reported to the married couples' quarters, Fort Holabird had been converted into a 'spy school.'

Officially it was a US Army Intelligence School and Counter Intelligence Records Facility. Upon induction, a fateful assignment decision was made. It was about the shape of Bishop's head. It made him look like a man from Northern Albania.[87]

At the time Northern Albanians were moving into Yugoslavia. They migrated to the part of Serbia adjacent to Albania. It was called Kosovo. There were more economic opportunities in Kosovo than in Albania. By the time Bradford was assigned to learn Serbo-Croatian, Northern Albanians were a growing presence in Kosovo. With language training, in a pinch, he could pass as a 'Kosovar.'

Language training was at the Defense Language Institute in Monterey, California. So, with the new post he was returning to California. Annette announced her pregnancy. She delivered a baby boy while at the Defense Language Institute, William Bradford Bishop III.

William Bradford Bishop Sr. and Lobelia could not have been more pleased. Old classmates of South Pasadena High heard the news and sent their congratulations. It was all very conventional.

And where did that leave Bradford? Bradford got to graduate as a military linguist in Serbo-Croatian. Afterward, and throughout his military career, he would be known as a "Monterey Mary."[88]

---

[87] It has been suggested that he had 'Bogomil' characteristics. Many of the Bogomil, in what would become Yugoslavia, converted to Islam.

[88] Monterey Mary was army slang for a translator who came out of the Defense Language Institute.

He got his Top-Secret Security Clearance on March 14, 1962. He'd work in a shift. ASA was operating a 24-hour, 7-day week radio surveillance and intercept operation. And, best of all, it was secret. ASA personnel were so secret that they could not discuss their work among themselves, unless they were in a secure location.[89] No fraternity secret handshake could match that. What's more, there were opportunities in this new field of espionage. America was far behind in the spy game.

* * *

American Intelligence operations did not have a good track record after the Second World War. Indeed, when it came to Counter Intelligence in 1945, America hadn't a clue. And Washington knew it.

At the time Bradford Bishop started in Counter Intelligence, American efforts were still dependent on the large espionage network set up by Reinhardt Gehlen, the former chief of Nazi intelligence from 1944 to 1945.

Major General Gehlen reported on Soviet activity. He reported directly to Adolf Hitler. He saw, more plainly than anyone, that the War was lost. In early 1944 he started planning for the future. He called his key men in and instructed them to copy and hide all files regarding the Soviet Armed Forces. His men concealed them in the Austrian Alps. When Hitler fired him on April 8, 1945, Gehlen put his plan in action. He started by surrendering to the Americans.

His interrogator, Captain John Bokor, was thinking the same way the higher ups in Washington were thinking. The next enemy would be the Soviet Union, and here was Hitler's Spy Master. The US took the bait.

America's leaders were practical. They set aside War Crimes investigations; and set Gehlen up in the same role he had under Hitler. The only proviso was that he was *not* to employ war criminals. This he pledged to do. It was a pledge that, at great cost to the West, he did not keep.

Gehlen knew that his spy service had to become as large as

---

[89] This was another aspect frequently downplayed by investigators, though not by the Bishop neighbors.

possible; and quickly too. The CIA was a fledgling organization at the time. Gehlen's reasoning was that the larger his agency grew, filling the vacuum, the more indispensable it became. Accordingly, he was able to hire former Gestapo, SS,[90] and SD[91] members.

As part of this, he exaggerated Soviet strength and, on a number of occasions, predicted a blitzkrieg-style Soviet invasion of the West. By the time Bishop entered into ASA training the CIA wanted more control. The CIA wanted independent operations of their own.

The situation got worse by 1949, when the North Atlantic Treaty Organization (NATO) was formed. NATO meant that all intelligence, along with plans and counter measures, were shared information. It was then that the Soviets came out with a counter intelligence masterstroke of their own. They would blackmail those Germans then working for the West.

The strategy was simple. America had a great many war criminals on its payroll. Soviet agents cornered those agents, showed them the damning evidence, and threatened to expose them. This was not an idle threat. There were still many in the NATO alliance who wanted to hang them.

For war criminals on America's payroll, there wasn't any choice. In any event, Gehlen had already been inflating the Soviet threat. Besides, America's espionage agents were new and few. How would America know it if it was being lied to?[92]

---

[90] The Schutzstaffel was a major paramilitary organization under Adolf Hitler, Himmler, and the National Socialist German Workers' Party.
[91] Sicherheitsdienst (Security Service), full title *Sicherheitsdienst des Reichsführers-SS*, or SD, was the intelligence agency of the SS and the Nazi Party in Nazi Germany.
[92] It has been estimated by some, that up to 90% of all the information passed on to the United States was incorrect.

1945 Photo

The Americans learned quickly. They had to. The odds were stacked against them. It was estimated that the KGB was "the world's largest intelligence and police agency, probably larger than all Western intelligence agencies combined."

After the Second World War, US Counterintelligence Corps (CIC) had to play it fast and loose. There were no guidelines, no rules. The CIC and the Soviet's KGB made up the rules as the spy game went along. It was a chaotic situation.

Included in this was SIGNET (electronic transmissions) and COMSEC (military communications). Cryptanalysis involved the enciphering and deciphering of messages in secret code. Continuing advances in electronic techniques and devices increased the potential of electrical warfare put the fledgling American espionage effort under strain. The Army's CIC kept up radio surveillance, often improvising and working out of the back seat of a car.

Ultimately, they folded this operation into the Army Security Agency (ASA). The ASA manned remote listening posts around the world. ASA sent out the call just before Bradford got out of Yale.⁹³

They needed US citizens of good character and discretion. They needed loyal Americans, with an emphasis on 'personal habits and traits of character unquestionable from a security standpoint.' At that point they didn't care about academics. They wanted enlistees who could pass the intelligence test.

There was more, much more. The ASA wasn't just secretive in day to day operations. It was secretive to the point where ASA personnel could *never* divulge any information. There was no time limit to this. ASA personnel were to take their secrets to the grave.

Bradford Bishop was sent to Italy and Austria. He was a non-commissioned officer and there to monitor radio transmissions from Yugoslavia. For many the 24-hour, seven-day a week watch could be tedious and hum drum. Bishop, however, worked his way into the confidences of undercover agents. He always seemed to be off to the side in huddles with them.

What is known is that he was assigned to infiltrate the Yugoslav Ski team while it was engaged in regional competition in Italy. A great deal has been said of this. Uncorroborated testimony has it that he, himself, claimed that he failed miserably. Witnesses who knew him said that he said that he was successful. He also is reported to have said that he was 'running a man' in Yugoslavia.⁹⁴

What is verified is that he posed as a student of Serbo-Croatian literature. The Yugoslavian Ski Team was in Italy for regional games. Whether he enjoyed any measure of success can only be verified by the authorities. Those authorities have not released any further information at the time of this writing.

There is something else that is noteworthy. There is some evidence that Staff Sergeant Bradford Bishop served on covert missions. Such a mission, or missions, could only be on a volunteer basis. It is highly likely that a risk-taker like Bishop would volunteer.

---

⁹³ ASA, in its turn, was ultimately folded into the National Security Agency (NSA). The NSA was, and is, more secretive than the CIA. This attracted Bradford, but it also would play a far more important role in his life than he could have anticipated.

⁹⁴ Both observations may be true. As the Cold War saying goes, 'You don't recruit ustaše, the ustaše recruits you.'

In such a case, he'd be on the inside of something bigger. It is entirely likely that he saw it as 'breaking the boredom' of listening to and analyzing routine Yugoslav broadcasts day after day. His language proficiency, training, and physical appearance made him an ideal candidate.

Such an incursion would almost certainly be directed at Yugoslavia, which at that time was under Marshall Tito. This was a time when World War Two operations of armed reconnaissance and infiltration, while winding down, were still options. Indeed, the CIA coordinated with ASA cryptographers. Those involved referred to each other in private as 'Wally the Spook." [95] Sneaky Pete, was the name adopted by earlier generation of covert warriors.

Typical of those who 'served in silence,' a Wally the Spook figure was sometimes pinned to the inside of their coats. When in the presence of another ASA veteran, they would flash Wally the Spook. Thus, nothing was said. The lifetime code of silence was not broken. Yet everything was said.

Sneaky Pete and Wally the Spook were two original nicknames for Special Forces soldiers before they were authorized to wear the Green Beret. For anyone analyzing what Bradford Bishop was doing on covert missions, his fluency in Serbo-Croatian and his Northern Albanian appearance can only point to the Croatian Coastline.[96]

---

[95] Inferential evidence holds that when anonymous agents debriefed Vietnam Generation soldiers, they referred to the man who debriefed them as "Wally." (As in, "did you speak to Wally yet?")

[96] There is circumstantial evidence for this. After the murders, Bishop's psychiatrist Frank Caprio attested that Bradford Bishop occasionally worked for the CIA. If so, he downplayed it and kept the rest in doctor/patient confidentiality. Dayton Lummis, Bishop's roommate during his senior year at Yale indirectly supports this contention. The author respects Mr. Lummis' commitment to remain silent on some of the important details.

ASK YOUR US ARMY RECRUITER ABOUT THE

UNITED STATES ARMY SECURITY AGENCY

AN ELITE ORGANIZATION OFFERING THE FINEST IN TECHNICAL TRAINING AND CAREER OPPORTUNITIES FOR THE SERVICEMAN INTERESTED IN HIS FUTURE

Wally the Spook

The Incursion

> In individuals, insanity is rare; but in groups, parties, nations and epochs, it is the rule.
>
> —Friedrich Nietzsche

Yugoslavia, or the South Slav Nation, was a complicated country in 1963. It was a country made up of many peoples. In 1914, the Imperial Habsburgs who ruled from Vienna, in what is now Austria, controlled much of it. At that time, Serbia was on the border of the Habsburg Empire. There was tension along that border. So much so that the First World War erupted along that, divide, with the assassination of the heir to the Habsburg throne.

Part of that Empire was Croatia. It was, and remains, a staunchly Roman Catholic area. Nearby Serbia was Orthodox Christian. When the First World War erupted Croatian units, serving in the Habsburg Imperial Army, faced Serb forces. The War got ugly as German Armies joined in to support the Austro-Croatian units; Imperial Russia sided with their fellow Slavs, the Serbians. New weapons, such as mustard gas, brought the carnage and horror of war to levels never before imagined.

When peace came, the Austro-Hungarian Empire dissolved. Croatia and other Habsburg areas were handed over to the Serbs. The new nation "Yugoslavia" was a patchwork of nationalities under the victorious Serbs. Yet there were enormous fissures under the surface.[97]

As the old Empire disintegrated, the Croats found themselves occupied by the Serbs. The Serbian king became the king of Yugoslavia. Croats who had worn Imperial uniforms just a short time before suddenly found themselves in Serbian ones. If the casual observer could but consider that both sides were shooting at each other a year or so before; and that now one side was in

---

[97] The Croats were promised autonomy at the close of the First World War and did not get it.

charge, it is easy to understand the Croat's most common comment. When asked about the situation in the new country of Yugoslavia, the answer was, "It is complicated."[98]

While under what contemporaries regarded as 'foreign rule,' the curse of King Zvonimir (Reign 1064 – 1075 and 1089) grew. Zvonimir was murdered and, according to Croat tradition, the dying Zvonimir said: *"May God never give you a king of your own blood".* (Or, for the days of castles and feudalism, may God make you foreign vassals. Or, in some translations, a foreign language would rule over the Croats for a thousand years.)

The Croats of 1919 needed only look at their present situation to recall the legend. It came as no surprise that they were not unhappy when, in 1941, the German armed forces crushed Yugoslavia in six weeks. The Germans carved Croatia out of Yugoslavia. Now the Croats had a country of their own. There were, however, further complications.

This time it came in the form of the long-time Croat overseas opposition to Yugoslavia. For decades it was led from across the Adriatic Sea in Italy. This organization in exile was known as the ustaše (Struggle). They had been violent prior to 1941 and had collaborated with the Italian Fascists, that is until they assassinated Alexander 1st,[99] the King of Yugoslavia, while he was on a visit to Marseilles, France.

It was October 9, 1934 when the King got off the KJRM Destroyer Dubrovnik, the ship that transported him to the port of Marseilles. He got into an open car with the French Foreign Minister, Louis Barthou, on his left. A small escort of guards, armed with sabers and revolvers, rode on horseback behind their car. A huge crowd lined the street.

No one was prepared for the frontal attack launched out of the crowd. The assassin got off over ten shots. The King, who suffered from stomach typhus for years, died before he could get to hospital.

---

[98] There is striking evidence that the Croats may have been given independence had the Archduke Franz Joseph not been assassinated in Sarajevo in 1914, though under the Habsburg crown. That, however, would have taken at least another 20 years of peace.

[99] King Alexander lost three members of his family on a Tuesday. He refused to undertake any public functions on that day of the week. However, he had to keep to schedule when the Yugoslav Ship Dubrovnik docked. The day he was assassinated October 9, 1934, was a Tuesday.

The Chauffer was killed instantly and French Foreign Minister Barthou died of his wounds. All told 15 people were injured.

The triggerman was a member of a pro-Bulgarian Macedonian organization, and an expert marksman.[100] He traveled with three Croats who were ustaše. All were rounded up, but not before a mounted French policeman cut the assassin down. The crowd then beat the assassin to death. It was all very Balkan.

King Alexander of Yugoslavia on the KJRM Dubrovnik
As he prepares to debark in Marseilles on a Tuesday

Ante Pavelić, the ustaše leader, was Benito Mussolini's protégé. It was alleged that 'professional criminals' were 'trained in the territory of a foreign state.' Yugoslavia, Czechoslovakia, and Rumania charged Hungary with complicity. As at the outset of World War One, violence in the Balkans threatened the peace of Europe.

Ustaše leaders were rounded up and imprisoned. Among them was Ante Pavelić. He is quoted as saying, "Assassination is the only

---

[100] The assassin himself was a member of the pro-Bulgarian Internal Macedonian Revolutionary Organization (IMRO or VMRO) founded in 1893 in Salonika. Initially its aim was to gain autonomy for Macedonia and Adrianople regions in the Ottoman Empire, but later it became an agent serving Bulgarian interests in Balkan politics.(Bulgaria claimed the area as part of Greater Bulgaria) The Former Yugoslavian Republic of Macedonia, now an independent nation-state, is still the subject of similar international disputes.

language the Serbs understand."

For European observers in October 1934, the Great War was still fresh in memory. Although Americans did not think of this act as touching off the Second World War, there were many in Europe who saw the machinery of the next Great War put in motion. That it did.

A far larger risk-taker than Bradford Bishop moved to draw Ante Pavelić out of jail and out of exile. After the successful invasion, Hitler installed Pavelić as leader of the new state of Croatia. The Slavs would be slaves. And the ustaše were not sorry to see the policy executed.

This change in Yugoslavia leads us into a dark corner of the story, and to the dark corners of both the Second World War and the Cold War. For the Bradford Bishop murders this is the back story, and it starts with concentration camps and flows into the Cold War.

A salient characteristic, of the extermination camps in the former Yugoslavia was that the camps were filled with Orthodox Serbs. (Jews and Gypsies appear to have been added on the insistence of Nazi Germany) Ante Pavelić and the ustaše had their own agenda.

It dovetailed with the National Socialist agenda in Germany. This was particularly so in that they were settling old scores, not with the French, but with the Orthodox Serbs, dating back to betrayal of the treaty at the end of the First World War. (And earlier)

Hitler's new order planned to eliminate Christianity and replace it with a Nordic mix of beliefs, including pagan elements. Nietzsche, somewhat modified, would be the new Europe's philosopher general. As Nietzsche foretold, the National Socialist movement sought to displace the current religions of Europe. The Germans were not particularly anti-Orthodox. Ante Pavelić and the ustaše, were.[101]

Their program was to kill one third of the Orthodox Serbs, convert another third to Roman Catholicism, and exile the remaining third. Those they killed were often thrown into death camps with

---

[101] It is a curiosity that Hitler regarded the Roman Catholic Church as more threatening than other Christian denominations. This was because it was highly organized and potentially an opposition within occupied countries. Croatia was an exception.

Jews, Roma, and political dissidents. Vjekoslav Maks Luburić was the commander-in-chief of all NDH (independent state of Croatia) concentration camps. He particularly signaled out the Jasenovac Concentration Camp as highly efficient. Ante Pavelić trusted Luburić and personally instructed him on the extermination of the Serbs.

Jasenovac was established by the NDH, not Nazi Germany. The brutality of the NDH camps, were beyond anything found in camps run by the German SS. The camp guards tried to use gas, but mostly employed manual methods. They used sharp or blunt craftsman tools: hammers, knives, saws, etc. It is notable that ustaše were known for smashing skulls with sledgehammers. A German major observing the slaughter was so sickened by this that he filed a report, objecting to the NDH methods, and sent it to Berlin. (Gas was so much cleaner and more efficient.)

Concentration Camp victim

SS Handschar Division off-duty, killed with a hammer. Pictured here... 'just kidding around'

Yugoslavia liberated itself. The resistance to the Axis powers was more successful in Yugoslavia than anywhere else in Nazi Occupied Europe. Although most of the successful fighting was led by other-than-communists, it is now known that Soviet Agents in the British Secret Service manipulated reports to make it look like the Communists were the most successful insurgents. A Communist Marshal named Tito led the Communists these agents promoted.

Consequently, British weapons and materiel were sent to Marshal Tito. This war materiel, and the German withdrawal to confront the advancing Soviet armies, left Tito in command at the end of the War. In the aftermath of the Second World War, an urgent question surfaced: Who was Tito?

Josip Broz Tito, a captured Austro-Hungarian Sergeant Major of the First World War, later joined the revolution that formed the new Soviet Union. He then returned to the newly formed nation of Yugoslavia. When the Germans defeated the Yugoslavian Army, he became a partisan. The victorious Soviets, dominating Eastern Europe, thought that he'd support them. They initially thought Tito would do as they wanted. They were wrong.

Here is where the nature of Tito's rule and the Yugoslavian Espionage Agency (UDBA) come into play. Communist Yugoslavia was not going to be a Soviet Satellite. The Soviet KGB was violent. The UDBA, in comparison, was excessively violent.[102] It was as if they didn't just want to kill. They wanted everyone to know that it was they who did the killing. People who knew their trademarks, their 'wetwork,' would only mutter, "Only the UDBA kills like that."

* * *

Very little was known about the 1963 incursion into the Socialist Federal Republic of Yugoslavia (SFRY). There has always been more information available about the latter, 1972 incursion. The 1972 incursion was the one that Maks Luburić was planning, and anticipating, the day before he was assassinated in Carcaixent.

Mak's planned incursion was always brought forward by Tito's Yugoslavia. Tito would say, after the 1963 incursion, that the remaining fascists after the Second World War were a clear and present danger. Historians of the period now generally believe that Tito knew all about the 1972 incursion beforehand and played the NHB incursion for all it was worth in their propaganda.

The 1963 incursion was different. It was an incursion that took

---

[102] It has been said that the two people who kept Stalin awake at night was Tito with his UDBA, and Carl Gustaf Emil Mannerheim sixth president of Finland. (Who fought him to a standstill in the Russo-Finnish War)

the government in Belgrade by surprise.[103] It was to be staged on July 4, 1963. A team of 13 Croats originating in Australia was to assemble in Northern Italy and enter Yugoslavia through Austria. They would then disburse and spark a rebellion in Croatia.

At the close of World War Two there was considerable emigration of Yugoslavs to Australia. Among the Croat émigrés were ustaše members. Ustaše members trained in remote areas in the Australian outback. The site they used in the Wodonga Military Region in the state of Victoria, Australia, was particularly active.[104] They trained in the old uniforms. They trained with automatic weapons and high explosives.

Some formed active terrorist cells. There would be bombings of the Yugoslav Consulate-General, the Yugoslav Embassy in Canberra, and other targets. The cells used parcel bombs as well.

The 1963 incursion was code named Action Kangaroo. The Incursion, and later HRB activities, would pose serious questions for the Australian government. Action Kangaroo cannot be wholly disregarded in any analysis of the Bradford Bishop case.

Bradford Bishop was then an experienced Serbo-Croatian hand. He was stationed near the targeted area. At this point, the end of his tour of duty, Staff Sergeant Bishop was a valuable US asset. It was impossible for him *not* to know about this incursion when it transpired. After the Australian-based team went into action, it is difficult to imagine that he did *not* play a role in this.

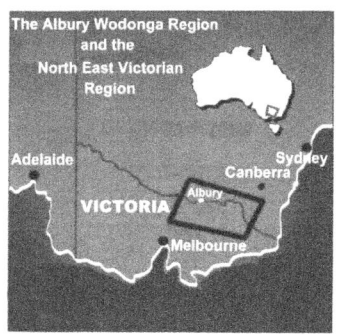

The Australian team included two HRB members and seven other Croatian-Australians. The organization that the average Australian of 1963 might have come across, in Australia, was the Croatian Liberation Movement, HOP (Hrvatski Oslobodilacki Pokret). HOP

---

[103] It appears to have taken the Western Powers by surprise as well. Although what role the West played beyond arresting one member of the incursion team is still an open question.

[104] Training Headquarters for Action Kangaroo was the Sydney Catholic Office, at 121 Queen Street, Woollahra. This office was run by a Priest, Rocque Romac.

became the leading body of Croatian movements. It was a widespread organization. It could be found wherever the postwar Croatian Diaspora settled: Canada, the United States, Europe, and Australia. The Australian branch alone had up to 5,000 members around the time of the incursion. HOP was a political organization.

The HRB, however, was a fighting organization. For the HRB, resistance and opposition were about assassination and rebellion. In Australia it was first formed with four emigrants who codenamed it, Command Post Number Four. Number One was in Croatia; number two in Europe (primarily in Germany and Italy) and number three in then fascist Spain. (Where Maks Luburić was)

The roles were that Area Command Four (Australia) would raise funds for the operations, Area Command Two (Europe) would stage the operations into Command Area One (Croatia). Their operational procedures were highly secretive. Members could not mention anything related in public places. Correspondence was coded, etc.

These and other operational procedures kept the group secret. They trained with relative freedom. HRB members were largely unknown within any of the Yugoslav communities, or by the Australian Government, until after Action Kangaroo played itself out. Indeed when the Australian Citizen Military Force (CMF or the Australian Reserve) were conducting exercises on a Saturday afternoon in 1962, in a remote part of Victoria State, they came upon a unit of uniformed ustaše.

The Australian reserve was surprised to see the ustaše trainees along the River Murray. The surprised members of the CMF were cordial. Indeed, the members of the CMF did not recognize the Ustaše or the uniforms they were wearing.

The CMF demonstrated explosives. The young ustaše trainees were interested in the Reserve's armored car. Obligingly the Australian Reservists let the trainees pose for snapshots in the CMF's armored vehicle. It later turned out to be what Americans call a "photo op," this one with pictures of uniformed ustaše holding sub-machine guns.[105]

---

[105] The picture appeared in the HOP magazine *Spremnost*. The caption read, "Today the River Murray; [Australia] Tomorrow on the Drina.' [in the SFRY] The local CMF commander had to back-peddle when confronted with the magazine report. He said that it was an opportunity for a low scale recruiting drive.

The secrecy of Action Kangaroo cannot be understated. Those selected would be secret even from those training along the River Murray in Australia. The team of nine was arranged in groups of three. Each group (cell) would have a commander, an intelligence officer, and an explosives expert.

To ensure maximum security, each cell was composed of relatives or close friends. The only person with any contact with the cell's other HRB members would be the commander. The nine were to recruit and spread small-scale operations within the SFRY.

Like the UDBA, the HRB wanted the SFRY to know that it was they who did the killing. The insurgents were instructed to leave "HRB," their calling card, in their wake. Whatever they sabotaged, or whomever they assassinated, there would be no doubt that the fascist style brutality of the Second World War had returned.

In this manner, it was thought, the insurgency would be unbreakable. The incursion would spread. And so, the members left sporadically for Stuttgart, in what was then West Germany. There they were further instructed in assassination methods, given targets for demolition, and the next phase of the rebellion.

Though highly secretive, and able to enter the SFRY without detection, all nine were rounded up by the SFRY militia within two weeks. One of the reasons for this was that the insurgents were woefully undersupplied. This is an indicator that the United States had nothing to do with the incursion. (Or did not want it to be successful) Were the US working with the three squads, there would have been adequate supplies for the insurgency.

Another reason for mission failure was that the team arrived unexpectedly. The Croatian population did not welcome the nine as anticipated. One of their instructions, to leave a card with HRB on or near any official they assassinated, could only have isolated the existing Croat population further. The Croats wanted independence; they did not want the return of anyone associated with the holocaust.

There were further setbacks. The early removal of a key cell leader destabilized the entire operation. The three squads (cells) tried to communicate with each other, but the attempts to coordinate the three were not successful.

It is here where the ASA comes in. Action Kangaroo was a

secret, too secret. Then it became public, too public. Given the resources the ASA had at the height of its involvement in monitoring the Cold War era SFRY, it is highly likely that the ASA's Defense against Sound Equipment (DASE) was on top of the situation once radio signals from the cells were transmitted.

This crisis was tailor-made for Staff Sergeant Bishop. He was the man who could decipher and investigate the intricacies of the nascent rebellion. He was also accustomed to secret liaisons behind his wife's back and passed himself off as a descendant of a notable Mayflower Pilgrim. As one who was habitually in a huddle with the higher-ups, he was also a man who could make use of another deception.

The ASA plainly saw the drawbacks in Staff Sergeant Bishop's character. He was widely regarded in the army as a "screw-up." He was noted for security violations. By 1963 his superiors were exasperated. He simply didn't understand strict security; and was reprimanded for it. Because of this he never rose beyond the rank of Staff Sergeant.

Nor would he have a future in the ASA or any espionage organization. Yet he was a good man to have a beer with. (That Yale humor, and the easy-going nature he got from his father, carried him through). Yet like many an army goldbricker he could rally in a pinch. Now he was needed, and this was big.

Everything fell into place. Bishop was originally chosen because he looked like he was from Yugoslavia. He did not necessarily appear to be a Serb or a Serbian ally. He could pass as a Croatian ally, or even as a Croat.

He was fit. He had passed his army physical exam 13 days before. Not to pull him in to monitor and decipher this situation given his experience would have been negligent. Screw-up or not, he was the man on the spot. Such an emergency is what the US government was paying him for.[106]

---

[106] Staff Sargent Bishop, at this time, worked with the then new Defense Intelligence Agency. He could have been given false documentation as a cover, kept it, and used it in his escape.

The Best and the Brightest

Everything in this world is a reflection of the basic needs of man + nothing else –
—*An entry in Bradford Bishop's Diary*

"The true man wants two things: danger and play. For that reason, he wants woman, as the most dangerous plaything."
—Friedrich Nietzsche

After the incursion Bishop stayed on in Italy. He applied for, and was accepted by, Middlebury College's program in Florence, Italy. The University of Florence hosted the students. The recently discharged Bishop took 30 credits in Italian; he attended the summer session too. That wasn't problematic; it was what he did during spring break that got him into trouble.

Barely eight months after his honorable discharge, Bishop took his wife on spring break holiday to Yugoslavia. Although the Dalmatian Coast of Croatia is picturesque, and he was a Serbo-Croatian linguist, this visit was flirting with danger. Nothing he could have done after his honorable discharge could have horrified ASA more.

Had anyone recognized him he could easily have been jailed for spying. At this time, anyone with a top-secret clearance who crossed into a Communist Bloc country would have been detained at the border. The KGB and UDBA kept files on anyone in military intelligence at that time, however lowly their grade or status.[107] Given that the nine would-be commandos from the previous year's incursion were in custody and awaiting trial, a military intelligence specialist could have scored Marshal Tito a propaganda coup.

In 1964 the U-2 incident of 1960 was fresh in mind. Francis Gary Powers was the pilot who flew a U-2 spy plane for the American CIA over the Soviet Union in 1960. The high-altitude plane was equipped with cameras, which could focus on, and take photos of, Soviet installations with astonishing accuracy and detail. As it flew too high for missiles to shoot down, it was regarded as a secure and reliable way of gathering information.

---

[107] The KGB was the intelligence and internal-security agency of the former Soviet Union, organized in 1954 and responsible for enforcement of security regulations, protection of political leaders, the guarding of borders, and clandestine operations abroad.

The Soviet Union's technicians, however, had developed a missile that could shoot the U-2 down. For some time, they were hoping to get their shot at one. On a reconnaissance mission during the Soviet May Day holiday, the target presented itself.

The flight path Francis Gary Powers was assigned was the longest flight thus far attempted by the U-2. It is notable that President Eisenhower, himself an ex-military commander, said of the lengthening U-2 flights; if you fly in a straight line long enough, you will be shot down. Francis Gary Powers *was* shot down over the USSR. Soviet Premier Nikita Khrushchev was livid over the violation of Soviet airspace during a national holiday. He then, cunningly, set a trap.

Soviet relations with the West were thawing. It looked like the United States and the Soviet Union would be able to live with each other in peace. A four-power summit (US, USSR, UK and France) was long scheduled for May 7th. Parts of the downed U-2 were displayed. Convinced that a U-2 pilot could not have survived the crash, the United States came up with a cover story that a weather plane strayed off course. The US went on to say that the weather plane had difficulties with its oxygen equipment.

Khrushchev waited. At the conference he pounced. The American president stated to the international press that there were no such spy flights. Khrushchev called the American story 'silly,' and produced Francis Gary Powers.

Eisenhower had to appear before the US Congress to explain. If Action Kangaroo and the pictures along the River Murray were embarrassments for the Australian government, America had tripped into one of the greatest intelligence embarrassments of the 20th century. This was an international disaster.

Powers got a cold reception when he returned to the US. He had been heavily interrogated. He had been tried in a Soviet show trial and was exchanged for a Soviet spy caught in New York City.[108] Powers claimed he did not divulge any critical information. He was discredited for years thereafter.

This is what Charles Peterson, Intelligence Operations Specialist,

---

[108] This was the plot of the movie "Bridge of Spies."

had to relate in his April 16th security evaluation of 1965. He knew Bradford Bishop well. He had to be diplomatic. Bishop was a man of low standards, yet fun to be with during informal gatherings. Just one year prior to this, Staff Sergeant Bishop was given a dressing down for failing to secure classified information. He had put it in a colleague's desk drawer. The next day he was asked where he had put it. He had forgotten. When it was found Bishop simply said that locking it up in the safe was 'too much bother.'

In picturing the situation, it might be helpful to visualize Bishop as a proto-hippie. This came at the time of America's first 'love-ins' on the beaches of California. California has always been a harbinger of America's changing mood. After the military, and while in school in Florence, he decided that 'love' was the central motivating force in his life. Italy, like most of Europe, took in American movies. These films were crafted for constant titillation but contained no nudity. They were aimed at the same 'passion pit,' drive-in circuit that screened teen movies, with wink-wink titles like 'Beach Party' (1963).[109]

These brief few years were a transitional stage to the 'love-ins,[110]'which sprang up in America shortly after. Like many, Bishop responded to it by imbuing the concept of love with already established beliefs. 'Love is compatible with ambition, egoism, and, special destiny,' he concluded. Digging even deeper was the bedrock layer of success both California and his mother put there. Bishop can be more easily understood if viewed in this context.

Bishop was a known quantity in the ASA. At this time of his life it would be difficult to find anyone who would put him in charge of anything. But, by touring an area of the Communist East, where he could be recognized, had shocked those who had worked with him to the core.

With the U-2 incident still stinging American surveillance operations, just the thought of Bishop and his wife detained, and associated with a Nazi-revival incursion, was chilling. Nikita Khrushchev was still in power in the Soviet Union at the time the Bishops toured Yugoslavia. For Tito, a similar American

---

[109] American International Productions (AIP) movies
[110] A love-in is a peaceful public gathering focused on meditation, love, music, sex and/or use of psychedelic drugs.

embarrassment would be as welcome as Maks' assassination.

Peterson wrote a stiff evaluation. In polite, yet unmistakable military jargon, he pointed out the candidate's flaws. No amount of California laxity could excuse them. In true government fashion, the list of Bishop's flaws started with security.

The incident of two years prior to Bishop's entry into the Foreign Service was still fresh in Peterson's mind. Losing a classified document had endangered his colleague in whose desk it was later found. Bishop had left classified containers unlocked and unattended. This alone would have been enough to sink a promising career in the American Foreign Service.

There is additional evidence that Bishop traveled to Germany, both officially and *on his own,* and there contacted someone he should not have spoken with. It is tantalizing to speculate who this might have been. It could have been Reinhardt Gehlen or someone who was a part of the Gehlen Organization. It could have been a person or persons associated with the Anti-Tito movement there, some of whom were former members of Gehlen's prewar spy network (or both).[111]

While politely noting that Bishop was not without research and administrative abilities, Peterson saw Bishop as someone without a great deal of common sense. Recommending Bishop 'for closely supervised field work' and noting that Bishop was incapable of selecting, training or supervising a staff spoke volumes. Anyone reading this would have been blinded by the number of red flags popping out of this letter of reference. Not so State.

The US Department of State simply noted that his candidacy for Foreign Service Officer was terminated due to a possible heart murmur. His background investigation was ordered on November 12, 1964. The Medical Clearance was denied on Christmas Eve, 1964. That should have been that.[112]

To get the candidacy process back on track, Bishop appealed

---

[111] It is notable that this was around the time of Reinhardt Gehlen's estrangement with Conrad Adenauer, the Chancellor of the Federal Republic of Germany. The potential for yet another embarrassment was enormous.

[112] It is entirely possible that State Department bureaucracy saw the heart murmur as an easy and diplomatic way to dispose of Bishop's application. If so, it backfired stupendously.

for and received a medical clearance. Once he got past that the background checks reopened. It was then immediately noted that the candidate already had a top-secret clearance. This always actuates State Department bureaucracy. With so much paper to shuffle through, and very little time to do it in, a preexisting security clearance is a time saver.

Thus Bishop, with red flags streaming, was inducted into the Foreign Service two months later. He started his Basic Officer's Training Course in Room A-100 in October, 1965. He got his first promotion in November 1965. This was a simple administrative move. He then enrolled in the Foreign Service Institute Consular Officers' Course.

In terms of time, the whole induction and vetting process was rapid. State Department concerns are more about prestige than effectiveness. The oft-quoted old saw, 'State gets what it wants, not what it needs,' explains the dysfunction that characterized State Department intake in a nutshell.

Thus, it appeared to all that William Bradford Bishop Jr., Yale Graduate and linguist, was a prime example of what the 'Best and the Brightest' were all about. What did other government agencies know about life abroad anyway? Indeed, what did other government agencies know at all? It was all very Foreign Service.

William Bradford Bishop Jr. as he appeared
in his Official 1965 State Department photo

* * *

The American Foreign Service Association (AFSA) addresses each new A-100 class. It is named after the room the inductees first meet in, A-100. Course titles are not recalled, just the room number. The speech each new class is given seldom varies.

The American Foreign Service Association inculcates the new Junior Officers (JO's) with the flaw of anticipated grandeur. (Instead, a slow death in obscurity - and the culling of Alpha males – that is more the order of things to come.) Notwithstanding, they are told they are the elite (*not survivors*). They are told that for every one accepted into the Foreign Service, five or more finalists are rejected. Indeed, they are a 'select group,' yet the reasoning that the A-100 class is the best of the best, and indeed the best and the brightest, can be nocuous.

The induction speech was much like what William Bradford Bishop heard at the freshman picnic at Yale. They were the elect. As this was the second time Bradford had heard this at his induction into an elite group, he could conclude that he was now 'the elect, of the elect.' It was what Bradford wanted to hear.

The representatives of AFSA were not wearing a cloak of ermine, nor were they carrying a mace. State's dignitaries, however, did include Dean Acheson and Cordell Hull.[113] State hosted world leaders and headliners as well. The message was clear, and it was the same.

The class would be among the men who intended to steer American Policy in the world, while largely regarding their political masters as a nuisance. William Bradford Bishop Jr. was embarking on a career as a statesman. Unlike Yale, where friendships were forged and alumni were helpful, colleagues at State would compete with each other in a system of bureaucratic measurement. On a deeper level, it meant that he had a second chance.

This was all in the future. For a few brief months a surge of triumph, and the sustaining glow of rosy future prospects mixed with glory, filled the A-100 class. Each of them had a 'special

---

[113] Both of whom were honored on US postage stamps.

destiny.' Then, before Christmas 1965, the graduates got their first assignments abroad.

Bradford got an exotic assignment. He was going to a faraway place. He would go to a country with an emperor and a royal court. He'd go to a country with a good climate and excellent scenery. It had its own alphabet and a formidable, if little known, ancient history. He was going on a voyage of discovery. He was going to Ethiopia.

The Fair-Haired Boy

Afoot and light-hearted I take to the open road,
Healthy, free, the world before me,
The long brown path before me leading wherever I choose.

Henceforth I ask not good-fortune, I myself am good-fortune,
Henceforth I whimper no more, postpone no more, need nothing,
Done with indoor complaints, libraries, querulous criticisms,
Strong and content I travel the open road.

—Song of the Open Road by Walt Whitman
Found in Bradford Bishop's Diary dated
October 9, 1965

The elation a new Foreign Service Officer feels is sometimes difficult to express. For those with an adventurous spirit, and a yen to explore faraway places and cultures, it doesn't get much better than this. For Bradford it was a new life. Yale had not worked out, nor had the ASA. This time he would focus. (As much as he had while playing chess games with Jacques.)

Today the Foreign Service (FS) wants diversity abroad. Nowadays the FS is recruiting people who "look like America." This makes a show of it abroad. During the time Bradford Bishop served, the Service was, as many retirees would later put it, 'very white bread.'

Indeed, this was what America looked like in 1965. America would continue to become more 'white bread' until, in the then future year of 1970, Washington would publicly fret over whether there would be no language other than English spoken in the United States.

Bradford had 'all his bases covered.' His Italian language proficiency was an asset. (In the land of the blind the, man with one eye is king.) His other asset went beyond his Yale degree. He had a traditional FSO name: William Bradford Bishop Jr. His son was William Bradford Bishop III. This was another Old Service pedigree quietly and unobtrusively appreciated by State's elder elite. He could also pocket the Plymouth Rock story; and bring it out at strategic moments, such as during the promotional process.

Women were not allowed to serve as Foreign Service Officers in 1965. A female was allowed to enter the Foreign Service, as did

Bradford Bishop and the men. She could not, however, remain a Foreign Service Officer if she got married.

Even given the rare case of a single female FSO, ambassadors would openly wonder what to do with a female Foreign Service Officer. There had already been a case in Brussels, Belgium. This did not happen in Africa. Moreover, Ethiopia was mountainous country, and set deep into that continent. If need be, if a female showed up at post she could be tucked away and out of sight.

It took a full day to get to Ethiopia. A stopover and change of planes in Europe was required. June through August was quite chilly and wet. September through May was gorgeous. The Bishops landed in the Ethiopian capital, Addis Ababa, in early December. The contrasts they encountered were breathtaking.

Ethiopia was unlike any other African State. With the exception of the 1945 Italian invasion, counted more as Second World War occupation than colonial settlement, Ethiopia had not been colonized by any European power. Indeed, it had an emperor whose linage went back to King Solomon and the Queen of Sheba. The Ethiopians even claimed custody of the Arc of the Covenant.

Ethiopia was then an Empire with a myriad of distinct tribal groups. The Emperor built two impressive palaces. His residence in the nineteen-sixties was the Jubilee Palace (known to Ethiopians as the Gannata Le'ul Palace). The gardens and the fountains of Addis Ababa University's main campus surrounded it. (The Emperor, Haile Selassie, was a great advocate of education for all.)

The Emperor seldom failed to impress. When Bradford Bishop rode on horseback, as many American Embassy staffers did, he could see a lion on the palace ramparts. Lions roamed free at the Emperor's court. He had other animals, such as cheetahs, as well.

The oft-told story at that time was about Kwame Nkrumah, the first president of Ghana. When first visiting Haile Selassie, he was ushered into the palace by the Ghanaian Ambassador. When he entered the throne room, he saw Haile Selassie seated on his throne with a couple of lions walking around. The Ghanaian ambassador said, "Mr. President, just ignore the lions or pet them."

Nkrumah was startled and replied, "Pet them? You're out of your mind! I know better. I'm an African."

Emperor Halie Selassie, "Now, Now, did that big, bad man frighten you?"

The memories of imperial banquets at this time need no burnishing. The china and crystal alone were dazzling. When entertaining the Queen of England, the Emperor's dining room was stretched out farther than, any of the attendees from the American Embassy had ever seen. On that occasion, no detail was left unattended. There was a servant in 18th century satin livery standing behind every two guests. Their every need was attended to. Here was Foreign Service life as the A-100 class envisioned it.

It wasn't just the opulence of the imperial court. Bishop was in the right place at the right time. Nineteen-sixty was the year of Africa. There were then newly independent countries all over the Sub-Saharan Region.

For anyone who planned to make it to ambassador before he turned 50, Africa was the place to be. It had nearly 50 countries about which no one seemed to care. The previous Kennedy administration focused on Africa as the Cold War heated up. The new president, Lyndon Baines Johnson, followed suit. As American representation abroad expanded, it could provide the ambitious FSO the opportunity that he sought.

There were novelties as well. For any Foreign Service Officer abroad there was the novelty of discovery. High adventure beckoned; and Ethiopia in 1966 was filled with both.

A harbinger of both was Tej, a notable feature of the Emperor's banquet. It was something the venturous junior officer discovered long before his first visit to the palace. Tej is what Ethiopians call wine.

Ethiopian wine is made from honey. Honey wines are found in ancient cultures. (Mead is a honey wine that is marketed in the West to this day.) There are many varieties of Ethiopian honey wine. The many varieties of Tej were available at banquets through the Emperor's liveried retainers. Sampling Tej is one of the great joys a first tour Foreign Service Officer in Ethiopia experiences.

Ethiopia had a tobacco industry as well. The Imperial Ethiopian Tobacco Monopoly started out with a single brand, Nigusu, and then Nyala (named after the African Antelope). This was a cheap brand, though not as ego-enhancing as the American brand, Marlboro. Smoking foreign (local) cigarettes enhances the Foreign Service Experience. Nyala sold for less than three Ethiopian Birr a pack. In the 21st century the Birr hovers around 10 Birr to the US Dollar. Smoking locally grown leaf was more than affordable.

Surely, an outdoor café, a cup of Tej, an Ethiopian meal served on a mesob,[114] and the lazy luxury of watching strikingly beautiful women walk past, is contentment. Addis Ababa, the capital of imperial Ethiopia, was a comfortable stop along a lifelong path on the open road, which is the US Department of State. For first tour officers, the comforting feeling of permanent employment and support settles in.

It is a life of charm and beguiling variety, with each rosy dawn bringing forward a new present to be unwrapped. It is part of what Walt Whitman was writing about in the poem Bradford, the Junior Officer, so loved, *'to see no possession but you may possess it, enjoying all without labor or purchase, abstracting the feast yet not abstracting one particle of it.'*

The Bishops lived in an Ethiopian neighborhood. There was no privileged diplomatic enclave in Addis Ababa at the time. As one

---

[114] A traditional table woven out as a basket

drove down the street the Bishops saw squalor next to grandeur. The dramatic experience of exotic scenery burst upon them when they got out of town.

The mountains were breathtaking. The poverty was shocking at first, but the Bishops got used to it. Nearly every visitor does.

The upside to poverty is that everything is inexpensive. A routine of servants to staff the US government housing is easily acquired. Often a staff comes with the premises.

Most countries in Sub-Saharan Africa are early rising, agricultural cultures. What little nightlife there is in 'Addis' gets stale after a while. Therefore, the little diplomatic colony made its own nightlife. The American Embassy Staff put on a production of the 1960 musical, 'The Fantasticks.' Brad auditioned for, and got, the lead and the spotlight.

He and Annette were an outstanding Foreign Service family. They embodied California for so many 'Africa hands' (as long-time FS analysts of the Region were called). They arrived at the right place, and at the right time, for 'career-enhancement;' and Brad took full advantage of the family's sparkle. So attractive were they that they stood out in the diplomatic community as 'eye-candy.'

"California Dreaming" by the Mamas and the Papas had just come out the year they arrived. The band, The Beach Boys, had been singing about surfing since 1961. Their hit, "Good Vibrations," came out in 1966 with their arrival at post. All of this helped the Bishops as they surfed to popularity.

The United States Ambassador in Addis Ababa at the time was Edward Korry. He was a Kennedy administration political appointee. George Ball, then Under Secretary of State for Economic and Agricultural Affairs, brought him into the State Department.

Ed Korry and George Ball were friends. That was how Ed Korry became the US Ambassador to Ethiopia. Shortly after his arrival in Addis Ababa he developed a reputation for being hard to deal with.[115]

Smart and articulate, Korry took a dim view of Foreign Service Officers. He felt that they were primarily interested in promotion within the State Department hierarchy. For their part, the Foreign Service Officers stationed at the Embassy developed an aversion to, and/or dislike of, their ambassador. Not so Bishop.

William Bradford Bishop saw his ambassador as just another situation to exploit. He understood that Ambassador Korry had to be right. It was his modus operandi. This ambassador thought he had all the facts too.

Bishop understood that he could talk back to the ambassador

---

[115] "A lot of the Kennedy Administration despised the State Department in general." (Rosenfeld, PAO Ethiopia)

when the situation warranted. If Bishop had the facts, and if he timed it properly, he could carry the day. He learned that social awareness at State is vital. Sensitivity to a situation in office politics is important. This went a long way toward his becoming the ambassador's favorite.

The other big plus for Bishop, in the Ethiopia of the 1960's, was Kagnew[116] Station. Kagnew Station, established in 1953, was American's base and listening post. Radio reception at the base was considered the finest in the world. Indeed, it has been said that a huge part of the globe could be listened in on from there. Radio transmissions were so good that, by the 1960s, the rock-and-roll programming on Kagnew's 1,000-watt AM station was heard as far away as Australia, Finland, and Brazil.

'Tract C' as it was coded, was *the* top-secret area at Kagnew. It was by far the most important US listening post in the horn of Africa. Tract C was what kept Kagnew running. It drove US policy; and it was run by the ASA.

Here was where his Italian language skills came into play. The Italian colonial legacy left behind some fluency in the language. The port city of Asmara features art deco buildings. Asmara's architecture is attributed to Benito Mussolini. The Italian dictator had an artistic bent, and the design he thought, would showcase the 'Second Roman Empire.' Today Asmara still contains the highest concentration of intact Modernist architecture in the world.

It is notable that, when Italian troops were sent to Somalia during the intervention in 1992, Radio Ibis FM Mogadishu was set up for homesick Italian troops. It drew a huge audience. The local population listened to it far more than the American broadcast. Radio Ibis' logo was a singing banana emerging out of a map of Somalia.[117]

The Italians had only three off-duty soldiers running the station part-time. They played pop tunes, punctuated by health

---

[116] "Kagnew" was the name of the warhorse of Ras Makonnen, Menelik II's General and the father of Haile Selassie, during the First Italo-Ethiopian War. Military units from imperial times would often adopt a name of a favored military commander and Ethiopian warriors were often referred to interchangeably by the names of their warhorses.

[117] On 89.7 MHz FM

advisories and public service announcements. Radio Ibis featured opera singers like Luciano Pavarotti as well. Even Somali warlords hunted by the Americans called in to the station to say how much they liked it.

Eighty Americans in the American Embassy building ran Radio Rajo (Hope). They produced a newspaper as well. Radio Rajo opened up with the theme music from the movie *Raiders of the Lost Ark*. This was followed by a broadcast of politically correct verses from the Koran, local folk songs, and army communiques.

To their puzzlement and dismay, the Americans at the embassy simply could not compete with Radio Ibis. Their first reaction was to try to kick Radio Ibis off the air entirely. The off-duty Italian soldiers somehow managed to assuage the Americans at the embassy and a deal was struck. The American station conceded the airwaves to Radio Ibis. In exchange Radio Ibis would carry a few hours of the American station's broadcast. The regular programing would come back on after a few hours of Radio Rajo.

Later, a survey showed that Somalis turned off Radio Ibis when the Indiana Jones theme commenced American programming. Somalia switched back on once the time was up. And the banana sang on.

Those romantics traveling to this Italianate region of Africa could still ride in the littorina railcar.[118] The littorina was a functioning period piece. The railcar looks like a cross between a bus and a train. It was co-produced by Mussolini and then Fiat President Agnelli, the new train type proudly displayed the symbol of the Fascist party on its front.

Although the bulk of Italians in Asmara left after the Second World War, some remained. With a background in things Italian, Bishop was able to coordinate embassy efforts down to the slightest detail. As he honed his social skills with notable alacrity, Bradford Bishop soon became the Ambassador's man. Not only

---

[118] The name 'Littorina,' came from the city of Littoria (now named Latina) founded by Benito Mussolini in June 1932, and was bestowed to all railcars of Italian origin, regardless of gauge. Three of these classic 'art deco' Fiat vehicles remain, as of this writing, on the 950mm gauge Eritrean Railway. (Minus the Fascist party symbol which was affixed to the front)

could he speak with impeccable authority on ASA operations, he could discuss sensitive information as no other FSO could.

'Suddenly I have new powers," he thought, while he delighted in the still vibrant Italian colonial charm. He noted that the effects of serax still made him sleazy. He would have to work on that. Yet everything else seemed to fall in with Nietzschean philosophy. His perceived 'new mental powers' were, what he understood to be, 'the sense of becoming.'

Bradford rode the littorina to the coast, along with military personnel. The littorina railcar crossed 65 bridges and 39 tunnels on the Italian standard narrow gauge railway. The highest point on the line is 7,854 feet just before Asmara. From there it drops steeply to the coast. The ride could make your teeth chatter. Yet when the Bishops arrived (in one piece) at Asmara, they could swim and engage in water sports with their friends from Kagnew.

Relations with Ethiopia were progressing nicely as well. So vital was Kagnew Station that the US generously sent the Ethiopians military equipment and ammunition. There were plenty of communications and economic benefits as well.

Ethiopia needed all of it. There was an insurgency brewing in the coastal province of Eritrea. Eritrea had gone from Italian rule to British rule to Ethiopian rule. The autonomous rights Eritrea had when the British left were pruned, then eliminated. By 1961 an armed rebellion ignited. Small at first, the revolt grew into a 30-year war for independence. That was where the Cold War stepped in.

In January 1961 Nikita Khrushchev, then premier of the Soviet Union, delivered his secret 'sacred wars of national liberation' speech. It suggested that Moscow intended to undermine Western influence in the region by fanning war and subversion. The Cuban Missile Crisis aside, this manifested itself in West Africa. Ghana, Guinea, and Mali were by then the Soviet focus.

Khrushchev extended a 'friendly hand' to moderate African countries as well. By 1963 that hand had reached the Horn of Africa. Just prior to Bishop's arrival, the Horn had entered the Cold War.

This was the second element of success for the first tour FSO.

Ambassador Edward Korry had his hands full. He had been in Addis Ababa since March 1963, when the Horn erupted like a hornet's nest. The Soviet Union had offered the then moderate Somali government an arms deal. Ethiopia was alarmed; and Emperor Haile Selassie said so.

Ethiopia had a border dispute with Somalia. The Cold Warrior mentality of the Kennedy administration held that a balance of power in the Horn of Africa was desirable. The role of 'balancer' might have looked good from Washington, but it wasn't clear-cut on the ground. Unlike Cold War Europe, there were more than two sides.

By the time Bishop became a player, the issue intensified. The Soviets 'upped the ante' on the arms deal. The US did not match it. America had already offered Ethiopia an arms deal within a consortium of Western countries. Yet Haile Selassie demurred. At first Ambassador Korry wondered why.

He saw that the key to politics in the Horn was an understanding of the constituent pieces. These Bishop understood well. Where the FSO succeeded, was in explaining that the sum of the parts of the Horn were greater than the whole.

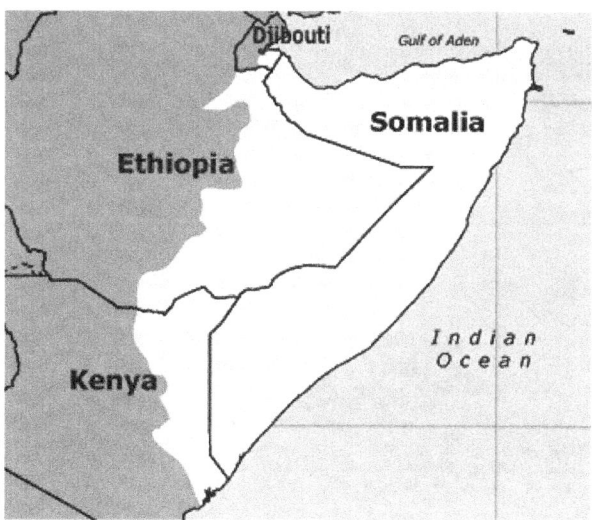
Distribution of Ethnic Somali people in the Horn of Africa

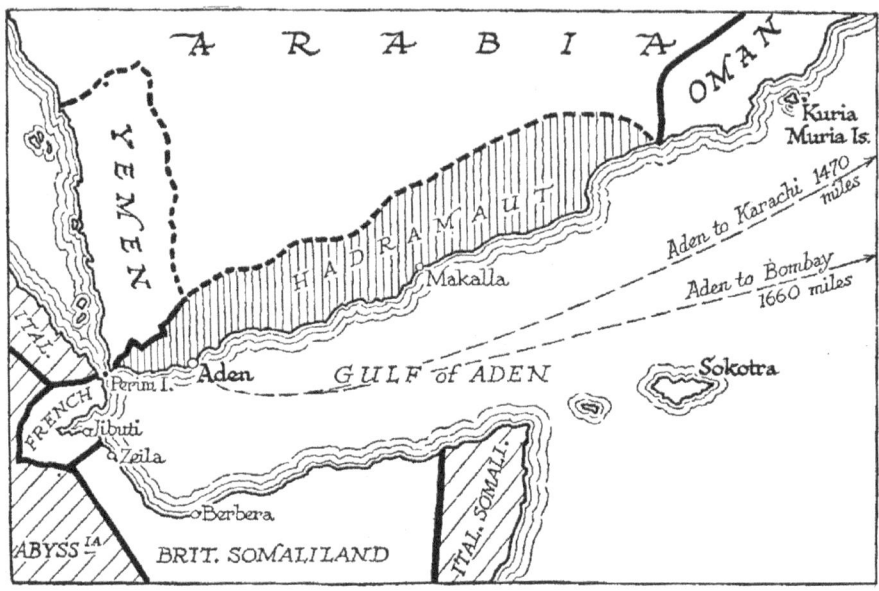

Kagnew Station Tract C, or in military slang: "the Funny Farm"

A littorina railcar at Asmara train station

The Somali Republic included the former British Protectorate of Somaliland. The British policed the area so that meat products could be shipped to the more important protectorate of theirs, Aden.[119] Indeed, with little interest beyond supply, checking slavery, and foreign interference, British Somaliland was once ruled from British India. Britain policed Somaliland because their colony in Aden across the Gulf needed a cheap source of meat. It was this trade the British policed, and by default made Somaliland a protectorate. The British called the protectorate "Aden's Butcher Shop."

After losing the city of Berbera, in the protectorate to the Italians in 1940 (It was the only Italian victory over the British during the Second World War) the British returned in 1941 and first occupied Italian Somalia, then retook British Somaliland. Britain gave both protectorates independence as one country in 1960; and wasn't unhappy to bid their Somali possessions farewell.

The situation when the Bishops arrived was that the newly independent Somalia was making claims on neighboring countries' territory. Somalia's official position was that the five points of the star in the Somali flag represented the five peoples to-be-united in a new Somalia. Somaliland was one of those five points drawn into the new country upon independence.

The other three points of the star were the Northern District of

---

[119] Present day Yemen

Kenya, the French colony of Djibouti, and the adjacent Ogden region of Ethiopia. This would make up the future 'Greater Somalia.' Few viewed this aggressive plan with contentment, least of all Haile Selassie. The Ogden region was one quarter of Ethiopia. It was at that point that the Emperor responded to Khrushchev's friendly hand, and Korry was perplexed.

Korry was the European editor for *Look* magazine. He was a United Press correspondent in post-World War II Europe prior to that. It wasn't just that his background experience was about a Europe that was divided in two. He also had to deal with the turmoil in the Horn instead of just observing it.

Haile Selassie, on the other hand, had considerable diplomatic experience. For the Emperor, the Somali claims were just a flank opening on the expanding chessboard of his long reign. The Emperor made his move.

Haile Selassie opened by receiving military aid from the Soviet Union. He then told Korry that he wanted the US to close Kagnew Station. These two moves put Kagnew in check.

With the Cold War priority for the US was to keep its listening post open and functioning; the ASA operation in Tract C was considered non-negotiable.[120] To many in Washington it looked like checkmate.

There was only one officer at the Embassy that had any training in the official language of Ethiopia, Amharic. Those FSOs serving at the time spoke French or Spanish. (The US Department of State sent new Foreign Service Officers out, seemingly at random.) Like so many ambassadors before him, the frustrated Korry had to make do with those FSOs he was sent.

This transposition intensified just before Korry arrived at post. The Stonehouse project at Kagnew was underway. This was sensitive. The Stonehouse project was a highly secret deep space probing operation. The Department of Defense was installing two huge parabolic antennae, to be used to intercept Soviet space

---

[120] In retrospect, some analysts have said that Kagnew station was not necessary after 1961. This was due to advances in Technology. Kagnew was closed in 1973. Others would agree with Ambassador Korry, who said, "...in order to maintain access to Kagnew Station, the Pentagon would give the Emperor his $10 million in military aid in 'solid gold Cadillacs' if he wanted it that way."

telemetry. It would, they hoped, assist in the development of ballistic missiles. The weak square in this chess game was Kagnew Station itself. Kagnew was highly visible from a distance.

A spy on the ground could easily garner information. It was so visible that Ethiopia's cooperation in cordoning the area off was vital in order to keep the project concealed. This became all-the-more urgent when the intercepts went operational.

The Stonewall Project was put in operation in 1965, just prior to the Bishops arrival in Addis Ababa. This situation was tailor-made for an ASA veteran. Further, previous experience in covert operations was a plus.

It was this waiting move that propelled the newly-minted Foreign Service Officer into the Ambassador's good graces. Korry, the old journalist, butted heads with the Public Affairs Officer (PAO) at Addis Ababa; while Bishop became the 'fair-haired' boy[121] (His blondish/brown hair notwithstanding). This dynamic at the embassy was rooted in Korry's editorial background; and that an ASA veteran was essential.

Even though things were going well for Bradford, he chided himself for being lazy in the morning. It was a side effect of the serax he was still taking. On this, his second chance, he wanted to be spectacular. "Only relax on weekends or vacations," he thought to himself, "...not even on weekends."

Bishop had another source of relaxation, an unlikely one: The Swedes. There were many Swedes in Ethiopia at that time. They were doing NGO (Non-Governmental Organization) work. That is to say that they were building schools and improving agriculture and health care in the country. They struck a chord with Bishop. He could relax around them.

The Swedes spoke softly and calmly. Excess, flashiness, and boasting were abhorrent to the Swedes. They worked hard, but not too hard. They did not discuss work at dinner and were notable for

---

[121] It is notable that Bishop's modus operandi had not changed. He received a Security Violation (LOU – Limited Official Use) on April 20, 1967. This did not affect his relations with Ambassador Korry. The Ambassador overlooked it, not knowing how vital it was to future FS promotion. Bishop got a promotion, yet he operated as he had in the military. Once again, he slipped through State Department oversight. (It was all very Foreign Service) At this point, it should be noted that there are reasons the military then took, and still takes, a dim view of Foreign Service Officer effectiveness.

enjoying themselves. The Foreign Service was largely the reserve of the East Coast establishment, and not a place where Bradford could let his guard down. It was, at that time, very Ivy League as well. The largely egalitarian and relaxed environment among ex-patriot Swedes, blended with the new California ethos that was broadcast in pop songs over Kagnew's AM station.

This is not to say that Junior Officer Bishop wasn't a typical FSO. His Yale credentials instantly made him a member of the club. His yearning for the type of eminence that would put him on a US postage stamp qualified him as well. Yet the first and foremost trait among FSOs is romanticism.

American diplomats are romantics. They yearn to see the pyramids and ancient places of the world. They prefer that their fellow Americans back in the States keep their heads down, and do boring and repetitive work, while they themselves prove their worth through the cultivation of their own tastes in cuisine and literature. It was a way of demonstrating their worthiness to be upwardly mobile. To the FSO way of thinking, such pursuits place them above the visa officers, their Marine guards, and motor pool clerks.

Consequently, junior officer Bishop read the *Rubaiyat*, by Omar Khayyam,[122] late in his tour at 'Addis.' Like many, he was struck with awe when faced with such places as the Mountains of the Moon, the Blue Nile, and the savage beauty of an African sunset over deep and trackless forests.

In an ethereal moment Bishop saw his situation in the seventh quatrain of the *Rubaiyat*... 'The Bird of Time has but a little way -- To fly and Lo! The Bird is on the Wing.'

---

[122] The Edward Fitzgerald translation

Coffee Ranks Tea

Rosenfeld says, "Galbraith liked me because I put my feet on the desk and didn't 'yes man' him. – Same thinking as concerns the Ambassador apparently –[123]

—Bradford Bishop's Diary concerning Senator Kennedy's visit

The United States International Exhibition came to Addis Ababa in 1966. It showcased American products. It was pitched as 'the ideas and manufacture from a new country that was built out of the wilderness of North America.' The exhibition opened with a recorded message, 'the Americans were a people who had a dream, a dream of progress.'

The Exhibition played to Haile Selassie's program: to teach, to communicate ideas, to keep cars and trucks moving, to help Africa build. It was something heard in 1960, 'the year of Africa,' but by 1966 the message was fading.

Among other things, the Americans brought machinery: to help sort coffee beans, to create new industry, and a machine that would create 200 building blocks in an hour. The automated hen house the Americans brought to the exhibition was astonishing. The hardscrabble population, bussed in from rural Ethiopia, had never seen anything like it. The eggs rolled off a custom-made wheel and onto a conveyer belt.

There was a fashion show with local models as well. The background music was soft jazz cocktail music from the 1940's. Most popular of all may have been the black and white American-made televisions on display. Halie Selassie, now called the 'wise Emperor' throughout Africa, had introduced television to Ethiopia in 1963.

The entire contingent of Amembassy Addis was involved in the exhibition in one way or the other. It was thrilling for Annette and other wives who pitched in to make the show a success. For a new officer with a young family, Addis Ababa was a frontier outpost

---

[123] Rosenfeld was then Public Affairs Officer, PAO, in Addis Ababa. John Kenneth Galbraith was US ambassador to India from 1961 to 1963. He was a close Kennedy family friend.

with all the excitement of the new and the exotic. America was on full display. It made the resident Americans temporary celebrities.

A large photo of President Lyndon Baines Johnson was set up. Young, often American-educated Ethiopians spoke to, and demonstrated exhibits for, the crowd. There was a Short History of the United States in a walk-through tunnel. A young Ethiopian, wearing a coonskin hat replete with a tail, guided the onlookers through while speaking in Amharic.

Those young men hosting the exhibit sported suits or white dinner jackets. Here was the future. There would be peace and prosperity (and plastic).

The Exhibition displayed items made of plastic. It was a notable innovation given priority, among many innovations during Halie Selassie's reign. Henceforth Ethiopian schools would have plastic desks.

Foreign Service Life was different for the wives. It was assumed that the men would go to post and that the wives and children would quietly walk behind. The term 'spouse' was not used. There were no spouses, only wives.

Officer evaluations referenced the performance of the wives. Wives were expected to help out (without compensation). This was especially so when a VIP arrived at Post, or when a cultural event was scheduled. A wife was a team member. Officers got extra points on their Employee Evaluation Reviews (EER) for the efforts of their wives.

A few years prior to the Bishops' posting to Addis Ababa, Foreign Service wives were given formal evaluations along with their husbands. Wives who weren't good at planning and hosting representational events could negatively impact their husband's careers. Brad Jr. made sure his home was open for cocktail parties and receptions. Indeed, he cheerfully volunteered to host whatever, wherever, and whenever a social occasion needed a venue.

William Bradford Bishop Jr. was mindful of this. Every advantage he could muster, including his 'Old Foreign Service' sounding name, was part of his meticulous game plan. Such indicators of diplomatic aristocracy still held sway on promotional selection boards.

People brought their elderly relatives along with them too. Previously the FSO didn't have to show an IRS form. The parents just arrived. It wasn't unusual for parents to arrive at post as dependents, as some parents still do today. Later a Foreign Service Officer had to have proof of dependency. An IRS form was required demonstrating that your parents are, actually, dependent; and that you contribute at least 50% toward their support. Then the Department of State would pay for their transportation and housing.

There was a time when Foreign Service Officers would pay their own way and find their own accommodations for their dependents as well.

There was plenty of protocol, of course. When the family arrived they first paid a call on the ambassador. At that time, the protocol was to notify the ambassador and request that parents or children (or both) were coming. There was a specific edict concerning this. The ambassador, as a matter of course, would never say no to the request.

Families in the Foreign Service compounds at the time were close. They were concerned over the health of the children. They were able to get good household help cheap.

There had been women's clubs at post for years. These had a long history of doing useful things such as volunteering to work to help the local population or improving the diplomatic community. There was home schooling for the children to do as well.

If there wasn't a suitable school at post, the Calvert system was often used. Calvert Education sent out material to 'home school' children in hardship posts.[124] There was also an education allowance for those who wanted to send their children to boarding school.

Saint Stephen's in Rome was just such a school. Classes were in English. It was an American-supported school. Cairo American College is a high school, though the word College is used. The use of the word 'college' isn't uncommon for high schools abroad.

The American Embassies in Africa, at that time, had more flexibility as to the manner of housing embassy personnel could use. Many places in Africa were like 'Addis,' where strong-smelling shanties were sometimes positioned alongside palatial mansions.

---

[124] The Calvert system is still active to this day.

There was nothing in between. There was no middle class in Africa in 1966. In many places in Africa this remains so, and Foreign Service Officers are now tucked away in manicured enclaves.

Annette threw herself into the role allocated to the wives. She hosted receptions and dinner parties. Indeed, Ambassador Korry commented that she was the most active of the embassy wives. This was something that her ambitious Foreign Service Officer husband probably urged her to do. (It was also an indicator of how competent she was.)

Like so many women of the nineteen-sixties, Annette, with her maid, regularly cooked meals from scratch. She served peanut dishes common throughout Ethiopia. The peanuts of Ethiopia became Brad's favorite snack. There was also 'Kolo,' a roasted grain mix. Like so many discoveries made by first post junior officers, he carried this first-tour passion throughout his adult life.

His son, William Bradford III, then only five years old, was notably spirited. Brenton was a baby. Both enhanced their father's image. Their father was further pleased as the family image enhanced his overall rating.

It was troubling, however, when Bishop confided to his diary that he did not know how to love. He saw his family as beautiful; and they were certainly useful. Yet he had an inkling that something was amiss. He didn't love them. He loved Brad III's spirit, but then nothing.

He would have to ask what love was about. He would confide in a friend, a young staff member, Richard Masters, at the Embassy. Richard would know, Bishop confided to his diary. He would ask Richard how to love.

After a talk, Bradford mulled it over. His conclusion was that love is compatible with ambition, egoism, and premonitions of special destiny. As Nietzsche pointed out, the Übermensch can hurt people, he is allowed to hurt people. However, the superior man should help the weak. "Compassion is your saving grace," thought Bradford. His conclusion was in keeping with his religion.

As with every embassy community, there were the comings and goings of very important persons (VIP). Notable for 1966 was the arrival of Robert F. Kennedy, who was doing a rapid tour of Africa. Kennedy was elected US Senator for New York in 1964. Now he was planning a presidential bid. This tour was about getting some foreign policy experience, as had his brother John before him. For the embassy staffs in four African countries, the visit became a nightmare.

For Amembassy Ethiopia it started when Kennedy's staff did not show up to help out with advanced planning. No one at Post knew who was going to go where, or when. The Embassy didn't even know how many cars were needed to transport the party when it arrived.

The worrying thing was that the Kennedys had a reputation, at the time, for being impervious. Now Bobby was going to meet the Emperor. If Haile Selassie could outdo the Kennedys in anything, it was on being impervious. This was a no-win situation for the Public Affairs Officer (PAO).

At this juncture, there was one thing Annette had going for her; she didn't have to deal directly with Bobby Kennedy. Bobby decided to discuss Ethiopia's problems by getting a casual conversation going. Such small talk may have gone over well at Annette's receptions, but not in the Emperor's throne room. It is regrettable that Bobby started the audience with "I understand that the Emperors are supposed to be descendants of the Queen of Sheba."

The Emperor nodded. Then Bobby went on, "Is there any validity in that?"

It has been reported that the Emperor was momentarily in shock. The audience wound up rather quickly after that. It became one of the great gaffes of 20th century African diplomacy. At a time when unrest was brewing on Ethiopia's Addis Ababa University campus, a US Senator had questioned the Emperor's validity.

This faux pas is an all-too-common dilemma foisted on Foreign Service Staff worldwide. An opinionated visiting US Senator can be destructive. To put it mildly, working with the status quo in the host country is an embassy's prime directive. Any US Senator trying to influence an American election by making headlines while abroad, is regarded as dangerous. The Kennedy tour highlighted this for a generation of FSOs.

At the beginning of his tour Robert Kennedy visited South Africa. Neither State nor the then apartheid government of South Africa had wanted Senator Kennedy to visit in the first place. The storm was such that the South African cabinet met over the visit. It denied *United Press International, Reuters*, and the *Associate Press* the usual courtesies for news coverage. It turned away four journalists who traveled to cover Kennedy's speech at the border. The University at Stellenbosch, which initially invited the Senator, cancelled the invitation. All of that only fanned the flames of protest. Nearly a thousand people were at the airport to greet the Senator as he landed.

He visited Chief Albert Luthuli, recipient of the Nobel Peace Prize. Luthuli was also the leader of the African National Congress (ANC) which opposed apartheid. That wasn't all.

The Senator gave a polite, but inflammatory speech on this, the first stop of his African tour. It was given at the University of Cape Town in South Africa. It has gone down in history as 'The Ripples of Hope speech.'[125]

As predicted, Kennedy gave hope to those students and journalists opposed to the ruling elite. He donned a patina of justice which encouraged and ennobled the young South Africans who heard him. The South African government said they would not let him into the country again.[126]

It reverberated across the continent. A prominent Afrikaans speaking industrialist invited him to the University town of Stellenbosch afterward. (It was all part of fence mending.) The next country he visited, Tanzania sent him to a faraway Peace Corps outpost. The locals declared it a public holiday as he was mobbed by thousands of jubilant Africans.[127] Tanzania, with a sigh of relief,

---

[125] The upshot from the Senator's visit was that he was acclaimed upon his return to America and invited back to South Africa by a private organization backed by concerned industrialists interested in improving South Africa's image abroad. Both the Foreign Service and the South African Government viewed the suggested next visit with all the anticipation of anyone, with hyperacidity, in the waiting room of an ulcer clinic.

[126] From the Afrikaans language paper, *Die Beeld*. Front Page, quote: "This is the firm stand of the Government after his behavior in our country and his remarks in East Africa."

[127] The Tanzanian government was wary. Kennedy was sent to a remote village where the US Peace Corps

then gingerly passed him on to neighboring Kenya.

The leadership in Kenya was horrified. They lodged an official complaint to the US government. Now as the tour wound down, and after putting the wrong foot forward in the throne room, Bobby's entourage arranged for him to speak at the University at 11:00 the next morning.

This was the last thing the Ethiopian government wanted. There was enough stress accompanying what should have been an unremarkable stopover as it was. After Kennedy's gaffe the tension intensified. The head of the University feared a large and unruly student body might spark some real trouble. The Embassy PAO stepped in with a solution. Why not move the speech to a time when fewer students were on campus?

Bobby was unhappy about not giving his inspirational speech on his schedule. He would have to move his speech to 4:30 PM. He had come to expect newsworthy attention, and spontaneous adulation, during his largely unplanned and improvised agenda.

Like many Americans, he could not see that Africa was not homogenous. As with all four countries he visited, Ethiopia was different. The PAO could not get that across, and now had to work out damage control.

He counted himself fortunate that the Senator was impervious. Kennedy had not noticed that security was at the ready, and the Ethiopian Civil Service was anxious. What he and his entourage did notice was that there weren't many students around. The Senator complained about it to the PAO.

Nevertheless, the Senator gave another good speech. Security breathed a sigh of relief, and the PAO made up for it by getting Kennedy an interview with the 'Voice of the Gospel' radio, which was run by American Lutherans and heard all over Africa. To the relief of both the Embassy staff, and the Kennedy entourage, this made up for the skimpy attendance at the University speech. It fit into a concerted media campaign which started with the furor in South Africa and would be capped by one last, rousing speech before returning to the United States in triumph.

---

was active. The entirety of that remote village turned out, and the celebration spread. The Tanzanian government was relieved to send him on to the next leg of his tour.

The Kennedy tour ended with a speech to the Organization of African Unity (OAU). Nearly all of Africa was represented. This was the anticipated crescendo, now enhanced by the senator's continent-wide Voice of the Gospel radio appearance (with no real thanks to the PAO who made it possible.) The most notable part of his final speech was the middle of his oration. Kennedy was just warming up – striving to make this OAU appearance part of a truly inspirational speech - when the power went out.

It was an embarrassment for the Ethiopian government as well. Then it got worse for both the Kennedy tour and the Emperor. During the OAU conference the Eritrean Liberation Front attacked 17 towns in Eritrea. The Ethiopian government was embarrassed, and the Kennedy speech was further eclipsed in the press. Only the media coverage of the Kennedy departure went some way toward ratcheting down the tension.[128]

Robert F. Kennedy with the Emperor's kitty

---

[128] The author takes this opportunity to define the Foreign Service term "wheels up." The term originated from the military for when an aircraft takes off and the mission has officially started. For the Foreign Service handling VIP visits, the term 'wheels up' means that their mission is officially over and that the VIP on the plane will no longer bother them. Usually Wheels up entails refreshments at a tavern. The 1966 Kennedy visit is a prime example.

Annette had taken State Department sponsored courses in protocol. Her volunteer and support work covered all such social/political events; just as Lobelia's had in South Pasadena. Indeed, she outdid her mother-in-law.

Unlike Lobelia in 1950's South Pasadena, Annette had a more than ample local staff. She could direct extensive house parties. Brad was a convivial and humorous host, very much like his father had been with his guests. Annette's guests genuinely enjoyed her husband's company. Here Brad was, once again, the bon vivant of his Yale days.

The JO even got to talk with Robert Kennedy one-on-one. It appears that RFK had an appreciation of language; and the Italian language in particular. He spoke of euphony. The recent Alliance for Progress program in South America was Robert's brother's initiative, when US president, in 1961.[129] In Spanish it was *Alianza para el Progreso.* Robert felt that the Italian "*Alianza para il Progreso,*" sounded so much more euphonic.

This was a triumph! It was Bradford's personal accomplishment. Brad had done what all junior officers dream of doing. He had a personal interaction with a historical figure while abroad. Surely the aims and goals of the Foreign Service abroad were now justified. For Brad, as for most junior officers, such a smooth exchange made his entire diplomatic tour in Ethiopia fall into place.

The young JO was generous with his entertainment budget and beer from Kagnew's commissary. Annette supervised the wives and the clean-up. The house the US government gave the Bishops was ample; and the gardener kept the yard neat. It was all part of life in the Service.

The Embassy at that time managed a housing pool. The pool had "Representational Housing." These consisted of larger houses where the occupants were expected to entertain, invite people, and host embassy occasions. The Bishops had fulfilled this role in their 'Representation House' amply. With it Brad put another accomplishment on his EER. Annette could look back as well. Many retired Foreign Service Wives still have sets of plates leftover from

---

[129] President John F. Kennedy

years of those functions.

Seal of the Office of the Chief of Protocol

And here there was yet *more* protocol. When the wives purchased their own extensive dining sets, bread and butter plates were encouraged, so that guests would never be hungry. It was also advised that male waiters be employed, so as not to inadvertently excite their mostly male guests. When entertaining a large group, the wives served coffee and tea with the meal. When they walked around the table to offer either, the wives of higher-ranking Foreign Service Officers served the coffee. The wives of lower ranking Foreign Service Officers served tea.

Traditional Coffee Pot

Traditional Tea Glass

Milan

"Italia"…you stand on the threshold…"
—Bradford Bishop's Diary
November 12, 1967

Bishop got his promotion before he departed 'Addis.' He was ecstatic, and either called and/or wrote everyone he knew about it. He had risen as fast as any Foreign Service Officer could in any comparable time period. Now he won his bid to fill a slot at the US Consulate in Milan.

The Foreign Service has a system of 'bidding' on job vacancies, much as American union labor goes through. Union labor bases 'bids' on seniority and skills required. Foreign Service Officer 'bids' are made according to officer rank. If an officer is ranked at level four, then an O4 ranked officer bids on level four ranked positions. The officer then chooses five posts. A review board then decides who will fill each post among those who put themselves forward for that post in a 'bid.'

There are times when a post has one bidder. The Review Board usually gives the sole bidder that post, then eliminates the bidder from other posts he or she bid on. This makes it easier for the Review Board. It clears out the competition for those posts with many bidders. Then there are some posts with no bidders. This can be problematic for Human Resources (HR).

Hence, Foreign Service Officers often put themselves forward with a higher ranked bid in hopes that they can fill 'bigger shoes' in a future bidding cycle.[130] The review boards are largely concerned with filling all the open slots; and everybody has to have a job. So, in many places if no one bids, the lower ranked officer can fill a higher ranked post.

At the end of that 'tour' the lower ranked officer can say that he or she performed the duties of the next grade up. (Thus, warranting further consideration for a promotion.) This is what the Foreign Service, calls a 'stretch.' It is also what ambitious people in the Foreign Service call 'career enhancing.'

---

[130] They are not paid more to do the higher-ranked job. It is all about boosting their careers.

Bishop won the bid for the Economic/Commercial Officer posting to Milan. The Milan post is a consulate. In less populous countries without significant commercial activity there is one Embassy. In more populous countries with significant trade relations, the workload often calls for a larger and more widely situated workforce. Thus, large cities, such as Milan, have American consulates.

At the US consulate in Milan the newly promoted Bishop saw his appointment as ideal. Milan is the business and financial capital of the Italian Republic. It is in a part of Italy Bishop cared for more than any other. He had operated in the area before, while with the ASA, and loved the ski slopes at Bormio, north of Milan, in the province of Sondrio.

Lobelia could not have been more pleased. She visited the family there and was warmly greeted by Annette at the airport several times. Here Lobelia could use the Italian she had studied in her spare time in South Pasadena. Together they would travel to Tuscany too. Their base in Milan made for side trips to Florence; where they both delighted in the scenery.

Milan is the home of La Scala, one of Europe's renowned Opera houses. There was ballet too. The dance tradition at La Scala goes back to 1778. It wasn't expensive either; and Lobelia could dote on her grandchildren. Indeed, her company was more important for Annette than it was for her son.

The marriage had not been going well between the Bishops for some time. Bradford was notably short tempered while posted at the Milan consulate. Annette wasn't fulfilling his demands. He grumbled that she was from 'the wrong side of the tracks' back in California[131]. He regarded himself as the only son of a wealthy and prominent family. He posited that his father explored for oil, and the resulting gushers were worth millions.[132]

---

[131] This is astonishing. Brad was from South Pasadena, a mainly 'working class' community. (A wise choice for Brad's parents, as it would still be affordable if their oil wildcatting business went bust.) When Brad and Annette went to High School together, Monterey Park was merged into South Pasadena High School. The wealthier community was San Marino, Annette's home. It is likely that, when San Marino High School reopened, Annette would have been districted into that upscale High School, and not into South Pasadena High.

[132] Annette's father was a salesman.

Part of his image was that of a Yale man. This was at a time when ancestors, and Old-World pedigrees, counted for something among European diplomats. It dovetailed with the image he was building for himself.

It is likely that this image lessened the pressure from the 'old foreign-service' Consul General in Milan. His 'managerial style' was never to lose an opportunity to castigate his staff. This pernicious style got to everyone at the Consulate. Often Bishop went home frustrated.

It has been said that a tour as a consular officer is 'the price you pay for a career.' It was just as well that Brad started off in Addis Ababa where Korry adored him. The Consul General in Milan was a curmudgeon. He was treated like a god by his browbeaten staff. In part this was because he would use much of the consulate's staff meeting time to berate the consulate's officers in the presence of their peers.

It was only months before Bishop's arrival, that the Consul General stopped opening up his officers' mail from home. The Consul General cut the stamps off of all incoming mail. The excuse given was that the Consul General's father-in-law was a stamp dealer in Switzerland.[133]

Nevertheless, the dual posting to Milan as a Political/Commercial Officer was a good start for Brad's career. Not only could he hone his skills at political reporting and protocol; there were enormous American business interests in Northern Italy to serve as well.

Foreign Service Officers often remake themselves for each new tour. When they get a new post, they often morph into whatever compliments the image they want to project. As the Political/Commercial Officer posted to Milan, Bradford had a chance to shine at diplomacy. The second posting for a Foreign Service Officer often is an opportunity to 'ply one's trade,' as it were, and Brad was now out of the consul function.

It was just as well. With over 10,000 Americans living in the area, consular officers had a huge work load, none of it 'career enhancing.' Handling the odd American death was especially

---

[133] It is noteworthy that cancelled stamps are of little or no value in the world of stamp collectors. Yet this was a time when the ink used to cancel American stamps could be washed off if the stamp was soaked in dishwashing liquid. The washed stamp looked as good as if it were unused. It could then be glued onto a letter and mailed.

difficult. While American cities saw no difficulty in scattering a cremated person's ashes wherever the last will and testament dictates, The City of Venice and other Italian municipalities, were aghast when the consular officers made a similar request on behalf of a deceased American.

Brad was probably grateful to dodge yet another unpleasant consular assignment that surfaced. Although she died in 1952, the body of Eva Peron (the revered wife of Argentina's Juan Peron) was moved. In 1957, with the covert assistance of the Vatican, the remains of Eva Peron were taken to Italy and buried in a Milan cemetery under a false name. In the course of Argentinian politics, she was first discovered to be in Milan, and then disinterred.

The Italian Ministry of Foreign Affairs was appalled. It was decreed that henceforth all foreign corpses had to be personally identified by the deceased's consular representative prior to burial or shipment to another country. From that day on, once or twice a week, an American consular officer had to go to the local city morgue and identify American corpses, using the late citizen's passport photo as a means of identification.

Misery loves company. Other consular officers from other foreign consulates in Milan usually joined the American consul. Far from a hardship post, it also stands as a reminder. Just because young people in the Foreign Service get to go to the region and country of their dreams, their duties there might be far worse than anticipated.

Venice was a bonus. The American Consulate in Venice was closed. The building itself was on the Grand Canal. The State Department doesn't sell such buildings. These are usually kept just in case a consulate is to be reopened at some future date. Long term, the policy can save the US government money. Thus, the American Embassy in Rome let the building to Wake Forest University for one dollar. (The then US Ambassador to Italy, Graham Martin, was a Wake Forest alumnus.)

The Venice Consulate still had a motor boat though. The City's Fire Department kept the boat for the Milan Consulate. Whenever Bishop, or any member of the Consulate in Milan, needed to visit Venice, the firemen made the boat available. It was great transportation. The firemen would pick up the visiting FSO at the train station, and then they'd sail away on the Canale Grande.

There was a further benefit to being posted to Italy at this time. In June 1968, the Economic/Commercial Officer post at the American Consulate in Naples was vacant. The work was piling up. Brad got himself assigned to temporary duty (TDY) there. It was good for him, as he could get away from the frustrations of family life. It was a relief to get away from the American Consul General in Milan, as well. He also got to know the area around Naples better.

Naples is a big port, and Sorrento to the south is important as well. An emphasis on Trade and Commerce was increasing at the US Department of State. There was also a great deal of smuggling and corruption along the Bay of Naples. Although the most notable part of smuggling in 1968 was the small-scale smuggling of cigarettes and drugs, a minor international issue could come in handy for a Foreign Service Officer in front of a promotion board.

This assignment would give Brad plenty to put on his Employee Evaluation Review (EER). There would be less 'employee exaggerating and rambling' as the EER has sometimes been called. Bradford was thus covering sections in two, diverse consulates in 1968. He even got a cryptographic clearance on March first, before he departed for Naples. (It is always convenient for any consulate to have an extra hand cleared for cryptography.) Together this demonstrated flexibility and industriousness at a time when the consulates abroad were short-staffed.

He also had an old school Consul General in charge at Naples: Consul General Homer Byington.[134] The Consul General was a no-nonsense, patriarchal figure. Working for a less curmudgeonly member of the 'Old Foreign Service' was another opportunity for Bradford to shine. Here his Yale credentials, and his son's very foreign-service name, "William Bradford Bishop III (the third)" dovetailed neatly into Brad Jr.'s goal of becoming an Ambassador by age 50.

The Byingtons liked to entertain both officially and privately on their boat, the *Zio Sam* III (*Uncle Sam the third*). They were

---

[134] Homer Byington was born in Naples. He spoke the Neapolitan dialect. His father was Consul General before him. It was a Foreign Service dynasty.

always on the lookout for a young officer to sail with them when they were entertaining. The FSO helped with the guests. Brad the comer, was in the right circles.

It was always a refreshing break from work to sail the Gulf of Naples on the *Zio Sam*, with fascinating people. These could be either Italian guests or high-ranking American visitors from the United States. A short cruise with the Byingtons could hold surprises, and perhaps - just perhaps - yet another way to ingratiate oneself to 'old service' stalwarts.

There was an American Air Force Base nearby as well. Foreign Service families could purchase groceries at a discount. Base privileges (the commissary) helped to make a tour abroad an inexpensive and rewarding experience.

* * *

Life in the refined city of Milan held much more than cultural opportunities. A curious incident occurred one evening during the Bishops' tour at the American Consulate in Milan, which could have come right out of fiction.

Patrick K. Murray was a consul in Milan at the time. He invited his co-worker, Bradford Bishop and his wife over to dinner. Patrick's other dinner guests were Mr. and Mme. Gérard Amanrich.

Gérard was the French Consul General in Milan at the time. The dinner was good, American hospitality; and the sort of intimate gathering that furthers quiet diplomacy. By this time both Bishops had honed their dinner engagement skills.

As it turns out, both Bradford Bishop and Gérard Amanrich became little known footnotes in the field of psychological research. Killing one's son or daughter is called filicide. Killing one's entire family goes beyond that and is now called 'Family Annihilation.'

The two men at Patrick's dinner table were upwardly mobile, each in his own Foreign Ministry. It is expected that Foreign Service Officers live for their careers. What was missed was that both Amanrich and Bishop were notably ambitious.

The French Consul General's wife Mme. Amanrich was from a

prominent French family. The family lived in the 6eme arrondissement, on the left bank of the River Seine, in Paris. The family had lost most of its money; and she was forced into taking a secretarial job in the *Quai d'Orsay*. It was there that she met her future husband. As with the Bishop's, theirs was often held up by their foreign ministries as the ideal family.

Amanrich, like Bishop envisioned himself on the threshold of great things. He had become a 'high flyer' in the French Foreign Ministry. He was later appointed to the most prestigious Ambassadorship within the French Foreign Ministry, the French Ambassador to the Holy See, Vatican City.[135]

He was a friendly person and likeable. He and his wife were great company at dinner. The entire family was appreciated. Indeed in 1975 his daughter, Ines Amanrich, then 16, was one of four women to give an oral presentation at the canonization on the life of Elizabeth Ann Seton.[136] Each spoke in a different language, as part of the canonization ceremony, before the Pope, 23 Cardinals, and over 100 Bishops. She spoke the French part saying, "She [Seton] is a Christian woman for our times."

There were so many attendees that the ceremony was held outdoors. The diplomatic corps turned out, particularly the American diplomatic corps. Here was an American saint. The pomp and ceremony in front of tens of thousands was glorious. Amanrich basked in the glow of appreciation. After all, it was his daughter reciting the praise in French; and he had the ear of the Pope too. French diplomatic life did not get much better than that.

Unfortunately, it was short lived. Two years later, following the election of President Valery Giscard d'Estaing, Amanrich was recalled to Paris. Ambassadorships, after general elections, to places as posh and prestigious as the Holy See are often awarded to political allies. Two years in an ambassadorial post is about what one could expect; and many career diplomats consider themselves fortunate when they remain in an ambassadorship for four years.

Not so Amanrich. He was crushed. He was 56 but did not have

---

[135] Traditionally the most prestigious Ambassadorship for America is that of American Ambassador to France.
[136] Elizabeth Ann Seton was the first native-born citizen of the United States to be canonized by the Roman Catholic Church.

to retire. It has been reported that he was offered ambassadorships to other places. Nearly every other diplomat in the world would have been flattered and pleased to get a second ambassadorship. (Any second ambassadorship *to anywhere* for that matter.)

None of those on offer were acceptable to him. He "walked the halls" of the *Quai d'Orsay* for the next six months. He was trying to secure a post that was not 'beneath him.'

The life he had become accustomed to was expensive. For nearly all of it, the French government picked up the tab. He was then living on the 4th floor of a well-kept building in a quiet, upscale neighborhood, 35 Avenue Bugeaud, Paris-16e.

On February first, 1977, while watching the television news in the Paris apartment building he and his family lived, he pulled out a pistol. He shot his wife Chante, age 52, dead. He shot his son Stephane, age 16, and daughter Ines, aged 18, dead. Then he went to the upstairs apartment, where his mother-in-law lived; and shot her to death.

He later claimed that he had emptied his pistol in the process. There were no more bullets. After killing his entire family, he got into his car and drove through the streets of Paris. Sometime in the wee hours of the morning, and about an hour's drive from Paris, he turned himself in to the police. He claimed that, had he more bullets, he would have taken his own life as well. In his statement he also claimed that he stopped at the River Seine and tried to throw himself in, but then lost his nerve.

The French authorities put him in the psychiatric ward of Saint Anne's hospital. On April 19th the attendants at Saint Anne's found him dead. He was hanging from a water pipe by his bathrobe belt.

Status Anxiety

"That's the news from Lake Wobegon, where all the women are strong, all the men are good-looking, and all the children are above average."

—Garrison Keillor

What do you regard as most humane? To spare someone shame.

—Friedrich Nietzsche

The Foreign Service is riddled with periodic and universal anxiety. It is not about what others think about Foreign Service Officers. If it doesn't affect their 'upward mobility,' it follows that what anyone beyond the Main State building thinks isn't worth a passing thought. Nor is this universal anxiety about how FSO's appear to anyone who doesn't hold their feet to the fire. Indeed, status anxiety does not usually strike until the typical Foreign Service Officer has passed the eight to twelve-year mark.

Prior to that, being an FSO is often a job with pleasures, perks, and comradeship. At the third or fourth post, after the eight to twelve years of service, Status Anxiety begins to take a toll. This is because it is about how Foreign Service Officers compete with each other.

Imagine a colony of koala bears. Suddenly at the same time each year some grow claws and fangs. Then they start to claw each other. After the promotion list comes out they morph back into a cuddly colony. Status anxiety goes back into hibernation until the next cycle.

Americans are particularly vulnerable to this anxiety. It isn't about being envious of those far beyond one's station in life. (By example, it is hard to find any FSO who is envious of the status held by the office of President of the United States.) This desire to 'climb the social ladder,' is more a condition suffered by people toward those of comparable rank. Working at Main State only sharpens the malady.

The Foreign Service has been called the steepest hierarchy in America. Foreign Service Officer careers excel or sink according to their Employee Evaluation Reviews. These reviews can be unfair. By example, if an officer contracts a tropical disease on his or her first tour there isn't much to evaluate as the stricken person could be in his or her bed for much of his or her tour of duty.

So how then to bloom in a world of the "Best and the Brightest?" It has been said that for every new officer accepted into the Service, one hundred applied. It has been further said that of those deemed qualified, decisions on whom to admit usually get down to three or five for every open position. The final choice is usually said to be a close call. For Brad it was Yale all over again.

Although few competing FSOs are aware of it, the environment they serve in has always been a very American one. It has been drilled into every one of them that the State Department is all about meritocracy; win or lose. Just like America itself.

The Foreign Service prides itself on merit. An intrinsic part of each officer's self-proclaimed superiority is a universal insistence on merit. Foreign Service Officers will tell anyone who will listen, that they are where they are by being brighter and more adaptable than others. (Or so the subscript goes.) This is a two-edged sword. In the steepest hierarchy in America, if you slip it is your own fault. No excuses.

Bradford Bishop wasn't going to slip a second time. He threw himself into this competition. Like so many of his peers at State, he was certain that he was better than all the others. Indeed, one of the constants during his time at the US Department of State was his utterances about "putting [this or that person] in his or her place."

What is notable about him is not how different – even unique – he was. It is how very similar he was to all those he saw as not measuring up to him. Bishop wanted to emerge from his assignments as a matchless emissary. Instead, he returned to Main State, registered at the Foreign Service Lounge, and was melted down to a humdrum bureaucrat with a few exotic stories.

His anticipated glory gone, he did not return the conquering hero. People did not see in him the next Howard Nicholson. They did not even consider his rapid rise up the ranks. And so, he grumbled.

This sort of grumbling is all too common among Foreign Service

Officers – especially prior to the posting of the promotion list.[137] This isn't just about the Foreign Service. The fact is that the United States *was built* on meritocracy. It is supposed to be about equal opportunity for all. The US Department of State only amplified it to a notably high (and some would say unbearable) pitch.

Equal opportunity for all in a system with annual winners and losers doesn't make for a great deal of comfort, or a happy working environment. A hierarchy is a pyramid. Only a few make it to the top. People are left behind. Careers are cut short.

The stress is all about what Foreign Service Officers think about each other. It is about avoiding controversy and not making a mistake. The safe way is usually the best way to get a promotion. Thus, displaying versatility along with deference to the 'appropriate' people is key.[138]

Bradford Bishop was at the top of his A-100 class at the outset. He analyzed what it took to succeed at State. Thus, he showed versatility, taking on whatever tasks he could, displaying a willingness to put in long hours. Yet he was unable to shut his eyes and sleep because of this tension. This time he envisioned the glittering prize, and the means of 'making good.'

Yet he never really squared meritocratic dogma with the obvious reality: State had an aristocracy all its own. State's assessors took him in as a Yale graduate, to flatter themselves.[139] The term the Foreign Service retained over the years, 'the Best and the Brightest,' could be bolstered by C students from prestigious schools, like Brad. Yet what the Kennedys and the Korrys of this world thought and desired were obstacles for State to get around, not for State to heed or cater to. State had its own measures and folkways.

At that time, State was similar to a private club.[140] Those who had parents who served at State before them were part and parcel

---

[137] Foreign Service Culture would, for a time, be called 'The Culture of Complaint.'
[138] The e-mail arrangements that tangled Secretary Hillary Clinton in her bid for the US Presidency are an example of the US Department of State's history of laxity and supplication to the boss. Better to let things slide than to say something that will displease someone who could make or break a career. Security is not a priority.
[139] This was at a time when the Oral Entry Exam was not blind. An applicant's credentials were closely examined.
[140] There is an oft-cited book on the topic, "A Pretty Good Club," by Martin Well, which examines this in detail.

of this. (At Yale, they are called 'legacies.') Every advantage was given them, as the aristocracy of old Europe was advantaged in their own Foreign Ministries. The failure of the State to grasp this paradox would have tragic results.

State aristocracy was reinforced by an intriguing 'Old Boy's Network.' Being social and getting along is all important. It was something Bradford Bishop excelled at while at his post in Addis Ababa. At a time when politicians were questioning the 'private club,' being social was a way that the tables could be turned. As an old European saw goes, a Napoleonic Officer once said of those with an 'ancient regime' pedigree, "You may have ancestors, but we are ancestors."[141]

Further, no one wants to be a 'loser.' This is particularly true when one is told at the outset of a Foreign Service Career that one is special. Indeed, the US Department of State is the only remaining agency of the Federal government still using taking the term 'the Best and the Brightest,' seriously. Considering that Foreign Service Officers are flawed to begin with, and that the term is specific to those who were handed so much and produced so little, Ambassador Korry's evaluation that FSOs are too concerned over their own promotions has some validity.

For William Bradford Bishop Jr., the news of yet another promotion in May 1971 came as a personal validation. It came before he left Milan. (To him, in the difficult environment the Consul General of Milan created, it meant that he had passed the 'private club' test.) The C average at Yale no longer mattered. It only mattered that he had been to Yale. True to form, he telephoned everyone he knew to present the news.

By the time, he returned to Main State after Milan he thought he was on his way. He saw his tour as properly navigating the requirements of a Foreign Service career. He wasn't going to relax now that he had done so well in Italy; yet he didn't see that he was just another card in a stacked deck. It was just as well that he was the joker.

After constant and careful examination, Bishop thought his

---

[141] The State Department, therefore, is a deadly combination of a Shame society and a purported meritocracy.

way through the process. The system had to be somewhat pervious. He reckoned that with a son named after him and ranked Bradford Bishop III (the third) no less, he could create a place for himself as a grandee. He wouldn't be denied.

So, he told everyone that the rate of promotion was, by his own estimate, the most rapid among those who started out with him (his A-100 class). He told everyone he knew (and whomever he could find as well). Let them try to deny him when he excelled among equals.

He thought that he, the little bird, had nearly flown to the summit, only to come plummeting down again. In both Addis Ababa and Milan, he did well; but afterward he was yesterday's man. Now he was going to *'go for broke.'* Despite State's habitual lack of applause at the completion of both tours, he would push on to an ambassadorship.

In order to distinguish himself further he took on a hardship post. A hardship post is a post with few amenities and a skeletal staff. Often the post is recommended for 'singles only,' as the term was then used. For an ambitious Foreign Service Officer such a posting shows a willingness to go wherever State sends him or her. At this time, in the early nineteen-seventies, too many Officers preferred the comfort and prestige of Western Europe. Too few were willing to do the difficult jobs (far from chandeliers and chamber orchestras) at hardship posts.

In small, often short-staffed, posts not only did the FSO multitask, but he could be the DCM (Deputy Chief of Mission). That position is the number two slot at an embassy. Outstanding service as a DCM goes a long way toward an ambassadorial appointment one day. Enough of those DCM slots, and years of standing in for an absent ambassador, is a strong suit to hold when seeking the US Foreign Service's glittering prize, an ambassadorship.

This time Bradford Bishop saw himself as getting in on the ground floor. He bid on the former British protectorate of Bechuanaland. Bechuanaland got its independence five years earlier, in 1966. There had been as of yet no American Ambassador there. Another Foreign Service Officer was holding down the fort while the matter was being sorted out. Indeed, the place was so unappealing that the aforementioned Foreign Service Officer serving while on

TDY (temporary duty) was posted there for only six months. The man could not be asked to stay in such a desolate place much longer.

This was an added incentive for any ambitious Foreign Service Officer. As Main State put it together, the ambassadorship to the new country was accredited to two other countries as well. The new and small enclave nations of Lesotho and Swaziland were thrown into the bargain.

Any ambassador assigned to one would be ambassador to all. No one could ever be in three places at once. That meant that whomever ran one of the three Embassies on a day-to-day basis would, de facto, become the chargé d'affaires (The diplomat in charge) in the Ambassador's absence. It would look good on a resume, and even better in front of any future promotion panel.

For a careerist, Africa was a place of diplomatic and bureaucratic growth. It had many new countries in need of US Ambassadors and staff. With continued rapid promotions, a pattern of taking charge, and covering every function in an embassy, the review board would be hard pressed to deny him his upward, and accelerated, ascent. This post had potential.

The new country had a new name too. The new name was far less cumbersome than Bechuanaland. It had a blue and black flag too. None of the flag contained that pesky communist red.

The new name fit in with the other new African countries as well. It would be an excellent place to work hard and build a career as an Africanist. The new name had a regal ring to it. The new country was named Botswana.

Bechuanaland

Blue and Black Botswana National Flag

Gaborone

> ...and still you stand on the threshold. Outwardly your accomplishments are great = My, such symbols = promotions, citations, languages, degrees. Still you stand on the threshold.[142]
>
> —Bradford Bishop's Diary - October 23, 1971

The country that looked so good for the aspiring Foreign Service Officer was one of astonishingly low expectations at independence. The territory was so desolate that it was administered from the outside. It was the only new country with its administrative center in another country. It was ruled from Mafeking, South Africa, which gladly passed the burden on to the new capital, Gaborone.

National Assembly Building at Gaborone

Gaborone at the time was not far from Mafeking, which was about all one could say for it at the onset. The capital was so small that, by January 1972, with newly constructed buildings, it could easily be mistaken for an American shopping mall. There were only a few thousand residents.

---

[142] It is noteworthy that Bishop penned this thought in his diary a mere 21 weeks *after* his latest promotion.

The American Embassy was above an Indian dry goods store. It was a rented space in that little, dusty desert town. The National Assembly building was in the middle of the small settlement. That was it.

The country itself was largely made up of scrub and bush. There were less than three people per square mile. The northern part was made up of the vast Kalahari Desert. Rutted tire tracks were what passed for roads, and a four-wheel drive vehicle was required to drive anywhere. There were only 5,000 licensed radio sets in the country.

There was a cattle industry that was largely brought into the territory by settlers, who traveled in covered wagons, pulled by a yoke of oxen. However small the economy, optimists noted that there was plenty of room to expand. That was about all anyone could say about the new country's future prospects.

Although there was an ethos of cooperation, and a single tribe making up most of the population, the few who bothered to take note of Botswana contemplated catastrophe. This was poignant because Botswana at the time was suffering through drought and famine.

The World Food Program (WFP) had been dealing with both since 1962. That was four years before independence. The United Nations had drawn up a scheme for emergency relief. The famine was so pernicious that the relief was ongoing. That part of the population without a family member employed was issued 10 ounces of maize (corn) and one ounce of vegetable oil per head per day. It was estimated that sixty percent of the new nation's population survived on these rations.[143]

Nothing was free, and there was plenty to do. With a minimal and monotonous diet, the recipients of emergency aid were put to work. They cleared land, built small dams, and improved what passed for roads. All of this was for that little bit of maize. The only positive thing to say was that the population was helpful and worked together. At the time observers wondered if there were even enough hand tools to go around.

The national herd suffered through the drought and famine as

---

[143] When made into a course flour, this came to be known as "mielie meal." Maize is the African term for the American plant commonly known as corn.

well. About a third of the cattle in Botswana were 'downers."[144] The drought got so bad that some of the cattle were chewing on the ears of the downers. This was to draw out some moisture from whatever was at hand. The WFP put on a special livestock-feed relief program to save the rest.

Tax revenue suffered as well. Most of that came from the sale of cattle. Many of the men of Botswana left for South Africa. In South Africa there was work to be had in the gold mines. It was difficult and sometimes dangerous work, but it was better than starvation.

The only outsiders to come into this difficult situation were Peace Corps workers from the United States and some British. Some of the American Peace Corps workers lived in brick buildings with tin roofs. These dwellings made the inhabitants bake from dawn to dusk. Others wound up in local housing.

The predominant form of housing is called a rondavel. A rondavel is a circular (often thatched) building with a conical roof. It features an outside latrine. (Large cockroaches and flies in the latrine were also a part of domestic life.)

It bears repeating that the posting to Botswana was originally 'recommended for singles only.'[145] Indeed, Bradford Bishop had to persuade State to agree to his family accompanying him to a post so hostile to family life. The previous chargés d'affaires concentrated on his own housing issues and privileges. Like Byington, the previous Charge had a similarly 'old foreign service' sounding name, like Byington, he had a lengthy Foreign Service pedigree as well. When he left the US mission to Botswana to the Bishops, he also left a load of unfinished projects and paperwork on his desk. It was all very much how the 'pretty good club' operated.

Into this world landed the Bishop family. Like most Foreign Service families, they expected to find vibrant African art and culture. Instead, they saw soul-deadening poverty, disease, and cheap mass-produced souvenirs. Gaborone wasn't Milan.

The US government controls most of one's life abroad. While ex-servicemen readily adapt to this situation, most wives find it an

---

[144] An old or diseased animal, especially an animal that cannot stand up
[145] Today such posts are referred to as "unaccompanied posts."

occasional nuisance. During the nineteen-sixties and early nineteen-seventies simple requests could take weeks. Sometimes a request could take months to process. The bureaucracy of the US Department of State, and other foreign affairs agencies, have logics all their own. There was no US base nearby to assist in amenities and in which to shop at discounted prices. This was not Addis Ababa.

The Americans at the embassy in Addis Ababa were living in an American/English speaking bubble. In Ethiopia, there were plenty of American contacts to network with. The term "Trailing Spouse" has since arisen to describe the straits the wives at hardship posts found themselves in. [146]

Rondavel dwelling on the winter farm Koedoesrant, South Africa

For an upwardly mobile minded Foreign Service Officer, despite the daunting anticipation of famine and drought, Botswana was an opportunity. Consider the logic. Africa was now comprised of nearly 50 newly independent countries - with more on the way.

Political appointees showed little interest in the Dark Continent. Standing in place of the traveling ambassador, a young officer could represent the embassy at the opening of the host country's Parliament, and in any other ceremonial capacity. Indeed, Botswana wasn't just a sizable place and a manageable host country, Botswana was strategically located. For any mid-level Foreign Service Officer, being the 'chief cook and bottle washer' at Amembassy Gaborone was a solid move.

---

[146] Later a mimeographed newsletter circulated called the "Spouses Underground Newspaper" or SUN.

Yet the Gaborone gambit was worrying for Bishop. The posting could become just another place where he was still 'on the threshold.' He was past his opening moves on State's chessboard. Hitherto he had played his pawns well.

Like most new mid-level officers, the strategy now focused on his knights - the only piece on a chessboard that can move over other chess pieces. He had to jump over his colleagues. When facing his adversaries - and he wasn't the only officer to view them this way - at the next Promotional Panel he would have his knights in the center of the chessboard. Mid-game is the most dangerous for any careerist. With his two knights, the Cold War and Apartheid, he was with the times. In front of any Promotional Panel he would be 'protected.' In any countermove by a peevish panel member, he could afford to make a quiet move, and thereby justify his next promotion.

He would not be a billiard ball. Nor would he be an advanced pawn, overextended and weak. Each of his two knights would be like an octopus, pieces covering eight directions. With no reason not to promote him, Bishop's performance rating would move him forward to the next level.

At this time, Independence and Apartheid were the two huge international issues facing the Region. These were Bishop's two knights on State's promotional chessboard. To the east, a White Settler minority ruled Rhodesia. Their capital was Salisbury. When the mother country, the United Kingdom, insisted on majority rule Rhodesia first balked, then unilaterally declared independence (UDI). The United Kingdom declared Rhodesia to be in a state of rebellion. That was eleven years before the Bishops arrived in the region.

To the South, where the European population was more numerous, lay the Republic of South Africa. Its parliament was self-confident and stubbornly defended Apartheid. There were good reasons for this. There were two nationalisms in one country. There was a White Nationalism and a Black African Nationalism.

The Foreign Service found the decolonization issue straightforward. Yesterday's issue was comfortable. State could take a back-seat view of South African and Rhodesian troubles. State could continue to luxuriate in, and repeat ever after, the pro-independence policies that successive American administrations since the Second World War had adopted. It was safe.

Brad, however, didn't want to be safe. When the Bishops arrived in January 1972, all the great colonial powers had quit Africa – except Portugal. So, the old men at State had his back.

From his post in Gaborone, Bishop was positioned hard by the focus of the previous generation's concern. Yet Bishop knew that the future was not about seeing colonialism off, but in turning the tide of the Cold War.[147] In Botswana he could say that he was involved in both.

There had been long and drawn out wars in the Portuguese colonies overseas. The two biggest of these were Mozambique and Angola. Together they geographically insulated South Africa from insurgents in the Region. As 1972 began, White South Africans could comfort themselves in the very intransience of the Portuguese government in Lisbon. "Without the colonies Portugal would only be a province of Spain," the Portuguese papers proclaimed.

Other borders were covered as well. South Africa was in control in South West Africa, a former German colony to the west and north of Botswana.[148] There were skirmishes, part of a low-level bush war, but nothing large scale. The insurgency in "South West," as it was called among the Whites, was sporadic and in desert areas. The insurgencies were far from the newly independent nations of Africa. South Africa could see itself as insulated in 1972; the former ASA linguist found the news stimulating. He pondered how he would spin all of this (and his heroic role defending the American way) on his next EER.

The minority Whites in the Region could take further comfort in the presence of then US Ambassador to South Africa, John Hurd.

---

[147] What he did not know, and where he made the same mistake as others at State, was that then President Nixon would change the diplomatic landscape by going to China. Nixon dismissed State's Cold War African focus as a diversion from the 'Great Game.'

[148] At this time the United Nations had recognized South West Africa as 'Namibia.' The South-West Africa People's Organization's military wing (SWAPO) or the People's Liberation Army of Namibia, a guerrilla group, had begun their armed struggle for independence. There was diplomatic action here as well. In 1971, acting on a request for an advisory opinion from the United Nations Security Council, the International Court of Justice ruled that the continued presence of South Africa in Namibia was illegal and that South Africa was under an obligation to withdraw from Namibia *immediately*. It also ruled that all member states of the United Nations were under an obligation not to recognize as valid any act performed by South Africa on behalf of Namibia.

Hurd was a Texas oilman. He was comfortable with Apartheid. Indeed, he got along so well with the South African leadership, that he went pheasant hunting with the then South African Minister of Transport. This would not have been of any note except for the venue. They went to Robben Island to hunt.

Robben Island was a prison island. It is situated in Table Bay, two miles away from the beaches of Cape Town, the second largest city in South Africa. At this time Robben Island was known as the location of a maximum-security prison. The bird shoot was within easy view of that prison holding a generation of political prisoners, including the future president of South Africa, Nelson Mandela. Even former US Attorney General Ramsey Clark was denied access to the Prison Island in 1970. Now Ambassador Hurd was hunting there. A pack of beagles lead the hunt, and two men from the prison picked up the birds from behind.[149]

Prisoners lined up on arrival at Robben Island

Ambassador Hurd was so friendly with the all-White South African Government that he was invited to the grand opening of Cape Town's new opera house – and he accepted the invitation. The opera was funded by all South Africans but only seated Whites. When the press covered the story Hurd's use of the term "Nigras"

---

[149] Later the South African Transportation minister insisted that the prison help he had were employees of the prison, not prisoners. However, reports persisted that at least some of the helpers were prisoners.

did not soothe the situation. The State Department stepped in to deal with the diplomatic gaffe. The department discreetly arranged for Hurd to be away from Cape Town during the event.

The Botswana post contained another plus for Bishop's assignment. His ambassador was Charles J. Nelson, an African-American. Ambassador Nelson was appointed six months before the Bishops arrived. Nelson had been with the Peace Corps and the US Information Agency (USIA). He could not have been more different from Ambassador Hurd.

The staff was scattered as well. Where Hurd's operational responsibilities were large and concentrated, Nelson's were sprawling. The Economic Assistance program (USAID) director was in Swaziland. The US Information Service USIS program director was based in Lesotho. Only the US Peace Corps had directors in all three countries.

By necessity, Nelson was often in motion. He was so mobile that he was often mistaken for the US Ambassador to the Union of South Africa itself. South Africans turned to him with their grievances... and he had to repeat that he was *not* the Ambassador to the Union of South Africa.

Needless to say, managing US relations in three countries at once is not easy. A great deal fell on Bradford Bishop's shoulders; and he was glad about it. It could only be surmised that he did not have much beyond paperwork to occupy himself at his home base, Gaborone.

There was Botswana's National Museum and Arts Gallery in town. It was only three and a half years old when the Bishops arrived. It featured a yoke of oxen and a covered wagon from the early pioneer days. This wasn't going to stir Annette or the children. There wasn't much to spend one's money on, nor anything to do. Indeed, the Bishop family's life there was frontier life itself.

There are breathtaking national parks in Botswana. The Bishops dashed off to them. Somehow Brad would unexpectedly come up with some money. This was especially so when domestic rows threatened Bradford's tranquility of mind.

At such posts any serving Foreign Service Officer has to appreciate the great outdoors. This was tailor-made for Bradford Bishop. He could hike, ride, and explore the vast desert with the best of them. There were tennis courts too.

The Okavango Delta is now considered one of the seven natural wonders of the world. The Moremi Game Reserve covers much of the eastern side of the Okavango Delta. The vastness and grandeur of this part of Africa caused Bradford to ponder that God might actually exist after all.[150]

The great African outdoors was something that impressed the boys, but after a time, it got stale for Annette. There simply were no fine arts as Annette had come to know them. Even Cape Town, the picturesque city off Table Bay and the Atlantic coast, had little to offer her. The closest town of any note was 70 miles away, Mafeking. Cape Town was 782 miles away.

In spite of the improvements in DCM housing Bradford's predecessor had installed, living conditions were far from ideal. The novelty of national parks, wild game, and living along the frontier only lasted so long. The vast spaces made her feel ever more solitary and cheerless. Annette had neither parties nor social life to organize. Aside from picnics there weren't a great many gatherings to host.

Brad put the best face on things. The family was part of his resume. He had to keep up the façade at all costs. They were part of the career he was nurturing.

It is common for Foreign Service spouses to turn to a psychiatrist. Spouses have been known to go doolally[151] waiting to go home. There is no evidence of Annette's seeking out psychiatric services before the Bishops were posted to Gaborone. It is not surprising that she sought psychiatric services after they returned.

No work even close to the education level of Foreign Service spouses was readily available in places like Botswana. The volunteer culture among the peoples of the new Botswana was admirable. It was admirably adaptable to Peace Corps goals as well.

---

[150] The Okavango Delta (or Okavango Grassland) (formerly spelled *Okovango* or *Okovanggo*) in Botswana is a very large, swampy inland delta formed where the Okavango River reaches a tectonic trough in the central part of the endorheic basin of the Kalahari. All the water reaching the Delta is ultimately evaporated and transpired, and does not flow into any sea or ocean.

[151] (British) Driven out of one's mind by boredom, the reference is to men in the military whose enlistments had expired, who waited there impatiently at post for transport home. The post it was named after was Doolally, India (Devlali or Deolali) the site of a former British army transit camp.

For Foreign Service wives it was not always as helpful.

Annette began the long journey that so many women in the early 1970's pioneered. Was being a housewife and mother all there was to life? With surrounding drought, disease and widespread poverty, depression is far more likely to strike than it is in places like Milan. Without a doubt, the 'Trailing Spouse' blues had set in.

Botswana Coat of Arms

To start with, the female Peace Corps volunteers (PCV) differed from the Foreign Service wives in outlook. PCV's saw their work as useful. Long before the women's movement took hold in America, Foreign Service wives pondered the concept of useful roles. Some even resented the household help. This was tempered by the real need of Botswana's people for employment.

In such circumstances, the wives had to create a role of their own. It had to go beyond being a hostess. Further disenchantment with Foreign Service life took on a new dynamic when Lobelia came to visit.

It is important to be busy when abroad. Some wives have feelings of worthlessness. Part of combatting this is for women to try to make their lives, and the lives of their children, as American as possible.

Bradford's view of his family had been souring for years. It wasn't working out as it had in Ethiopia. Hopping on a horse and riding beyond Gaborone's city limits was only a temporary respite. (As it had been in South Pasadena when he and Ron Currie took off for Mexico, and the desert, during his high school days).

Since his post-ASA service, and while studying in Florence, he pondered what love was. He simply could not understand it. He simply could not bond with his wife and children. It was sufficient, and so much easier, to see his family as part of his success. Now they were becoming an unexpected drag on it.

He once wrote 'your family grows more and more beautiful every day' in his diary. It was another misleading clue that perplexed law enforcement and psychologists alike. The 'beautiful family' and their services to the US mission is what scored points in his efficiency report. There was no such meaningful score in Gaborone at that time.

This became more ominous in his dealings with the Soviet Union's Ambassador to Botswana. There was then a real interest in South African affairs on the part of international communists during the Cold War.[152] The Soviets backed and armed substantial opposition groups to Apartheid. Bradford's contacts with the Soviets were questionable. He may even have paved the way for an alternative life's scenario at this time.

For their part, the wives as a group had mixed feelings. On the one hand, many thought that what they were doing for State was a good thing. They understood that their husbands would suffer, and be judged on, what spouses did or did not do. Yet they didn't want to feel that they were being watched (which they were).

The wives worked hard for the US Government. They gave it many hours of unpaid labor. For these efforts, they were barely recognized. Accomplishments either were credited to their husbands (the employee) or not at all.

Bishop's quest for an ambassadorship was on course. With this dingy assignment, he could claim to be an all-around FSO, capable of nearly anything any far-flung outpost demanded. He had it so well planned that he could almost see the next promotion on the

---

[152] It had spread from Guinea and Mali, to the horn of Africa while he was there and, in a timely progression, south. It played nicely into Brad Bishop's middle game, and next EER.

horizon. It was within his grasp. Yet his family was no longer compliant. Lobelia was thwarting him with a concept of the family that was diametrically opposed to his Foreign Service assumptions.

It is curious that, while Ambassador Nelson was in one of his two other posts, Deputy Chief of Mission (DCM) Bishop *without authorization and on his own*, was in contact with the Soviet mission to Gaborone. It was September 22, 1972, about ten months into his tour there. This only raised eyebrows at State *after* the murders. At the time State simply rolled on. Correspondence and traffic from Botswana was not closely scrutinized. Any questionable actions were overlooked.

It is also noteworthy that DCM Bishop reported his State Department ID lost in July, toward the end of his tour. It could, of course, be that Bradford was as careless at State as he was in the military. In retrospect, a genuine State Department Identification during the Cold War period was a valuable item on the black market. This was another element not considered as part of the puzzle.

Bishop in Botswana, picture from the pilot
license he earned while in Gaborone

The China Card

"I was traveling through South Africa to reach the capital of Botswana…" "…in terms of Black Africa, it was in a sense more distant, but in terms of southern Africa – South Africa [had] significant control vis-à-vis Botswana and Botswana's access to the world.
—Ambassador Charles J. Nelson from ADST Oral History Project 31 October 1981

"… all the money in this world is either Red or Blue. I do not have my own Green money, so where can I get some from? I am not taking a cold war position. All I want is money to build it."
— Julius Nyerere, PRO, DO183/730, From Dar es Salaam to CRO, No. 1089, 3 July 1965. (Concerning the proposed Tamzam Railway)

There was a kicker to the assignment. There had been a turn of events that concerned the West. In the 1950s and thereafter, the West had been concerned over Communist influence in Africa. There was a real concern over Communist-oriented rebel groups in the Portuguese colonies. Africa and Rhodesia had always used this ploy to edge closer to the West.

Now there was a real Communist presence in Southern Africa. It wasn't an invasion. It wasn't subversion or guerilla groups. From the point of view of the West it was far worse. Mainland (Communist) China had agreed to build a railway in Africa.

The Chinese, under Mao Zedong, were already estranged from the Soviet Union. There had even been serious incidents along the Russia-China border in Siberia. Mao was competing with the Soviet Union for leadership of emerging nations in Africa and Asia. Zambia, north of Botswana—penned in by forces beyond its control—drew Mao's attention.

Zambia's wealth at the time was copper. An aerial survey conducted by the Canadians and the British found a plausible railway route north, through neighboring Tanzania. It would, however, be costly. None of the Western Countries were willing to finance it.

Zambia's then president, Kenneth Kaunda, did not want to strain relations with the West. The West was Zambia's primary market for copper. The main rail route was jointly owned by Zambia and Rhodesia. Diverting the valuable freight north by building an access route through Tanzania, and its port at Dar es

Salaam, would complicate relations with the West even further. Nor was the Soviet Union interested in the project.

The opening phase of African decolonization was not complete. Phase one was about independence; combined with a united African voting bloc in the general assembly of the United Nations. Both game plans were either frustrated by, or incomplete due to, the Portuguese in their African territories and the White-ruled south.[153]

Africa north of the Zambezi was in a chokehold. (And Kenneth Kaunda's Zambia felt it intensely.) As in chess, the minority-ruled white knights' 'octopus' position covered all options.[154] How could Africa move forward to decolonization's endgame: prosperity financed through mineral wealth?

When the Bishops arrived in Botswana in January 1972, the 'Great Game' in Africa was intent on the second phase of its priorities. This, the middle-game, was increasingly about the position Central and East Africa found itself in. This was about getting Africa's mineral wealth to market. It was about isolating South Africa and squeezing Rhodesia; and it was not working. What was needed was a tactical move to achieve some gain.

South Africa had become the economic engine of the Region. Rhodesia continued to be prosperous after a decade of its Unilateral Declaration of Independence (UDI) from Great Britain. Rhodesia shipped its produce through the Portuguese colony of Mozambique by rail. There it was loaded onto ships bound for world markets.

The terrain and the dense jungle made shipping by any other route nearly impossible. All lines of transport and communications ran north/south. This put African nationalists throughout the continent in check. Getting out of check was the overriding priority. There seemed to be no getting around geography.

* * *

---

[153] If viewed as a chess game, the White pieces always move first. In the African South, the "Black pieces" had yet to make their move. During Bishop's tenure outside forces, both East and West, would propose 'Black's' next move.

[154] So, called because on a chessboard a knight at midgame can strike and cover 8 positions. The combination of geography, modest military resources, and finances were the three knights for the "White pieces."

The new nations north of "South" (South Africa) were called the "Front Line States." This sharpened a divide that South African and Rhodesian policy would rather blur. Their policies became worrisome when Zambia and Tanzania sought a loan to build a railway through the two countries, thus avoiding the traditional railway routes south. That loan was turned down, and the minority ruled areas comforted themselves, once again, in their analeptic geography.

A cursory glance at the map told the story. It made neither engineering nor economic sense to build the proposed railway line. It was easier to say that it could not be done, even with massive cost overruns, than to broach the main reason for building it. Both Zambia and Tanzania were bereft - but only for a time.

In a surprise move Zambia and Tanzania turned to Mainland China. China was still competing with the island of Taiwan for recognition as the legitimate government of all China. To Beijing the support of poor nations in Africa was not only about spreading revolution, it was about getting votes in the UN General Assembly, to officially sanction their legitimacy. At the time both Zambia and Tanzania were governed by socialist governments. An aid arrangement with Beijing was ideal.

There were snags of course. The obvious one was the terrain. The proposed railway would have to climb 1,800 feet. The plan called for the construction of 18 tunnels and the crossing of four major rivers. The track would have to be laid over a swamp and span the Mpanga River Valley. (Ultimately three pillars of 50 meters, or 164 feet, had to be built to accommodate the bridge alone.) Although planned as a single-track railway, it was expected to carry two million tons of freight a year. It became the most ambitious rail project of its kind since the Second World War.

The West doubted that the Chinese could complete a viable project. The methods to be used were assumed to be makeshift and flawed. It would cost a half a billion American Dollars. For a time, it was called the "Bamboo Railway."

Further, the 1160-mile railway would have to be financed through advanced credits. These would be paid for through sales of Chinese goods in State-owned stores in both Zambia and Tanzania.

An even larger snag turned up when the math did not add up.

In order to finance construction, the economies of both Zambia and Tanzania would have to cease purchasing Western goods. Both would have to devote their entire consumer spending to Chinese manufactured goods. This came as a jolt.

Products such as Zambia's copper, and other raw materials, were being shipped to the West. The complete reversal of traditional economic outlets was impossible. America, in the middle of the Cold War took comfort in this.

The State Department, with no real mercantile expertise at the time, should have advised official Washington that the prestige of the three countries involved was on the line. Wiser heads, in other parts of the US government, estimated that it might take six or seven years to complete. Yet complete it Beijing would.

There had already been a shot across the bow. The French had spearheaded Mainland China's claim to the China seat on the United Nations' Security Council. That powerful seat was permanently in Taiwan's possession. The competition intensified as France, itself a member of the Security Council, brought the question before the United Nations in New York for a vote. Was Mainland China (the People's Republic of China) or Taiwan (the Republic of China) the legitimate government of China?

A stream of cables sent directly from the Secretary of State streamed into far flung outposts like Botswana. These cables urged the staff to lobby the Head of State to instruct their UN representatives to vote with the West. It was a real Cold War battle; and the US outpost in Gaborone was part of the worldwide, US effort. Lobby as US diplomats in Gaborone might, Botswana's vote went to Mainland China; and America's ally, Taiwan, vacated the United Nations seat for China.

Fortunately for the newly-promoted, midlevel officer, Bishop missed this defeat of the West by a few months. Defeat worked against him. Only success could burnish his Employee Evaluation Report. His EER would read better if Bishop was there for the rebound.

The West had already responded to communist advances by making simpler - and more immediate - plans for transport. America invested in roads. Bishop would ride this wave on his EER.

American reasoning was that a good road benefited everyone, just as a good elementary school education benefited society as a whole. This had been a key element of US Foreign Policy for decades.

Therein was the answer to China's Tanzania/Zambia (Tanzam) railway project. America would build a road north and it would outmaneuver the Tanzam Railway. It would include a leg to Botswana as well.

There was a narrow path around the minority-ruled countries. The entire roadway scheme converged on a roughly two-hundred-meter strip of land along the Zambezi River. Those two hundred meters separated White-ruled Rhodesia from then White-ruled South-West Africa. Zambia and Botswana had a common border. It was a 19th century cartographer's mistake.

The fact is that the maps of Africa needed more work. (Some say they still do.) The borders were drawn in 1890. Africa was so uncharted that much of the vital information on the Zambezi, one of Africa's greatest rivers, was guesswork.

Then German Chancellor, Leo Von Caprivi, negotiated a treaty with the United Kingdom to acquire some islands in the North Sea.[155] It was a land swap for the German-held Indian Ocean nutmeg islands of Zanzibar. A 280-mile-long strip of territory north of Botswana was thrown into the bargain.

The idea was to link up the then German Colony of South West Africa with the German Colony of Tanganyika (present day Tanzania) to the east. The Chancellor envisioned the Zambezi river as a commercial thoroughfare between the two. After all, the Zambezi reaches into the heart of the continent, doesn't it?

There were two inconvenient unknowns at the conference. The first was that the Zambezi was not navigable for much of that stretch of newly acquired territory. The second was that the Zambezi empties into Victoria Falls, the largest waterfall in the world.

---

[155] The Heligoland–Zanzibar Treaty (German: Helgoland-Sansibar-Vertrag; also known as the Anglo-German Agreement of 1890) was an agreement signed on 1 July 1890 between the German Empire and the United Kingdom. Germany gained the small but strategic Heligoland archipelago, which its new navy needed to control the new Kiel Canal and the approaches to Germany's North Sea ports. In exchange, Germany gave up its rights in the Zanzibar region in Africa, allowing Zanzibar to provide a key link in the British control of East Africa.

What concerned the Americans was the two hundred meters along the Zambezi, at Kazungula, where, what became known as the Caprivi Strip stops and Rhodesia begins. (It was the result of the 1890 mismeasurement.) This discrepancy in borders meant that Zambia had a narrow border along the Zambezi with Botswana. That was key. The two-hundred-meter border gap had a functioning ferry crossing as well.

What was needed to make it a major commercial highway, was good all-weather roads. Tire tracks (mere ruts in the desert) would not do. America's response to the Tanzam railway, would be the Tanzam highway. The highway would open up the route north with a network of roadways through Zambia. It would continue on to the Tanzanian coast.

Once the Chinese started to build their railway, promotion-conscious Foreign Service Officers quickly touted the highway project. Useful infrastructure efforts to improve Botswana's domestic roadways took a backseat. Bishop and others made the bridge over the Zambezi the focal point.[156] Their EER's would show that America's planned bridge exceeded whatever the Chinese were building; and would further eclipse Chinese influence in Africa forever.

The South-West African post office celebrates a famous Diplomatic blunder. It also shows the Okavango Delta, the aforementioned endorheic drainage basin in the desert.

---

[156] This was a prime example of the headaches those who have to evaluate Foreign Service Officers for promotion go through. They can be forgiven for looking up from this tiresome duty and wondering out loud how many Foreign Service Officers were responsible for the construction. (If any at all)

When Nixon visited China on February 21, 1972 the highway project went beyond the Cold War and entered into a three-way contest: China, the Soviet Union, and the West. This added a new dimension to the embassy's routine work. Of course, there was the anticipated outcry from South Africa. It came as expected; and it was immediate.

The South Africans were happy in their isolation. The Kalahari Desert was a natural barrier. The vast dry scrubland in northern Botswana was a hedge against possible insurgents. The South African papers reported that the construction of all-weather roads through the desert would create a 'terrorist highway.'

The outcry worked out well for America. Nixon was president. He and Henry Kissinger kept their own council on foreign relations. In a cagey move, Nixon had balanced the ambassadorial appointment of Ambassador Hurd with Bishop's direct report, African-American Ambassador Nelson, to Botswana. It was no accident that Bishop's African-American boss was highly visible. This would be a further check mark for the next (promotional) review board, Bishop was on the right side of the Apartheid issue.

A promotion after one year is too much, too soon. Nevertheless, what a China story he could dovetail into the Apartheid issue! Kissinger's trip to China was all the rage. Of course, he would be just another 'Employee Exaggerating and Rambling.' Nevertheless, like all successful FSOs before and after him, he had caught the diplomatic wave. He would surf in on it. Nothing could stop him now. He was a 'comer.'

He could see the middle game looming. It was taking shape. His willingness to bring his family to a hardship post would demonstrate that he was no epicurean. The long sought-after end game could be an ambassadorship to one of the new countries emerging from decolonization.

The timing was right too. Nixon wouldn't leave office until after the 1976 election. Bishop would be back at Main State in 1974. That would give him plenty of time to lobby and ingratiate himself to the higher ups.

He could just picture it too. The fun-loving Bradford Bishop of Yale was now the 'most likely to succeed.' He had shown what he could do. His 1974 EER would clinch it. It was a plan; and it looked like clear sailing to the next step, O3.

* * *

In Botswana, Bishop had the great outdoors at his doorstep. He could trek cross-country, ride on horseback, and camp under the stars. Conventional wisdom in the US Foreign Service has always had it that, in some posts, if you are not involved in outside sports you will not be happy. Gaborone in 1972 was one of those posts. The Bishop boys enjoyed the outdoors and the small-town atmosphere. Viewing it from afar, fellow officers thought the situation ideal.

Despite this, it appears that Bradford Bishop got bored. Even the initial thrill of being in charge four months a year wore thin. After all, he was alone. He was in charge of himself. And there was only discontent, after the boys went off to bed, to go home to.

As the time passed Bishop went another year without a promotion. Conventional State Department wisdom was that, even if the O4 FSO was the fastest rising member of his class, it was better *not* to rise *that* quickly. As an FSO has five years in each "time in class" (TIC) it is desirable to stretch one's service time out, thus guaranteeing a lengthy career.

And what if his career was cut short? For all his 'doped up' sleaziness on serax, he still planned in secret. The Americans did not mix with the Soviets in Botswana. That's part of what made Bradford's communication of September 21, 1972 to the Soviet Embassy in Gaborone questionable.

He could have been signaling that he was willing to collaborate. The expenses of an expanded family had to weigh on him. It has now become painfully evident that, selling out to the KGB was far more common in the nineteen-seventies than America could have imagined.

There was also a secret cloak-and-dagger aspect to it. Such exploits had always appealed to the ex-Yale prankster and ex-ASA operative. Besides, his post *was* boring and far from glamorous.

Gaborone, and indeed the entire Region, was behind the times. There was no television. The first real television programming did not appear in South Africa until the 1980's.[157] Even at that late date, clergymen railed against its adoption. The Bishop children accepted the situation, as all children do. Gaborone was not ranked as a 'singles only' post for nothing.

This came at a pregnant time for women back in America. There was a new domestic movement. Sometimes called "The Women's Movement," it burst onto the American scene in 1973 with an astonishing resilience. This was no fad.

A new magazine was launched for women, *Ms. Magazine*. It appeared that the female population of 1973-4 America had made a group decision. And the Foreign Service was at a loss on how to deal with it.

There were sudden (and to many) surprising assaults on women who stayed at home. The movement challenged the single bread-winner household. *Ms. Magazine* was the antithesis of 'Coffee Ranks Tea.'

Within the US Department of State, it ultimately meant the rise of female FSOs. Foreign Service rules appeared to be democratic on the surface, but they were also strict. A woman could be a Foreign Service Officer but had to resign when she got married. Prior to this about five percent of the women in the Service, were Foreign Service Officers. As often as not, they were not welcomed at Post.

This was successfully challenged just before *Ms. Magazine* came out. It could be argued that the Women's Action Organization (WAO) at State was a bellwether. When women working with 13 departmental task force reports, put forward repeated inequities at State, the male management officers were taken aback. There were no ready answers.

By the time, the Bishops returned from their posting to Gaborone, the shift had occurred. The change was everywhere, especially in the news. Annette could not have failed to notice it.

---

[157] BOP TV broadcasting was on a UHF band and commenced in 1984. BOP TV was broadcast from a Bantustan, Bophuthatswana. (A homeland set up to house Setswana-speaking peoples in 1983) It primarily transmitted imported programming, most of it from the USA and in an unedited form, allowing all comical references about White people to be aired to Black people.

The Tanzam Railway

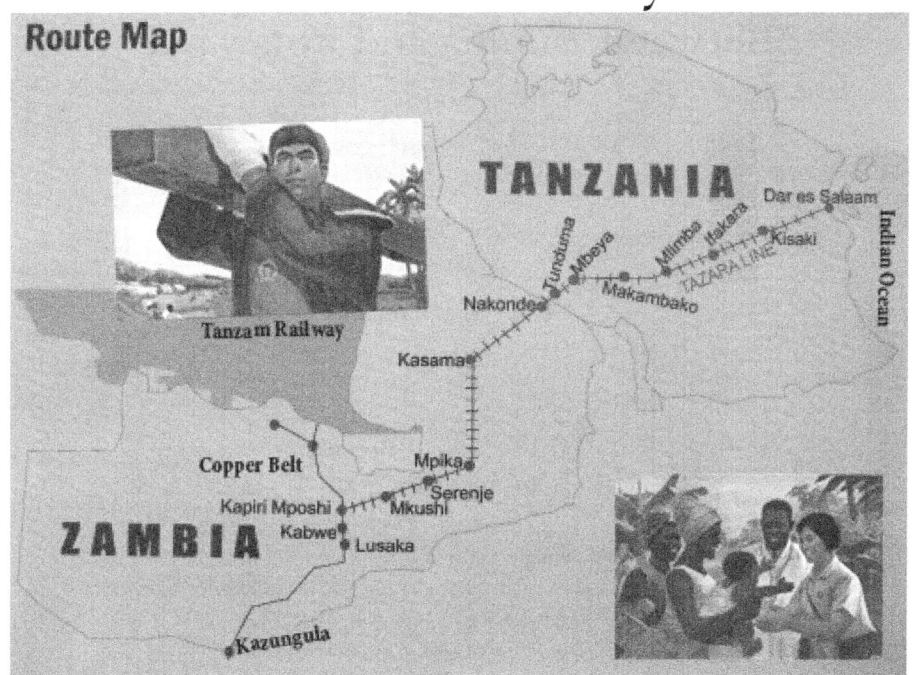

The Tanzam Highway

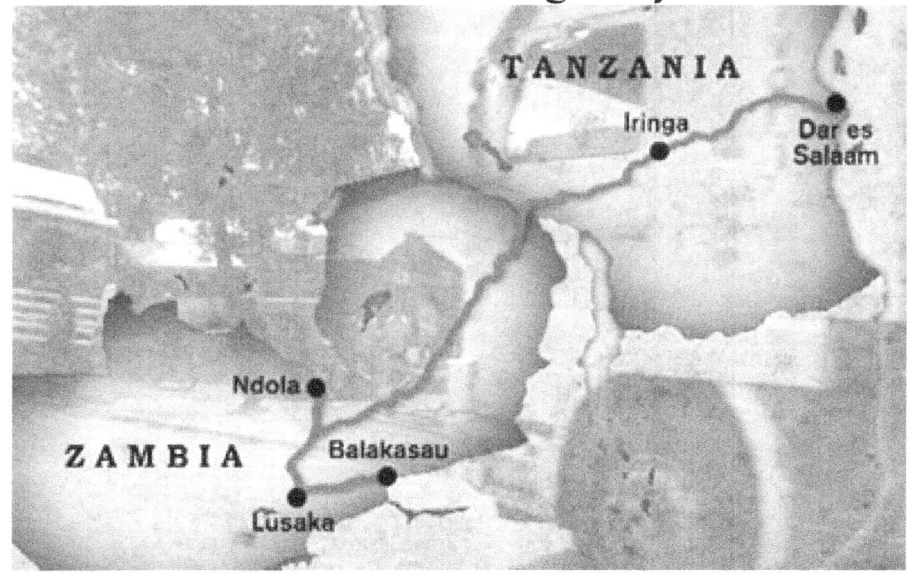

The Few Hundred Meters of Border Between Zambia and Botswana

This is where five African Countries came together on a 1972 map. In 1972 South Africa administered the Caprivi Strip. Both South Africa and Rhodesia (Today's Zimbabwe) had minority-controlled governments. Portugal still held on to its African colonies. The 200 meters along the Zambezi River was the only place where a link could bypass the White minority-ruled areas.

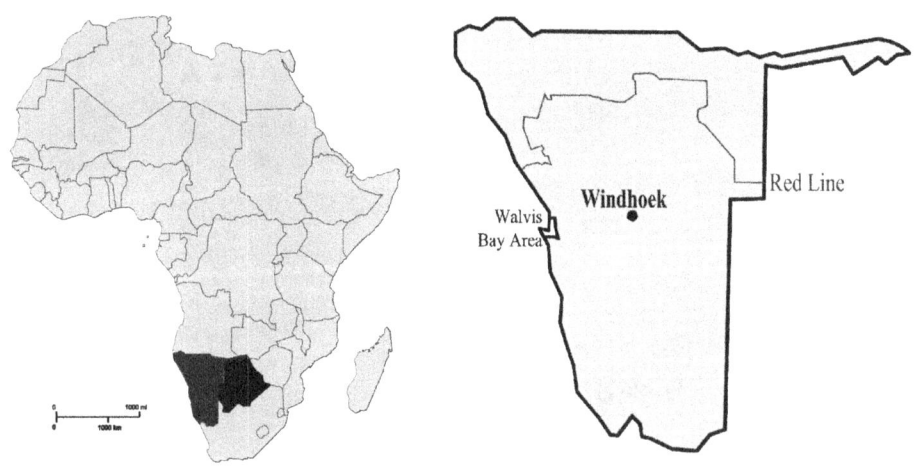

The Red line, originally drawn by the German colonial administration in South West Africa in 1911, became a fence during South Africa's occupation of the territory. Originally a veterinary cordon fence, it separated the more numerous African peoples of the North from the settlers in the south, and later became a factor in the ensuing border war

The Corridor Reputation

...timing social awareness and sensibility to a situation are important.
—Bradford Bishop, from his Diary

Nobody realizes that some people expend tremendous energy merely to be normal.
— Albert Camus

The return to America was truly welcome for the entire Bishop family. This was true for Bradford as well. He reported to the Foreign Service lounge and signed in. The Foreign Service Lounge connotes the camaraderie, as well as promoting the bonhomie, of generations of Foreign Service Officers. Once the FSO signed into the Foreign Service lounge his assignment was formally finished. Then he looked forward to rotating on to his next assignment. Bishop could look forward to more training at FSI and then working amidst grandeur.

The Foreign Service lounge was in the Main State Department building on "C" Street in Washington. Main State was completed in 1941 and was renovated in the early 1960's. The renovation was designed in the 'international style.' (Just as the United Nations building in New York City is.)

The Ben Franklin room, the largest reception room at Main State, is arguably the best reception room in Washington. Some would add, 'in the world.' The backdrop of American Art and Architecture is astonishing for anyone familiar only with Main State's drab outward appearance.

The area is a suite of 42 rooms of about 28,000 square feet. The diplomatic reception rooms hold antiques, including the desk from which Thomas Jefferson is reputed to have written the Bill of Rights. All together the collection is valued at US 100 million US dollars (Give or take a few million). With all that grandiosity and prestige in their background, the Bishops took a flight to California.

* * *

Sometimes it isn't easy returning home. Nineteen seventy-four was the 20th anniversary of South Pasadena High School's graduating class of 1954. It was held at the Newport Beach boat basin. It featured a barbeque, as had other reunions. The high school president of the class of 1954 oversaw the celebrations. All of Bradford's primary and high school friends were there. It was cozy. For Brad and Annette, it was like a big family reunion.

While Annette reconnected with her friends, Brad circulated among his old buddies. It was time to flaunt his success in the Foreign Service. The reunion quickly became uncomfortable when he learned that every one of his fellow classmates was making more than he.

He asked them what they were making. They were open about it; after all they were fellow grads. He sought out each one; and each time it was the same. At $21,500 Brad was making from $5000 to $10,000 less than his old classmates.

Everyone noticed this but pretended not to. It was hard *not* to notice. Brad went from old high school classmate to classmate flailing his arms after speaking with each. William Bradford Bishop Jr. came to the reunion as a triumphant diplomat. Just as he returned from Yale during school breaks, just as he would later speak of his undercover days at ASA, just as he presented himself at society parties as a diplomat, so he returned triumphant, important and basking in glory. Now this.

His classmates owned their own homes. These houses had appreciated. The sudden inflation the Bishops had missed while in Botswana was part of the conversation. He could talk about Milan and the Bay of Naples, but his life was not about that. It was about winning. Here he was behind his entire high school class. What had he done wrong?

Annette had reconnected with an old school friend. Her friend had married another class friend, and the Bishops were invited to their pool party. Annette and her friends spoke about the children. With three beautiful boys and still attractive, Annette was quite accomplished and comfortable in her high school circle. They were all full-time homemakers, yet in private they questioned their roles. Annette had as wonderful an experience at the reunion, as Bradford's was belittling.

Brad's friends had accrued money and assets. Brad had collected experiences but had debt and growing expenses as well.

He had no house to return to. Was he a permanent tourist?

This was further unsettling when he got a tour of Annette's friend's house. He settled in by the pool, and as at the barbeque, regaled the men with stories of Africa. Of course, those who stayed behind in Southern California thought the stories Brad had to tell were not reasons to leave Southern California. Life there was about looking good and being prosperous.

Bradford was back in Southern California culture now. He saw what others owned and could not see what he had. Few Foreign Service Officers of the day understood that their free housing, free travel, and other benefits unattainable to their high school cohort, more than made up for the difference in wages.

Of course, one could make a case that champagne with a cabinet minister in an exotic land trumps an evening at the bowling lanes back home. Was a night out at South Pasadena's Rialto Theater, with Annette, better than a reception with an emperor? What so many in the Foreign Service did not grasp was that one does not really own things. What the 'owner' has is the use of needful things for a time. After that the FSO gets a fulsome government pension among other perks.

Brad had journeyed through the Okavango Delta. He had sailed the Grande Canale and the Bay of Naples. He had climbed and skied the Italian Alps. He had servants, subsidized transportation across oceans, no electric bills, and far more disposable income than his peers. He had three healthy sons. What he could not see, and may never have realized, was that State had also given him memories that would last him a lifetime.

The Rialto Theatre, South Pasadena, California circa 1960

It was while he was at the reunion in California that he was at his weakest. Annette told their friends that she was looking for a house in the Washington DC area. Yet with rising oil prices and soaring inflation, there wasn't enough money to house a family of five. That was when Lobelia made her move. "Why not move in with me," she proposed?

Lobelia did not want to live alone. She wanted an active role in raising the family. With her husband gone, she was frustrated. She offered to move to the Washington DC area and pay for the house. Annette was delighted. So were the kids. Brad was horrified.

* * *

Bradford bid on and received a posting at Main State with the grand title of... "Assistant Chief in the Division of Special Activities and Commercial Treaties." He would host diplomats and presidents in the Ben Franklin room and other posh venues. Nevertheless, Bradford continued to reevaluate his accomplishments in the Foreign Service: promotions, citations, languages, degrees. He was taut; and it showed.

He did not like being a bureaucrat. He saw no point in some of his work. His mother effectively controlled his household's purse strings. It was the third consecutive confinement in his life (The first being out-of-his depth at Yale, and the second being the constraints of the ASA). His resentment focused on the clear and present irritant, his mother.

In his self-analysis, Bradford concluded that he had performed well enough at Gaborone. Ambassador Nelson was an affable fellow, although his wife was not. None of that mattered. What did matter to a Foreign Service Officer was the next step up. He racked up the points he wanted on his EER. So, he thought to himself in the slang of the day, what gives?

Without an onward assignment, it got lonely. This is the recurring theme of every FSO: the euphoria of being a person of note abroad, followed by letdown after signing in at the Foreign Service lounge. This is the fear that one's efforts abroad were 'a flash in the pan,' and that no one at Main State cares.

Bradford's response was to 'try again, much harder'. He turned to "Prairie Songs,"[158] when he jogged in the morning to relieve stress. If he could live in a piece, or pieces, of music, a collection of Prairie Songs would be his choice.

Baby Geoffrey was born on February 12, 1971, seven months before the diary entry below. Bishop was promoted when Geoff was three months old. The American situation comedy "My Three Sons," was aired on CBS until April 13, 1972. The ensuing references, followed by the good will it generated at Main State, were obvious.

---

[158] The television series, "Little House on the Prairie," ran from 1974 to 1982. Prairie Songs are Midwestern Folk Songs. While Lobelia preferred opera, Brad's taste in music reflects the great outdoors and a pioneering spirit.

"…your family grows more beautiful, and you still stand of the threshold" Brad Bishop's diary. Passport photo of William Bradford Bishop III, aged 10, taken at the time of the diary entry (Left)

Main State is the place to be when one lobbies for upward mobility. A lot can be accomplished there. Officers in the field usually have to return to be noticed. The corridors are notably wide. FSO's mingle and, as the old departmental saying goes, "One's 'corridor reputation' is taken into consideration," when the promotion review board convenes.

Careers at State are precarious. They hang on the vital 'Time in Class' (TIC) system. The Foreign Service ranks an officer using the term 'class.' An FSO cannot remain 'In Class' for over five years. Bradford had been ranked O4 for over three years now. So, what if President Nixon left office before January 1977? China was still important. Brad just knew that the Kazungula Bridge was *the* talking point that would get him his promotion. So why was his career stalled?

This year he had to either get the promotion or bid into a stretch (An unfilled O3 slot that would take an O4 for lack of candidates.) By early 1976, if he did not move up and into open O3 slot he would be 'TIC'd' out of the Service by May. Oblivion.

If he won the bid on a stretch, he would live to bid another day. It would be a temporary promotion, a breathing space leading to another chance to move up. If he did an O3 job in a stretch, then he would have proved that he could perform as an O3. Like many Foreign Service Officers, he could comfort himself in that.

For reasons unknown to him, Bradford's stellar career had stalled. It wasn't long before it became plain that the Assistant Chief in the Division of Special Activities and Commercial Treaties position he then held, was a potential dead end. The Ben Franklin room experience got stale after a while. For all his cultivated charm and deference, to every jot and tittle of diplomacy, no one stumped up to further his career. It was one thing to admit a Yale graduate and a linguist into the Foreign Service, to flatter the entrenched old guard; it was another thing to let him pass through the now permeable strata to O3.

As the grim reality of not being 'old Foreign Service' took hold, he had to take a hard look at his options. With two promotion cycles remaining, any "port in a storm" had to be considered. If his carefully laid plans as a Junior Officer were no longer working, he would have to come up with something else.

That something germinated in 1975, but the seed was planted in 1974. It started a continent away from Washington, not in the bush wars of Africa, but along the Pacific coast. Without knowing it, by making her move, the ever-ambitious Lobelia had sealed the family's fate.

The State Department on the Couch

> The only thing that cannot be refused to these poor beasts of burden is their "holidays"— such is the name they give to this ideal of leisure in an overworked century; "holidays" in which they may for once be idle, idiotic and childish to their heart's content
> —Beyond Good and Evil, Chapter 2, the Free Spirit, Friedrich Nietzsche

> The job supports the family, not the other way around.
> —An old saw too often ignored at State

His family situation didn't make the pressure to get a promotion any easier. His mother had put up the $30,000 down payment on a house in the Maryland suburb of Caderock Springs. She would live with them of course. This suited Annette to the ground. Lobelia could side with her and check her husband during their domestic disputes. Their grandmother pampered the boys, and Annette enrolled at the University of Maryland.

Nothing was working for Brad: pills, cigarettes, hypnosis. So, Bradford turned to a psychiatrist. Indeed, he consulted with three, before he settled on Frank Caprio. Caprio had written the book, *How to Avoid a Nervous Breakdown.*

Caprio was a logical choice for other reasons as well. He had authored another book, *Healing Yourself through Self-Hypnosis*, a dozen years earlier. He had been an Army psychiatrist at nearby Walter Reed Medical Center in the District. This fit neatly into Bradford's experiences in the military, with self-hypnosis, and his anxiety-induced lack of sleep.

Another intriguing aspect was that Caprio had stunned the conventional world in the mid-1960's by talking openly about sex. His 1967 book *The Art of Sexual Lovemaking: A guide to a happier sex-love life for married couples* addressed the downward sex spiral of his marriage. Simply preforming and leaving a complacent Annette to herself during her pregnancies was no longer enough. Like most women of the mid-nineteen-seventies, she wanted more out of life. Like most wives, she wanted to know where her husband was when he was away, and what he was doing.

Once in passing, the desk-bound Bradford said to his secretary, "After 35 a man is no more good." She took it to mean sexual impotence, not the pressure the average mid-level officer at State feels to advance or die a career death. Either way he needed help. In a Service where appearing bright and substantial was at a premium, Bishop had no place to turn. [159]

Caprio was just the man Brad needed, or so he thought. What came out of his sessions on the couch astonished the new patient. Brad concentrated on the task, as he did with all things in his Foreign Service Career. Brad became more intense as his therapy progressed.

He saw Frank Caprio twice a week while at Main State. This in itself is telling. When a psychiatrist meets a patient twice a week, it indicates that therapy is progressing.

This was tricky as well. Bishop had to slip out regularly using whatever plausible excuse he could think of. This was because, at the time, the US Department of State fired employees who sought out psychiatric services.

He usually slipped away in the mornings. His customary cover was that he had a scheduled conference to attend. Of course, none of the conferences was scheduled.[160] As time went on, he appeared sleazier and sleazier, just as he had at Yale and while in the Army. He was balancing on the edge of a career abyss; and his family did not want to go abroad again.

This left Bishop twisting in the wind. The first of his two remaining promotion cycles had not succeeded. While those who should have been 'put in their place' long ago were further promoted. He had to 'suck it up.' For the fastest rising star of his 1965 FSI class, the lowest earner of is high school class of 1954, and an adult no longer supreme in his own household, it was intolerable.

When the anticipated promotion in the third cycle, 1974, did not materialize, the increased pressure took its toll. He played tennis more intensely. It was one of the few things that relaxed him. Still seeking the definition of love, he thought of tennis. He

---

[159] Susan Mosley, Bishop's Secretary from 1971 to 1972 was interviewed by the FBI and stated that she felt from observing Bishop that his wife and mother were "running his life." She further recalled a comment Bishop had made to her that "At 35 a man is no more good." March 18, 1976

[160] These absences fell heavily on his secretary's shoulders. FSO Bishop would pile an entire day's work on her desk just prior to the end of her shift.

concluded that love was 'love of strokes.'

Annette was a good tennis player too, yet after all these years he did not put Annette and 'love' in the same category. Tennis relaxed him. Annette caused stress. When a tennis player cut into his court time, Bradford reacted as if he hadn't taken his serax. In the jargon of the time, his acquaintance on the tennis courts noted, "He (Bishop) was always uptight."

Another aggravating factor was the IRS. The Internal Revenue Service was auditing his 1974 tax return. This should have been a straightforward matter. Foreign Service Officers are taxed as if they worked in the US. He had purchased the house the family lived in. Lobelia and the $30,000 down payment could be explained (The illicit sale of passports notwithstanding).

It is likely that Bishop's pattern of private consumption raised red flags at the IRS. Water, fuel, and taxes ate up half of his monthly paycheck. Yet he whisked his family away for impromptu ski holidays. Five people can run up a considerable bill in America. Even abroad, in a place like Botswana, a week's vacation for five on safari can be costly.

It is noteworthy that the family bank account had US $400 in it when Bishop fled. (It was less than his estimated mortgage payment.) Yet his mother shopped at Saks Fifth Avenue in Washington. The price of gas had tripled. Even Bishop's driving to work and back by motorcycle could not have made up the difference. The IRS wanted to know all about it.[161]

What Bradford did not know was that his past had caught up with him. It probably will never be known exactly when this happened, but it had to be sometime after his promotion to O4 in May 1971. It could have been something as simple as a routine review of his Top-Secret Clearance. Whatever triggered it off sometime after 1971, his past association with the ASA surfaced. He was not just a draftee who served in the 23rd Infantry. His MOS was listed as 'Military Intelligence Specialist.'

It could have been that warming relations between Yugoslavia and the United States brought something to light during the review

---

[161] His wife thought she would have to get a job to make the bills meet, further aggravating Bradford's vital image of his own self-importance.

process. The sprawling Cold War made for many strange bedfellows. In the seventies the old adage 'the enemy of my enemy is my friend,' might have been dropped from this part of foreign policy.

The UDBA, the Yugoslav secret service, may have come up with some damaging news. (As had the Soviets when exposing former SS and Gestapo agents in American employ during the post-war period.) Evidence of a hostile incursion into foreign territory by a Foreign Service Officer, during his previous employment, would have been even more toxic.[162]

Such a scenario is plausible amongst promotional panel members, as they sorted out the sometimes-nasty business of erstwhile cuddly koala bears. As one international observer at State once said, "An embassy without a basketful of spies is no embassy." It is no wonder Bishop was 'uptight.'

Similarly, his *present* may have caught up with him. His unvarying excuses for his midday absences were obvious. He *had to* conceal those visits to Frank Caprio. In the discreet terminology of State, if either scenario were revealed, it would mean 'Career Death.'

Even at that, law enforcement may never have known about his therapy, had Bishop not been so lax about not putting important documents away. When his secretary discovered a bill from Dr. Caprio on Bishop's desk at work, she said nothing about it. His co-workers, themselves concerned over their own prospects, seemed not to notice his absences.

It was no secret that he would be TIC'd out soon. At this time, his section was more of a holding pattern for FSOs with few prospects. It was not the kind of section that could be described, as "career enhancing," a term Main State 'comers' loved to roll off their tongues in eager anticipation of a *substantial* promotion. His co-workers may have thought his absences were about putting out feelers for a job outside of the department.

* * *

---

[162] The second HRB attempt to stimulate an uprising in Croatia, "the Bugojno Group," infiltrated into Yugoslavia on June 20, 1972. After a number of military clashes, the survivors were apprehended on 24 July. Those captured were questioned by the UDBA.

Toleration of secret agents by embassy staff has always been part of the Spy Game. Espionage is anathema to diplomats who pretend spies are not nearby. Indeed, Cold War espionage had gotten so pervasive that the State Department had to discontinue its annual 'Biographical Register' after 1974. The Biographical Register was a list of Foreign Service Officers by name. The very snootiness of State at the time undercut the entire mode of CIA operations.

State would not list a Non-Foreign Service Officer in the Biographical Register. The results were, for the years prior to 1975, that foreign agents could peruse the Register to see whom at any given embassy or consulate was a legitimate Foreign Service Officer. If an American was not listed as a Foreign Service Officer, then he had to be an undeclared American agent.

Bishop's world of the ASA, NSA, and DASE shrank in Frank Caprio's Office. Caprio put Bradford's stories of electronic espionage, cryptography, and visions of grandeur in perspective. During one of his sessions, Frank Caprio brought up 'involutional megalomania.' This came from an interdisciplinary paper presented in Canada in 1964. It was about middle-aged men 'thinking big.'

Bishop's thoughts, about being a latter-day Howard Nicholson and wanting to make it to ambassadorial rank by age 50, were pointed out as grandiose aspirations. This is a situation common among Foreign Service Officers. Frank Caprio cannot be faulted for gently putting it forward. How could he, or anybody outside of the Service for that matter, know that nearly all Foreign Service Officers at State were so afflicted? To analyze all of Main State would require a bullhorn or the public-address system.[163]

It had to be obvious to Caprio that his patient suffered from status anxiety induced by his job and, before that, unrealistic expectations at Yale University. The shame and honor society inside State was challenge enough. Bishop was wrestling with 'the Bitch Goddess Success' as well.

The good news for the patient was that the Bitch Goddess

---

[163] It would take another 25 years and a new Secretary of State to pronounce "the System is broken."

could be beaten. The Yale lesson was that a pile of dollars, and a stately place on State's totem pole, is not the ultimate goals in life. Like most Foreign Service Officers, the patient had lived a life most Americans would envy. He would have to come to that realization himself.

Psychiatry takes time. Bishop had more going on than a job crisis. He also had his mother to deal with. After all, the dynamism of his household shifted when his father died and his mother moved in with him. Now that she was a permanent presence, day-to-day life was confusing and often humiliating. Bradford was used to having his own way. Now both his wife and mother would, on occasion, 'gang-up on him.' Bradford's mental anguish only increased when Dr. Caprio analyzed his patient as having a "Mother Complex."[164]

Bradford Bishop Sr. had passed away on May 17, 1969 after a long illness.[165] He was one month short of his 70th birthday. As with so many entrepreneurs of the day, a lengthy illness forced Bradford Sr. and Lobelia to fall back on their own resources. With Bradford Senior's passing Lobelia was on her own. She could draw on a widow's benefit from the Social Security Administration. Yet the developing retirement culture in America did not appeal to her. She stayed on in the house at 920 Oliver Street.

Bradford flew out to California to attend the funeral. Along with his mother, he settled what remained of his father's business affairs. She kept the proceeds of B. Bishop Oil Company. He kept his father's 38 Revolver.

For the remainder of 1969,[166] and just prior to his assignment to Gaborone, Bradford was assigned to further training in nearby Los Angeles at the University of California. This time it was for African Studies. For his recently widowed mother it was a chance for the company of family. She was particularly pleased when

---

[164] Throughout his life it was always, 'her Brad.' Lobelia never let go. She had to have dominion.
[165] Heart disease
[166] All of tuition and incidentals paid by the US Department of State

Geoffrey Corder Bishop[167] was born in 1971, shortly before Bradford got his (US government paid) MA in African Studies. For his part, his mother's boundless energy and 'hands-on involvement' was getting on his nerves.

Bradford was pleased when he left Southern California for Washington to staff the Somali Desk. Each country has a 'country desk' at State. Information and cables from the host country are sent via the country desk to State. Brad was a good choice for the Somali desk. He spoke one of the regional languages, Italian. His first post had been nearby Ethiopia, which included ethnic Somalis. He understood the issues.

African issues however, were at most, 'background noise' for Capitol Hill. Good reporting and communication benefited a junior officer seeking mid-level responsibilities. Any mistakes or mishaps would not cause an outcry from the Hill. For someone fresh from UCLA with a degree in African Studies, it was promising. Lobelia could see Bradford's progress. Brad could not.

State is counterintuitive. Throwing money at Foreign Service Officers is not an investment. State does not develop officers. Training is something the bureaucracy issues as a matter of course, and without thought to long term utility. Bradford was on the brink of being 'TIC-d' out when he was sent to the 26-week Foreign Service Institute Economics course just prior to his dismissal. It is no wonder his mother could not understand why - after her son had done everything asked of him - the Department would throw him out on the street, without giving a reason or so much as a hearing.

The Department of Personnel simply processed the Standard Forms. These could be anything from applications for promotions to petty reimbursements. Although it is likely that the office staff at Main State worked harder and more diligently than many of the elite. They process paper. They do not come up with answers. And answers were what the increasingly puzzled FSO wanted.

As Bradford's May 1976 'shelf life' date loomed, there was no relief in sight. This was nothing new. He had been on edge over

---

[167] Lucy May Corder was William Bradford Sr.'s mother and Geoffrey's paternal great grandmother.

remaining in the Service and succeeding since his initial training at the Foreign Service Institute. His mother's puzzlement over the inscrutable movements of the Foreign Service, and his wife's insistence on staying put in Caderock Springs intensified. (Brad was the family bread-winner as well. That combined with State's shame and honor culture can be deadly.)

It is no wonder that Brad continued to lie to his mother about his performance. Passing himself off as an excellent student at Yale was easy. If she ever doubted his academic ability, she had only to recall his high school achievements. So, Brad's replies to his mother and wife's concerns left him twisting in the wind. As Lobelia and Annette grew ever closer at 8103 Lilly Stone Drive, he came to subconsciously view them as one.

The only thing Brad could do that he wasn't already doing was to trot out the most well-worn objection to ending Foreign Service careers. Foreign Service Officers seldom criticized their lavish educational benefits. When it came to career death, however, they ask a traditional question, "Why would the Service get rid of an officer who is fully trained and now knows how to do the job?"

Were all these years about being a permanent tourist? Was all the training and effort for naught? Wasn't this supposed to be a career? Would all this self-sacrifice go unrewarded?

Another element is that officers returning from Post encounter surprises. Brad had returned from Botswana to an America in recession. While he was away America plummeted into a Wall Street crash. It was an already depressed market economy that was still falling and would continue to sink for the rest of the year. The year he arrived in Botswana, 1972, had been a good year for the Dow Jones Industrial Average. It gained 15% in those twelve months. Indeed 1973 had been expected to be even better.

In the 694 days between 11 January 1973 and 6 December 1974 the American economy was turned upside down. The New York Stock Exchange's Dow Jones Industrial Average benchmark lost over 45% of its value, making it the seventh-worst bear market in the history of the index. Indeed when Brad opened up the embassy's long delayed copy of *Time Magazine*, it reported that 1973 was 'shaping up as a gilt-edged year.' Everything was going to come up roses. That was just three days before the crash began.[168]

The Oil crisis of late 1973 prolonged the bear market. The ensuing oil embargo lasted until March 1974. When the embargo ended it was easier to get gas for Brad's car. Yet with unemployment nearing ten percent, his friends noted that they were all lucky to have career-jobs. Brad had bested them with his federal job. Yet unlike his former Southern California classmates, he did not feel in the least bit secure.

---

[168] From the peak in January 1972 to December 1974, the American economy slowed from 7.2% real GDP growth to −2.1% contraction, while inflation (by CPI) jumped from 3.4% in 1972 to 12.3% in 1974.

God as a Verb

God is plausible, considering the ineffable wonder of absolute mastery of this phenomenal universe. But I cannot reconcile the total, absolute indifference of god to me – to my infinitely minuscule role on the stage of life and the irrelevance of "<u>GOD</u>" to this trite yet vitally important moment on stage...

—Bradford Bishop Diary Page 30

"After coming into contact with a religious man I always feel I must wash my hands."

—Friedrich Nietzsche

Bishop's thinking as he struggled to get to the next level in the Foreign Service is a leap into darkness. Like so many of his fellow FSO's, he could not understand how his plans for upward mobility were not being serviced by Almighty God. How could God be indifferent to Brad Bishop? Wasn't God supposed to be his helper?

The Foreign Service Officer had devoted every fiber in his body to success. He had done everything everyone, as well as the old hands in the Service, had advised. He had not relaxed for a moment and, if there was a god and that god was indeed his helper, he should have moved on to O3 by now. All significance and value seemed to drain out of his life.

Surely the god that turned his back on Bishop was cold. 'This little thing, this little thing,' has been muttered by so many members of the Service in moments of career anguish. If there was an Almighty Deity, why wasn't He at hand when needed, like spare tire?

The privileged, those who were envied for their international mobility, diplomatic immunity, and grace, could be brought low. Those in Bradford's position, who had visions of glory at the outset of their seemingly solid careers, cried out in private. Through the lens of an ambitious Foreign Service Officer falling short is not only uncomfortable, it is shameful. It is then when the shame subculture at State is the most visible.[169]

What no one seems to have considered was what this spiritual crisis looks like to the Übermensch. It is not about atheism. Atheism

---
[169] Public (particularly in this case, departmental) disgrace

is defined as the doctrine or belief that there is no God. This prevails among the partially educated elite in the West, many of whom hold doctorates. For this swath of human society - including many Foreign Service Officers - there is no God. Atheism is *not* the observable crisis of career disappointment, common among the Brad Bishops of the world. It is about antitheism.

What is antitheism? Antitheism can be quite polite and diplomatic. Schools of liturgical-thought strive to define the term. It often means direct opposition to organized religion and/or a deity. It could mean opposition to a specific god or gods. It often is put forward as the belief that theism and religion are harmful to society and its people. To atheists, even if theistic beliefs *were* true, these beliefs would be undesirable.

None of this describes antitheism, at the moment of extreme anguish brought on by career failure. It isn't shame, that comes later. It is the simple belief that there is a God, and you hate Him.

* * *

It is important (and grossly inconvenient) to understand that to be Croatian is to be Roman Catholic. It is advisable for any criminal active with Croatian gangs as a go-between or as a consultant to be Roman Catholic.[170] It does not have to mean religious devotion. It only means baptism and, in the case of the Balkan ghosts haunting Southeast Europe, choosing a side and ruthlessly sticking to it.

The ustaše of the Second World War, recognized both Roman Catholicism and Islam as the national religions of the Croatian people. They initially rejected Orthodox Christianity as being incompatible with their objectives. Any Croatian patriotic organization at that time had to be Roman Catholic with the optional inclusion of Muslim Croats. Baptism was the price of admission.

For someone who hates God, if only for the time it takes to murder a family and bury them, baptism is worth the price of

---

[170] An old Polish joke from the communist period illustrates this best. One man asks the other, "Are you a Catholic?" The second man replies, "I am an atheist." Then the first man says, "I know, but are you a Catholic atheist or a Communist atheist?"

admission. There is a steely logic to this. To Bishop, and to any other Foreign Service Officers so agitated, God can be used.

* * *

America had become far less religious while the Bishops were away in Botswana. Some of the innovative religious doctrines espoused upon their return would have been astonishing ten years earlier. The then new magazine, *Ms. Magazine*, had a revolutionary impact on American women in this as well. Among those interviewed in 1973 was Mary Daly, a feminist theologian who described herself as a "radical lesbian feminist."

Ms. Daly taught theology at Boston College, a Jesuit institution. She started teaching theology in the 1960's. By 1973 she called for the removal of 'phallocentric images and ideologies which have institutionalized into stereotypes [of] both male and female roles.'

She, too, spoke of 'Being.' Her new theological concept was God as a verb, not as a noun. She suggested that the verb, to be, is more appropriate to the task that both men and women face in becoming fully human, and in joining their lives in the unfolding of Being.[171]

This was only one of the changes that greeted the Bishops when they returned. Male and Female 'help wanted' sections in newspapers were then deemed discriminatory. These references were eliminated from the newspaper want ad columns

Title Nine was passed by Congress. Title Nine states that schools that accept government aid must make male and female sports budgets equal. This meant that suddenly there was a great deal more funding available for girls' lacrosse and softball high school teams.

Wonder Woman, a comic-book character who first appeared in 1941, was back. In the 1950's she was more a fashion model, movie star, and 'lonely hearts' columnist.[172] Now the character was updated. She appeared in a live-action television series. Indeed, the

---

[171] Take that Nietzsche! Both Daly and Nietzsche are difficult to read at first. They both, however, are cited and compared by university students to this day. The author offers his condolences to both University Students and the readers of this book.

[172] In the early days her comics featured bondage, which was distinctly sexual is nature. William Moulton Marsden, the comic character's creator, openly and unabashedly admitted to it.

actress depicting the action-heroine lived in Montgomery County at the time the Bishops moved to Lilly Stone Drive.

This came at a pregnant time for the Episcopal Church as well. Five women wanted to be ordained Episcopal Priests. They, and others, appeared before then Bishop Moore with their male counterparts. The men were ordained, the women were not.

The firestorm that ensued was *the* liturgical story of 1974. The Episcopal Church, long reaching out to both the Roman Catholic Church and the Eastern Orthodox Church was having some success. Given 21st century divisiveness, it is notable that in 1974 real ecumenical progress was being made. A unity of all Christians was a glimmer in the distance.

All of a sudden, the question of ordination of women surfaced. For Rome this was a deal-breaker. It did not go down well in the Eastern Orthodox Church either. Fiery rhetoric aside, when four Episcopalian Bishops ordained eleven Episcopal women into the priesthood in Philadelphia, the issue was forced. Charges were filed against the ordaining bishops, and pictures of the female priests distributing Holy Communion in the Episcopal Church appeared in newspapers.

* * *

While Lobelia's family were Roman Catholic, Bradford does not appear to have had any religious upbringing as he grew up in California. There is no evidence of his baptism. His only encounter with religion was as a teenager. A Presbyterian youth ministry was held on some evenings. Brad said that he attended but used the time to slip out of the house to see Annette.

Now that the family had settled into Caderock Springs, the boys were growing up. Annette saw the need for some religious background. While abroad this need was absorbed into the larger community at Gaborone. The economic pressures the family was under, when resettled into a liberal and bureaucratic federal-employed enclave, fed into this vacant space.

There was the local Riverside Unitarian Church that some families of Caderock Springs attended. Neither Lobelia nor Brad were drawn to it. Yet there was the local Catholic church. As with everything the ambitious Foreign Service Officer encountered; it would fit into the plan.

* * *

Given the arch Vatican bias in favor of the Croatian independence movement, any Roman Catholic could be welcomed into the ranks. Gangs in Yugoslavia on both sides of the religious divide would (and still will) cooperate in criminal activities. To be accepted, however, as a freelance smuggler or a facilitator, works better as either a Croatian Catholic or an Orthodox Serb.

Bradford Bishop had a ready-made excuse. He could simply report to a rural church deacon and say he wanted to convert to Roman Catholicism. He wasn't going to accept Mary Daly, or any of the new age theology. All of this would go down well at most Roman Catholic churches when he got back to Italy.

He could use female priests as the impetus. He could also confess to a priest in the privacy of a confessional booth. That would wipe the slate clean. For Bishop (and far too many others) attending a church service was for show. He would join those among the baptized who view God as a vitamin supplement to be taken every Sunday.

It is likely that Bishop became a "nay theist." A new term, a nay theist is someone who grudgingly acknowledges the possible existence of a god or gods. A nay theist usually refuses to worship or goes through the motions as a 'just in case' scenario. Should there turn out to be a deity somewhere, that deity might be angry, vengeful, or both.

In Brad Bishop's case it is likely that he held a grudge against God for what he expected God would do for him; and did not do. Although all available evidence indicates that he did not believe in God, he wasn't going to turn down a useful cover. Getting absolution for all his sins might have been attractive as well. He could go to a confessional booth just prior to, or after, executing a crime. If God is plausible, it might be better to combine the expedient with the convenient. It was simple business sense.

Molasses

"Against boredom the gods themselves fight in vain."
—Friedrich Nietzsche

Molasses. One word; molasses. The word hit Brad like a thunderbolt. The Assistant Chief in the Division of Special Activities and Commercial Treaties was in a meeting concerning, among other things, the OPEC embargo. His father's World of Petroleum was brought forward with that simple reference. It was a Proustian moment.[173]

What would later be referred to as the first "oil shock" continued to reverberate as Bradford Bishop attended the conference. Demand for the now pricy commodity had gone down by 10% and the world economy slowed. All industrial nations were concerned over job losses.

The war in the Middle East had turned oil into a weapon. Any nation supporting Israel was cut off. For the oil producing countries, the Petroleum Embargo was stupendously successful. The wealth of nations flowed to any country that could export oil. It also opened a lucrative field: 'fuel bootlegging,' or smuggling.

How was it done? Tons of oil were diverted. Much of it wound up in nations supportive of Israel anyway. The Petroleum Exporting countries did not care if a share of the bounty slipped through the net. The significant surprise was that they were suddenly rich.

Much of the smuggled oil was shipped in small tankers. The formula was simple. A sufficient cash bribe to a man on shore at ports on either end of a ship's route, then something for the captain and for a man aboard to fudge the bill of lading. With that an entire shipload of oil could evade the embargo.

It was then that someone, in a middle of a speech about smugglers getting around the OPEC [174] embargo, mentioned falsifying the of bills of lading. That wasn't all it took to slip out of port with a cargo of bootlegged oil. One needed to disguise the oil as

---

[173] Involuntary memory. It is named after the novelist Marcel Proust, who discovered that the journey of memory on which he, the narrator, went when he tasted a madeleine (cookie) dipped in tea was a process of involuntary memory. It has come to be called "the Proustian moment." See note 74.

[174] Organization of Petroleum Exporting Countries

something else. One needed to list a viscous[175] product as the cargo.

The word 'viscous' did not register with the honorable assemblage. The speaker then simply added one word, 'molasses.' Everyone giggled. So, did Bradford, but it struck a chord. It was light relief, but also an 'aha moment.'

Molasses is a by-product of the refining of sugarcane, grapes, or sugar beets into sugar. The quality of molasses depends on the maturity of the source plant, the amount of sugar extracted, and the method employed. It could be a product of anywhere sugarcane is grown and stripped of its leaves. Countries that grew sugar beets could also export molasses.

All petroleum smuggling took was a little organization and some money up front. Bishop already knew all about grades of oil. Mount Poso Field produced heavy crude. It had an API gravity of 13 to 16.

API stands for American Petroleum Institute. The API is an inverse measure of a petroleum liquid's density relative to that of water. Molasses was something that was dark and thick and could pass for oil so long as the port authorities did not get close enough to smell it.

That was why the key was in the bill of lading. People doing the inspection at busy ports don't usually look too closely at cargo. This is something Brad could easily connect with. Most of his fellow diplomats were career government employees. They had never gotten their hands dirty in private industry, much less the petroleum industry. (Even less by digging ditches.)

Since his return to Main State, each news bulletin concerning oil pricing was deeply disappointing. How would his father have advised him to prosper in this new environment? Brad pondered this as he came off the FSI (Foreign Service Institute) course in Economics.

His last chance at keeping his job was due. Still, he played by the rules. It would be fair to say that at this moment he was under severe strain, yet nevertheless undaunted. The Economics course was for 26 weeks.[176] He attended it from July 15, 1975 to January

---

[175] Viscous is defined as "of a glutinous nature or consistency; sticky; thick; adhesive."

[176] It was so compacted and rushed through that it has been called the 'Berlitz' course in Economics.

10, 1976.

In the 21st century a course in Economics is regarded as a firm foundation and (gasp) even necessary. For the Assistant Chief covering commercial treaties, some knowledge of Economics is expected. This, however, was the US Department of State. Anything to do with Economics was a career disappointment.[177] State's attitude toward economics only sharpened Brad's anxiety.

At this time (and there are those who would say to this day) State did not concern itself with economics. Anything to do with Economics was a backwater. So much so that the Commercial Section of State (a section devoted to American Business and Exports) was cut away and handed to the US Department of Commerce. Preferred careers among officers gravitated to the Political Section and to protocol.[178]

Bradford Bishop now found himself in a 'backwater' in the ebb and flow of State Department bureaucracy. He'd meet with State department attorneys as they went through treaties. They'd go through details that Brad never cared for. Detail was boring, yet it was part of the job. Now upon completion of the Economics course, he was assigned to the Economic and Business Affairs Bureau (R-2521 C).

International meetings and conferences were not going to get him anywhere. Nor would taking courses at FSI. Taking courses anywhere was not considered career enhancing. *FSI was delaying his vital career advancement!* He had citations. (These were paper awards that State distributes.) Yet the clock was ticking. The little bird was in flight. All of it was maddening. He told his psychiatrist so.

Brad kept his cool, though the strain was beginning to tell. He had that May deadline hovering over his head. As with so many Officers, to remain in the Service, and claw his way to prominence had become the only thing worth having. Brad hatched a plan.

With all this going on he would be sent to the January

---

[177] The situation changed not long after the murders. Economics and being able to be conversant on economic topics became, to the astonishment of many long-serving, upper level officers, highly desirable at State.
[178] These came to be called 'cones.' The political cone was the most sought after. It was the path to the top. (To Nicholson-like fame) It was regarded as 'real' or *substantive* work. The word substantive is used at State *ad nauseam* to this day.

economic conference in Geneva, Switzerland. It was routine. It was what an Economic Officer did. It was also the perfect alibi. He had everything worked out down to the last detail.

He had worked it through Albert Kenneth Bankston, a bank robber imprisoned in the Federal Penitentiary at Marion, Illinois. Bankston sent out letters from his prison cell to anyone he thought he could get an answer from. Somehow, he got Bishop's name, came up with a story, and sent out a letter. Bankston's plan was to escape with the aid of anyone he could con. He had a reputation of picking up prison-yard gossip and passing it on as fact. This time one of the Bankston letters hooked a big fish.

For Bishop it was ideal. Bankston was a contact far outside of his polite and conniving circle at State. Bishop saw Bankston as someone he could use, in exchange for a genuine passport and a new identity. Bishop was in control. He liked it that way. What Bishop thought up was a simple solution to his many problems. He wanted professionals to murder his entire family. Could Bankston locate anyone?

Bankston did. David Paul Allen, and an accomplice known as 'Sonny,' were part of the plot to murder the entire family. They would pose as workmen while Bishop was away. Bishop would tell the family that he hired them to do leader and gutter work on the house. He arranged for it to be at a time when all the Bishops were at home.

Brad left for the conference in Switzerland a few days early too. That way he could take in a little skiing on his 'Per Diem.' (That term is shorthand for the money the State Department pays out for one's hotel and expenses while employed and traveling.) Brad did complain that the Per Diem amount did not cover enough in costly Switzerland, but the same amount went much further in nearby Italy.

Courmayeur, on the Italian side of the Swiss border, is a lovely old village and one of the great skiing and snow sports communities of the Alps. One can walk along part of the ancient Via Romea Francigena, and enjoy its quaint shops, bars, and restaurants. It was here among the steep and narrow cobblestone alleyways that two Canadians attending that same conference saw Bradford. He was with a woman.

The woman was described as 'light skinned.' Others had seen him with young, female companions in social settings before; though none had spoken about it. What happens in the Service abroad stays in the Service. This time, however, two outsiders had seen something.

Had Bradford seen them he might have been concerned. Of course, when the anticipated bombshell of his family's annihilation struck, no one would inquire or care about what café or bistro he was at in Courmayeur at the time, and with whom. Besides the two were Canadians. The American Foreign Service of the day had distinct opinions on the Canadian diplomatic community.

To be fair, Foreign Service Officers felt that Canadians were fun to be with. They were people with whom American Foreign Service Officers could socialize. That, however, was as far as it went. The universal State Department opinion concerning Canadian diplomats in 1976 was that the Canadians were whiners. In any diplomatic setting they were insufferable.

Bishop and the officers of his day quietly saw their Canadian counterparts as having an 'inferiority complex.' They recognized that Canada was, in the world of 1976, a 'Middle Power.' This sounded good to Canadians at the time, yet there was one enormous drawback. As then Prime Minister Pierre Trudeau once famously quipped, "Living next to you (the United States) is like sleeping with an elephant. No matter how friendly and even-tempered the beast is, if I can call it that, one is affected by every twitch and grunt."

The one situation the Canadians found themselves in, where they were equal to the United States, Japan, and the European Economic Community, was when diplomats gathered in councils like GATT[179] and the Quad Process.[180] Canadians would talk about Capitalism, but this was undercut by the intricate subsidy arrangements they had at the time. That was how it stood when Bishop and his companion were spotted.

---

[179] General Agreement on Treaties and Trade
[180] The Quad Process is where the USA, UK, Canada, and Australia meet as equals to come up with a unified position in international bodies.

Bishop worked out of the old US Mission on the Rue de Lausanne in Geneva. Proctor and Gamble (A US Company) had put up the building and the US Government rented it. The Soviet Union and British Missions were located down the street.

The story about the Mission to Geneva was that nothing was secret, and that diplomats did not have any privacy. The story describing the Geneva Mission says that one night a US intelligence operative pried up a manhole cover in the Rue de Lausanne and went down the sewer. He was following the telephone lines. On his way he met both Soviet and British intelligence gatherers. They were all tapping each other's telephone lines.

Molasses, not oil, as it is poured out. It is viscous.

There were rules at State, or so Bishop thought. He did not want to be a billiard ball again; this time he'd lined up everything. As at Yale, a great deal was happening around him.

First it was State's de-emphasis on Europe and shift to the Third World. He went to Africa. Then the emphasis turned to China. He thought he had that covered.

The next focus shifted to the politics of oil. Any review by State would reveal that he had worked for his father's Oil Company. That should have been taken into consideration by any promotion panel. It should also have been considered during the hunt for the fugitive from the beginning.

The 1973 Yom Kippur (or October) War in the Middle East had

mixed results. In the depths of what looked like another defeat for the Arab powers, the oil producing countries of the Middle-East boycotted Israel's supporters by stopping all oil exports. Suddenly, everything stopped. Once the Organization of Petroleum Exporting Countries (OPEC) turned the spigot off the World economy sputtered, jolted, then slowed to a crawl.

The price of oil went up four times, from three US Dollars a barrel to twelve dollars a barrel, in a matter of months. Among industrialized countries, Japan was the hardest hit. It did a quick inventory and concluded that the entire country had about four days' oil supply in reserve. After that the entire country's economy would be at a dead stop.

Other countries fared little better. Factories slowed down, contractors had fewer orders to fill, and gasoline prices grew at alarming rates. Oil became the centerpiece of the department of international trade and commerce's conferences and concerns.

With so much money siphoned out of America and into OPEC members' pockets, the cartel and its actions were a recurring topic at State. OPEC had the West in a stranglehold. For the first time in the twentieth century the Arab world was on top; and it did not want to lose its grip.

Thus, at a post-Yom Kippur War meeting, OPEC decided to regulate the amount of oil exported to Israel's friends and allies. If a nation did not break ties with Israel - or actively take the Arab world's anti-Israel side - then there would be no oil exported. The price would be kept high by allocating each of the OPEC nations a certain quantity of oil production to export. Keeping oil scarce would keep the price high, or so it was thought.

Oil smuggling naturally spun off from this hugely profitable business. The new smuggling was secret, lucrative, and seldom policed. Indeed, it became part of the gray economy. This was unfamiliar – indeed unwanted – territory among those adventurous young men at State who fervently sought promotion.

There was no glamour and there was no glory in economics, let alone oil bootlegging. There were however huge, if illicit, profits in oil. It was something FSO Bishop, hearing the many credible stories of said profits, did not miss. At the conference he could contemplate yet another plus on his resume. Who else at State knew the industry as well?

Fuel bootlegging was coming into its own. The gray economy of preempted and smuggled petroleum ameliorated the OPEC stranglehold on the industrial world's economy. That was how the thunderclap burst over Bishop. It further reverberated through him when the process was explained.

It fell into place instantaneously, the small tanker diverted with the false bill of lading, the cash bribes, the inspectors standing at a distance. Unless they smelled it, any fluid that was black and bulky… 'molasses.'

This had been a moment of levity for the conference. Yet Bishop tucked it away. Later on, after Bishop's plan to pose as a mourning family man imploded, it would form the basis of an alternate career. In retrospect, it became part of another plan.

The only way to deal with an unfree world is to become so absolutely free that your very existence is an act of rebellion.
—Albert Camus

Part Three

The Hunt

Sketch of the Missouri Monster in 1972

Bishop Seen Everywhere

> ...the effluvium of the earth; the waste product of a nation.
> —Henry James' cable on expatriates
> Found in the Bradford Bishop Diary Circa 1967

Bishop had a ten-day head start. He could have gone anywhere in that time. That is, if he had the money and means to travel. After March 2, 1976, nothing was known. The only thing law enforcement had to go on was a strong hunch that he had a confederate, the 'Caribbean-looking' woman, spotted in Jacksonville, at Outside Sports. That was all.

Bishop went from missing to wanted. The fingerprint on the gas can and other evidence were enough to file for 'probable cause.' A warrant for his arrest was issued.

An All-Points Bulletin (APB) was sent out. All law enforcement agencies checked airports and shipping ports along the East Coast. The media reported that the police were attempting to check "foreign ports of entry."

There was a sighting at a Fort Lauderdale hotel by someone who said that Bishop had checked in and out. This fit in with the maps of Georgia and Miami discovered in the family station wagon at Jake's Creek Trail. All together the result was a wanted poster including the Florida details. From there the suspect was thought to have left the country by fleeing south. The State Department responded to requests by ordering wanted posters with Bishop's picture and description to be posted in every embassy and consulate throughout South America.

Later the police discounted the Fort Lauderdale sighting. (The poster still circulated.) Reports of sightings came in from Floridians as far apart as Tampa and Jacksonville. Sightings in Georgia seemed to add validity to the theory of Bishop's flight south. And, of course, there were continuing sightings in North Carolina.

* * *

It was at the Kettle Pancake House in Hanover County, North

Carolina, that two plain clothes detectives saw a man who they later said 'looked like Bishop.' After the fact they said that they were 'pretty sure,' of it. They weren't the only ones.

The waitress who served them corroborated their suspicions. She said that the man they described was misbehaving. It was about midnight on Wednesday, March 10th. This would put Bishop by Wilmington, North Carolina within the approximate timeframe.

The waitress reported that the man had been drinking. He was abusive to several African-Americans in the pancake house. She said that he had ordered sausage and eggs. He tipped her an additional three dollars as he left. Then the man said that he had to "get back on the road."

Other Wilmington and Hanover County residents reported sightings around the same time as well. This was enough to shift the hunt's focus to Hanover County. The waitress, one Barbara James, was shown a newspaper picture and said, "That's him alright."

If so, she was the only one living to have a good look at him since he left the Capitol District on March first. When she spoke to the detectives she said, "When he came in, he grabbed my arm. He gave me a two-dollar tip just to serve him."

She went on about the encounter in detail. "He couldn't make up his mind [on what to order]. He kept grabbing me and was obnoxious. He flipped [cigarette] ashes on me, and in the saucer," she said.

Miss James went on to say that the man was belligerent and "cussed out" several black men sitting in a nearby booth, using the "N" word, and other abusive terms. She slipped away and told the cooks that she was afraid that there was going to be a fight.

Later, when the police located the man, he turned out to be someone else. His manners were awful, but none of that was cause to detain him. There would be more false leads as people from North Carolina to Florida called in.

There was another false sighting at Atlantic Beach, Florida. The man was a sailor on shore leave from a tanker transporting fertilizer. There was a report from Spindale, North Carolina on March 12th. A Rutherford County gun shop store owner reported a man, looking like Bishop, with a loaded .38 to trade in, had been in his shop. The man wanted a magnum pistol in exchange. Although the dogs were brought to the shop for scent tracing, there was no reaction from the bloodhounds.

Speculation on what came to be called the 'Roy Rogers killings' focused on Bishop as well. The execution-style killing of four persons at a Roy Rogers Family Restaurant on March Fifth turned up few clues. A fifth person survived with a shot to the head. The survivor gave a description of the perpetrator as a man in his late 30's, 175 to 190 pounds, about six feet one, with short, brown, straight hair combed back, broad shoulders, and a muscular build. The sketch portrayed a man with a prominent chin, but the similarity to Bishop went no further.

About 20 32-calibur shells and 15 bullets were removed from the victims. The police received thousands of phone calls. None of them led anywhere.

The Restaurant was in Eastern Fairfax County, at a Junction with I-95 (6227 Little River Turnpike). From Little River Turnpike and I-95 a vehicle could have made a quick exit to anywhere. It was only one of a string of unsettling crimes in the area.

Just as the shaken community of Caderock Springs was settling into usual their routines, there were more killings. Two police officers were shot in the head while pursuing a suspect in the Potomac Savings and Loan Bank Association. The perpetrator fled to South Carolina.

When the shooter was returned to Montgomery County he was questioned about a shooting of a youth found lying dead in the middle of Seven Locks Road, in nearby Bethesda. The boy was shot in the back

When the alleged bank robber's residence was confirmed as 7602 Hamilton Springs Road, the community returned to shock. Hamilton Springs Road was in Caderock Springs (Indeed, in the same subdivision as 8103 Lilly Pond Road). If any of the Bishops' neighbors had returned to leaving their doors unlocked, they locked them now.

The FBI ultimately sent out flyers to more than 100 countries. When the authorities in South Africa received theirs, the police chief at Pretoria misinterpreted it. He thought the FBI had evidence that Bishop was hiding there. This was later dismissed, but not until South Africa was permanently listed as one of the places Bishop could have taken refuge.

The trail went cold, until July 5, 1978. An anonymous male caller telephoned the State Department claiming to have information he wanted to sell concerning Bishop's location. It was 5:10 AM.

The caller claimed that he had overheard two foreign nationals discussing Bishop in a bar in New York City. Bishop could be located close to or in a foreign embassy in the United States. He called back at 6:15 AM to say that he had verified the information through a female employee in a sensitive position in a foreign consulate in New York.

The man did not want money in exchange for more information. He wanted a passport. He said he was on probation and wanted to leave the country. The matter went no further, but the timing and the date, fifth of July, are data points in the long search for Bradford Bishop.

There was another notable tip-off that Bradford Bishop could be hiding in the United Kingdom. It was 1992 and Bishop would have been 56. It was important enough for Detective Chief Inspector Alan Wright, the head of Scotland Yard's extradition bureau to call in the press.

It came to nothing, or so many of Bishop's pursuers concluded. Yet this seemingly unfruitful announcement was another data-point. Then the trail went cold, but not for long.

The Migrant Trade

"That which does not kill us, makes us stronger."
—Friedrich Nietzsche

It starts simply. The spiral into organized crime usually does. It starts with a footloose man eager for travel and high adventure. It is fueled by a need to replenish the funds he no longer has in his pocket. Suddenly the money walks up to him and offers itself.

In Bradford Bishop's case it is likely that he was touring a coastal town, like Catania. Catania is a port city on the southeast coast of Sicily. It is also the seventh largest metropolitan area of Italy. Mount Etna, an active stratovolcano, is in the city's background. A wanderer who loved Italy and took to the open road wouldn't miss it.

Catania has beaches, as well as good local wine. There, most likely at a civic park or at a street corner, the wanderer recognized an Ethiopian refugee. It is highly probable that an ex-FSO who had served in Ethiopia/Eritrea would have enthusiastically greeted such a street vendor, or beggar; perhaps speaking a few broken words in Amharic or Tigrigna.

Of course, a warm welcome, and the memories of African chicken peanut stew, would ensue. Stories of the migrant's hazardous journey to Italy would follow. It is likely that the bearded wanderer would quickly discover (what is now called) land smugglers.

To get transport to the industrial north the migrants would be approached. The land smuggler then warns them that they will soon be caught. They say that the illegal-migrants will have to leave quickly before their fingerprints are taken. Once they were thus catalogued they would most likely remain in Italy as refugees from war and famine. (Economic migrants are turned away.)

The land smugglers sell newly arrived migrants bus tickets north, at up to five times the price. Simply knowing the bus terminal's location is a way to turn a few liras. For the middle-aged Bishop it is likely that such a transaction would be, at first, done as a kindness in exchange for an authentic bowl of Ethiopian cuisine and collegial company.

This meeting could have happened in Rome, or in any other

major way station on the migrant's trail north. Wherever and whenever it occurred it had to be another 'aha moment.'

Getting started as a land smuggler is simple. With almost no capital Bishop could, 'hippie-like,' set up an all cash operation. He could use his knowledge, and the trust it engendered, to service refugees of the Derg (Provisional Military Socialist Government of Ethiopia).[181]

Later he could expand his operations as his reputation for logistics and smuggling got around. For someone on the open road, with a yearning for the great outdoors, and a penchant to flit close to danger - only to pull away at the last minute - this small-time activity would be invigorating.

It fit in with his visa training (and presumed visa sales) from his Foreign Service days. Junior Officers have to know about tickets, flights, and transport. During their first tour, nearly all Junior Foreign Service Officers do consular work.[182] The training and experience the US Department of State provides can be translated into a promising career in human trafficking.

Such an illicit business is conducted under the radar. During the 20th century, human trafficking was virtually absent from the political discourse. Yet it went on in the Americas. It is notable that sugar and Banana boats engaged in small scale human smuggling for years.

Migrants were often hidden in a room by the driveshaft. The driveshaft is noisy. The migrants have to plug their ears, but two of them could make the journey without detection.

Boat captains could transport migrants once a year to enhance profits. In the 20th century, when discovered, the captains found that there were few sanctions, perhaps a slap on the wrist. Putting in to a small port at night was enough for the human cargo to offload, get into an awaiting vehicle, and depart for an urban center. All it took was organization.

Wars and poverty throughout Africa and Asia made for a limitless supply of refugees. Europe's prosperity was the magnet. The American military enforced stability. Old colonial ties insured a

---

[181] The Derg took power in Ethiopia from 1974 to 1987 and embraced communism.
[182] The work is typified by Visa approvals, passport review, American citizen services, etc.

small support population in the destination countries.

It is notable that all that was needed, for a European operation, was a 45 to 65-foot boat. An old motor with a capable engine would do, and not much more. Life jackets take up room. They are dispensed with so that more migrants can be crowded on board. Indeed, in the 21st century, one human shipment on a 65-foot boat could be worth as much as US $1,000,000. (No pesky IRS to deal with either.)

In a sense it was all working for the Yale graduate. It is easy to imagine building a small business as his father had and thriving in port cities around the Mediterranean. (After all, his father took up lodging in Long Beach Township, and started out as an independent geologist from there.) In short order Brad Jr. could have assembled a trusted network of contacts, some of whom would be notably loyal and subservient.[183]

Many were desperate. They would assure him that he wasn't a failure. If necessary, and for their frightened families, they'd go beyond respectful obeisance. If necessary, they would grovel at his feet. It is likely that any passing reference to State would evoke Bradford's evil grin. That, and the thought that: if only the jellybean counters at State could see him now.[184]

---

[183] He could have built up a network of illegal immigrants from Ethiopia/Eritrea who would keep silent on pain of discovery and/or deportation. Bishop would be in total control.

[184] It has been reported, but not confirmed, that the fugitive was teaching English as a Second Language in Italy for a time. This is entirely possible, even likely. In the 1970's it was easy to get such a job if one was a native English speaker. American Language instructors were highly valued on account of their desirable accents.

Petroleum

> Try again, much harder – one last great effort = come home.
> —Bradford Bishop's Diary – October 23, 1971[185]

There has always been organized crime on the edge of business activities. In long-established countries, such as those in the West, the line is somewhat clear. In transitional societies, such as Slovakia, the Czech Republic, and Croatia, the line between business and crime is not always clear. Indeed, the moral norms of such societies find it difficult to cope with such criminal groups. The police and the judiciary have neither the power nor the authority to deal with them. Often the necessary political will to fight organized crime isn't there either.

Such countries transitioning into the European Union view the line between what is legal and what is illegal as flexible. Their governments are not yet efficient enough to deal with organized crime. Courts are formalistic. There are parallel structures which have real power.

Organized crime is not just a problem of crime. It is the problem of a weak state doing nothing or not enough. In such an environment it is the smugglers who take-charge. In such a world the criminal element has reputations, not resumes. Grade point averages don't matter.

To piece together Bishop's life after the murders, seekers have to turn to reputation and acquired skills. A Yale degree could peg Bishop as a rogue with style. Yet the salient point in Bishop's reputation-resume is the family annihilation itself.

With that Bishop could be feared by spies and spy agencies. His reputation had spread worldwide. He was no one to cross. Even now the disquietude among his high school classmates in faraway California, surfaces when it is suggested that the Bradford they knew might return. There is a further downside to this.

There are legends about criminals who are notably vindictive

---

[185] He had just won his 'bid' for the post in Botswana at the time of this diary entry. It demonstrates the typical FSO determination to attain a promotion. His return was not the triumph he anticipated, however. The diary entry further explains his state of mind when he did not do better than his former High School Classmates at the 1974 reunion.

when crossed. There is a healthy awe and obeisance toward someone with that combination of control and violence. Yet because he killed his entire family, the Italian underworld would have nothing to do with him. In that lamina of organized crime, he was beyond the pale. That entire stratum would be horrified at his murdering his mother.

It differs from organized crime in the former country of Yugoslavia. There murders were not just a warning of what he was capable of. They were a clear message. In tough neighborhoods it is a form of protection. In Yugoslavia murder has roots in the past. The experience of communal violence in the 20th century placed Bishop's actions within the sphere of acceptability – although only just. What then was his logical path?

* * *

With some money to invest, and influence to use, Bradford Bishop could have set himself up in semi-legal activities. Some activities are not contrary to legal provisions, but the behavior and tools used are. These are risky situations, but also opportunities.

In the three months after the Organization of Oil Exporting Countries (OPEC) called an embargo of petroleum products exported to the United States the opportunity was enormous.[186] A gang led by a Yale graduate, and someone who understood incursions, has some distinct advantages in an uncertain world. The post-1973 oil shock world was a world of semi-legal activity.

The illegal transport of petroleum products across international borders could be compared with the international drug trade. Assessing the volume of both is difficult. The volume and profit margins are also hard to gauge. Gas smuggling, however, was always less risky than drug dealing. Most oil importers were more concerned with the loss of tax revenue than the crime itself.

Demand for fuel in the nineteen-seventies seemed limitless. Then the domestic gas racket alone, was estimated to cost the US Treasury up to eight hundred-million US dollars a year. (This does not count losses to state and local authorities.) This windfall was

---

[186] The official price of "Saudi Light" was at $12.37 a barrel for most of 1976

not overlooked by domestic organized crime. Illegal imports made for cheaper gas prices. Ultimately it made it possible for some illegal importers to buy gas stations, and even terminals, providing the means to launder their profits.

This was one avenue of inquiry overlooked by the authorities. It was the same type of facile excuse used by frustrated police; that Bishop's false trail into the Great Smoky Mountains National Park was reason enough for not taking up a more arduous investigation.[187] No one considered that there might be a connection between Bishop's father's occupation as a Petroleum Geologist and wildcatter, and the vast profits to be made as a facilitator in the oil trade.

Nor did the oil boycott by the Petroleum Exporting Countries (OPEC) against the United States help anyone much but the smugglers. Once oil is in a tanker, neither OPEC nor any civil authority can control where it goes. Oil that was exported to Europe during the embargo was simply resold to the United States or ended up displacing non-OPEC oil that was diverted to the U.S. market. Supply routes were shuffled but import volumes remained steady.

There were Yugoslavian gangs operating internationally in 1976. These gangs were accused of drug trafficking, illegal weapons trade, dealing in stolen vehicles, and murder. The ustaše were involved in illegal activities, both before and after, they were in power in the nineteen-forties. Where does political action stop and organized crime begin? Indeed, where nation states or resistance groups are concerned, where does the independence struggle stop and organized crime begin?[188]

Organized crime is a more systemic and sophisticated form of illicit enterprise. It differs from conventional criminality. Organized crime covers a wide range of profit-motivated criminal activities, *including* transnational smuggling. This international mobility coupled with a large diaspora make transnational operations

---

[187] The police found a map of the Great Smoky Mountains National Park from its own welcome center in the Bishop station wagon parked by Jake's Creek Trail.
[188] Foreign Service Officers often fall in love with the cultures they are in contact with. The phenomenon is called "clientitis."

easier. It does not come as a surprise that the Swedish woman who reported sighting Bradford Bishop in a Stockholm park, said that Australia was the other place he was likely to be found.

There is also a tantalizing connection to Bolivia, though it is not likely that Bishop fled there immediately after the murders. The legal processing of cocaine has gone on in Bolivia for over a century. This is common knowledge. What is *not* commonly known is that the cocaine business was started up at the turn of the 20th century in Bolivia and dominated by Croatians. Even today the producers (families with many generations who have lived in South America) still have Croatian names. They export to Roche, in Basel, Switzerland.

Sightings

> Do your own thing...
> —Bradford Bishop's Diary, Page 29

Annette had many friends. The Bishops were gregarious in Addis Ababa. They entertained widely and knew many in the ex-patriot community there. Annette's best friend while in Ethiopia, Barbara Egertie, was Swedish. She worked at the Swedish Embassy to Ethiopia. She had married an Ethiopian and she knew the Bishop family well. She was in her late thirties at that time.

Bradford had a great many Swedish friends too. Sweden's aid and presence in Ethiopia went back to 1954. Before and during the Bishops' tour of Ethiopia, the Swedish commitment to Ethiopia grew beyond technical assistance. The Swedes introduced new agricultural methods into ancient Ethiopia, bringing still more Swedes to serve in Addis Ababa.

Nobody disappears completely. Friends keep them in their memories. So, it was with the Bishops. People who knew them, and were entertained by them in Addis, remembered them well. They grieved when they read the astonishing news of the family's annihilation. Those who recalled happier times with the Bishops discussed this among themselves.

Those who had mutual experiences in Ethiopia came to a consensus. They believed that Brad Bishop would be hiding in either Sweden or Australia. He knew many Swedes. Those who knew him 13 or 14 years before in Africa were AID workers.

The American authorities, at the time, did not think that Bishop could be staying with someone *outside* of the diplomatic community. Then Annette's old friend received word from a mutual friend, whom she had known in Ethiopia, that Bishop might be coming to Sweden. It was 20 months after the murders.

Annette's best friend in Addis Ababa felt so strongly about this when she heard that Bishop might show up in Sweden that, in November 1977, she contacted the Swedish police. Of course, there wasn't much the Swedish police could do about her fears. They only took note of what she, and the friend who contacted her, had surmised.

It was the first of July, 1978. It was in kungsträdgården, the main park in Central Stockholm. She saw a bearded man as she strolled through the park. She came within six feet of him. She was startled.

It was Bishop. She saw him on the fourth of July as well. This time he was 30 to 35 feet away. He followed her; but she lost him.[189]

The FBI had cast a wide net worldwide in 1976. They handled the Pretoria announcement by saying that Bishop could be hiding in Botswana, or any other place he knew. They questioned Americans who knew him or had worked with him. They did not, however, notify the Swedish police as part of their investigation. Nor did they question 'any Swedish woman,' prior to Annette's friend's sighting.

This time Interpol got involved. The inspector was skeptical because the man she saw had a beard. Bishop had always been clean shaven. He was neatly dressed. In addition, it had been over ten years since the woman had seen Bishop in Ethiopia.

The American FBI was interested. This was the first time anyone who knew Bishop well had sighted and identified him. It was the first solid lead since Bishop's car was discovered in the Great Smokies.[190]

The Bureau (FBI) had jurisdiction due to the "unlawful flight" warrant it issued. Even with the evidence the Bureau had against Bishop, there could be nothing more than a warrant for unlawful flight, until Bishop was caught. Thus, the ball was dropped. There was no 'red notice' either.

A red notice is an Interpol (International Criminal Police Organization) 'arrest warrant' sent to member countries listing persons who are wanted for extradition. Indeed, no red notice would be sent out on Bishop for six years.

The Americans sent an agent over from the FBI's London office. Together with the Swedish police they conducted a covert search. It

---

[189] The timing for the sightings in Stockholm and the 5:10 AM call to Main State in Washington (presumably) from New York could be possible if Bishop had an arrangement with a foreign power. Getting operatives out of a situation is usually prompted by a call, a 'hello number,' as it is called in spy craft.

[190] What was then thought to be a sighting came in from the Netherlands in June 1978. A man being held hostage by South Moluccan terrorists was thought to be Bishop. The hostage turned out to be a Dutch taxi driver.

didn't work.[191]

The search was hampered by Swedish Laws and Customs. The American FBI complained. By example, radio stations could not broadcast the license plates of any getaway vehicle. To do so would be an invasion of privacy.

It was not helpful when the story appeared on the front page of Sweden's afternoon tabloid (*The Afton Bladet*). The newspaper's policy was not to run pictures of criminal suspects. (Pictures were only published *after* a conviction.) Other publications would not even use the name of the suspect.

There was another gap in the net. To travel back and forth through Sweden, no passports were required of citizens from the other Scandinavian countries. Sweden's borders with Norway, Denmark, and Finland were porous. This was the FBI's first serous lead since the discovery of the Bishop family car in North Carolina; and their quarry easily could have slipped away.

The Swedish police circulated Bishop's photo in all police stations and ports of entry. The computer network (such as it was in 1978) carried the details. Police methods at the time depended largely on the extensive Swedish bureaucracy. At the time purchasing a television set, or renting an apartment, required proof of identity. It soon became plain that FBI methods of relying on the public, and broadcast through the media, did not easily adapt to Sweden.

Ultimately the point man for the Swedish police hazarded a guess that "Bishop committed suicide and was eaten by bears in the Great Smoky Mountains." It was all very bureaucratic and predictable. It was just as Bishop had planned at his desk at Main State. The Great Smoky Mountains National Park continued to provide Bishop with a neat alibi, and law enforcement a convenient out.

This was the conclusion to the sighting. Six months of covert – and not so covert - investigation turned up nothing. It was the first such investigation. It would not be the last.

* * *

---

[191] The American newspapers reported that the FBI did not get a picture of Bishop to the Swedish authorities until a month after the July sightings.

The Red Notice

It was raining heavily around 5:30 PM in Sorrento. Sorrento is an Italian port not far from Naples, Southern Italy's most populous city. It was a cold rain. It was the New Year, 1979. It was January eleventh. Roy Harrell Jr. stepped into a public lavatory.

Roy worked for the United States Agency for International Development (USAID). He was on leave and would have to return to his posting in Africa soon. He had purchased a copy of the *Rome Daily American*, an English language newspaper. He stepped up to a urinal. That was when he glanced at the man standing at the urinal next to him. He said, "Say, aren't you Brad Bishop?"

Roy reported that the man, 'began shaking, trembling and backed up from me,' Harrell went on... 'And then, just before he bolted away, the man said in English, Oh, God, no.'

The man fled the restroom. Harrell chased after him calling out, 'Brad, Brad...". The man was wearing greasy clothes, dark (probably corduroy pants) and a grubby pullover sweater. Harrell would later describe the man he pursued as having long, unkempt hair and a beard.

The rain outside the public lavatory made it difficult to see. The man was running in the direction of the embarkation docks for boats sailing to the island of Capri. Roy gave up the chase and departed, as planned, on a bus to Rome.

Roy was shaken after the encounter. He was certain that the

bearded man he just saw was his former colleague at State. He got on the bus. He opened the *Rome Daily American* to read and calm his nerves. As he read and relaxed he came to page eight, *US Diplomat Hunted Worldwide for Killings*.

It was a report of the sighting in Stockholm. The Swedish sighting was over six months old. This was the first Roy, who was then serving in sub-Saharan Africa, had heard of the sighting.

He arrived in Rome about 10:00 PM. He called the American Embassy in Rome as soon as he could to report the sighting. At that hour only, the Marine guard was on duty. Roy is quoted as saying, "But the guard didn't consider it important enough to get the duty officer routed up at that time of night, so I went to bed."

The next morning, he reported to the Embassy. There he met the Embassy's security chief. He also met the legal attaché, who was an FBI agent. He was asked to describe Bishop, and then was shown half a dozen pictures of the fugitive. This was standard operating procedure. Roy identified the photos of Bishop.[192]

Roy had to keep to schedule. He had to get back to his post. That was when he noticed Dell Prendergast. Dell, an FSO posted to Rome, had nervously got up and started fussing with the copy machine. This sudden shift in behavior raised Roy's suspicion, but Roy had to get back to his post in Sub-Saharan Africa. Besides, the Security Officers and the FBI must have known that Dell Prendergast had Serbo-Croatian Language training. He had served in both Belgrade and Zagreb, Yugoslavia. Surely there was nothing to this.[193]

Prendergast wasn't the only one unnerved by this. As it turned out, Romano Argenio, a criminal investigator with the Italian police was on the case. There had been another sighting.

The newspaper *Corriere della Sera* got to the story before the police could comb the colorful port bars and hotels of Sorrento. It

---

[192] The Harrell sighting has since been discounted by police authorities in America. It is their opinion that Roy Harrell, like so many Foreign Service Officers, wanted attention and to be part of the big story. It may have been that he saw someone who resembled Bishop. The odds of his opening the newspaper to read about Bishop immediately after the encounter are long. Yet it has to be acknowledged that Bishop was familiar with Sorrento.

[193] Dell Prendergast was Brad Bishop's good friend and A-100 classmate. Dell took Serbo-Croatian language training and was posted to Yugoslavia when the Bishops were posted to Addis Ababa. There is no evidence of his being questioned about Brad Bishop.

published the story on June 20, 1979. (As it happens, this was during the second 'oil shock' of the nineteen-seventies, where the price of a barrel of oil doubled to $39.50 in the course of that year.)

The story claims that the sighting was on March second. Plainly exasperated, Romano confirmed that police received a report "sometime around Easter," that Bishop had again been seen in Sorrento. The FBI was contacted as well.

* * *

The Montgomery County Sherriff's Office never gave up. The warrant for Bishop's arrest was still outstanding. Once in a while the Montgomery County Sherriff would run Bishop's social security number through credit bureaus, just to see if something came up. One day in 1990 it did.

A man in the Los Angeles area was using it. He had a different name, but the Montgomery County police looked into it anyway. Too late as it happened. The man was dead. (This is probably why a credit bureau turned up the number.)

Reports from around the country came in. One secretive man was reported as bearing a striking resemblance to Bishop. When the Sheriff investigated, it turned out that the man was wanted in several states, but he was not Bishop.

For over 15 years' law enforcement had nothing. Reports still came in; and from all over the World too. Perhaps the most distant sighting was a report from Hong Kong. A fisherman claimed to have found Bishop drowned, and would the American Authorities please fly out to the British territory to confirm it?

This was a hoax.[194] Then the two significant clues turned up in the 1990's. They were the only clues after the discovery of the Bishop's station wagon in the Great Smoky Mountain Park that law enforcement, over the long investigation, considered solid.

It was routine really. It was September 19, 1994.[195] As soon as the report came in of a sighting in Basel Switzerland, the FBI went

---

[194] Who would commit such a hoax? Was it a lure? Or was it Bishop, who almost certainly traveled to Australia, baiting his pursuers and thus "putting them in their place."

[195] There is a record that the date was September 12, 1994, and not September 19th. Both days were Mondays. For The purposes of this book, the 19th is the date used.

into motion. They would review the cold case.

Jean Wadsworth and her husband were on vacation. They were waiting for a train in Switzerland's Basel train station. Jean said to her husband softly, "Don't look now. Turn slowly. Isn't that Brad Bishop on that train?"

She had 'felt him,' as one does when someone peers intently at one. He was watching her from the train on the next platform. Then her husband turned slowly, as naturally as he could, and looked into the face of Bradford Bishop Jr.

The man closed the window, put on a pair of glasses, and opened his newspaper. He partially concealed himself in it. The man's train started to move just as the Wadsworth's train was pulling into the station. As it pulled out of the station, he put his hands to either side of his head and waggled his fingers. As he put them down, he appeared both defiant and jubilant.

"Should we report it," Jean asked?

The Wadsworths were on the way home. Their train was about to depart. It was taking them to Italy, and from there they were scheduled to fly back to America. Mr. Wadsworth decided that it would be best to report it when they got back to the Washington DC area.

The young FBI officer who took the call was receptive and helpful. A few days later the FBI made a routine visit to the US Department of State. The visit was retracing the steps of the March 1976 investigation. There, as before, the FBI asked for any available records. To the astonishment of the Bureau, there were some.[196]

---

[196] At this point a dispute over when the evidence was uncovered should be mentioned. The US Department of State is filled with FSOs who rather law enforcement would take their silly questions down the hall. There are some reports that the 'smoking gun,' as the Bankston letter could be called, was discovered in 1992. The Montgomery County police are vigilant. They may have decided to return to the US Department of State 16 years later on a routine check as part of their task force operation. The author uncovered an Associated Press report in 1993. Other reports of recovering the Bankston letter in 1994 followed. The FBI would, as a matter of protocol, have gone to the US Department of State to see what records there were in 1994. Although the Montgomery County Police should be celebrated for their efforts, for the purposes of this book, the 1994 date is used as the date of discovery. The author apologizes if anyone is disturbed by the two-year discrepancy.

The Bankston Letter

"I did...relate to the Senator that a 'Cult' was responsible for these killings and that I and two other inmates had been told the whole bit and sick trip behind the whole thing. I also corresponded with some people in Minnesota and in the world of hippies. The cult is of Satan and blood is drawn from the cattle by hypo and their sex organs are taken for their fertility rites...I will say that this is a prelude to human sacrifice."

—Albert Kenneth Bankston's letter to Kansas State Senator Ross Doyen (January 23, 1976)

Out of an easily accessible filing cabinet came a certified letter, copied in triplicate. It was dated March 15, 1976, the day law enforcement arrived at Bradford Bishop's office to pick up any evidence out of the suspect's desk.

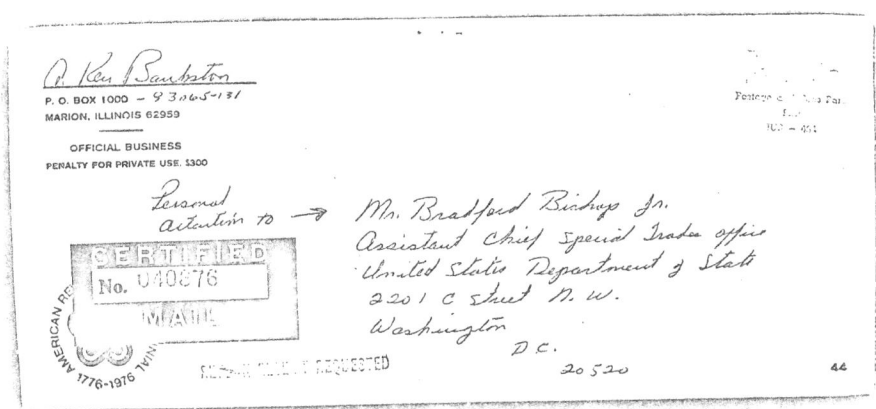

At that time the FSO's third class mail was discarded by State. First class mail was handed over. No one contacted the authorities when a certified letter arrived shortly afterward. Three copies were made. Then it went into a file and remained undisturbed until after the sighting in Basel in 1994.[197]

The return address was the Federal Penitentiary in Marion, Illinois. It was from a person heretofore unknown to the case, Albert Kenneth Bankston. It had passed through the prison censor and had Bankston's prison serial number on it.

---

[197] Here State's shame and honor culture meets State's bureaucracy. The shame and honor subculture does not readily assist the justice system. Yet the bureaucracy demands that forms be in triplicate. Thus, the police found all three copies filed together.

Certainly circumspect, the letter had just enough in it to tantalize the FBI investigators. It also was general enough to frustrate anyone who read it. Even more seductive, the letter was numbered

The only letter the police had was numbered 'seven.' There were references to letters four and five as well. It named names, though somewhat cryptically. Its tone presumably answered questions previously asked. It and the sighting in Basel were the first real, solid clues the authorities had picked up in years.

The easy part was running a check on Bankston. His rap sheet was long. Just for starts, Bankston was convicted of armed robbery. Yet there was far more to Bankston; and until this writing, most of it left unanswered.

* * *

Bankston entered the courtroom in handcuffs. The sheriff's deputy removed them as soon as he got to the counsel's table. The court cuffed him for good reasons. For one thing he was convicted of armed robbery, but that was not all. He was convicted of jailbreak and kidnapping the local sheriff and two deputies.

This was what he was appealing. He wanted a reversal of the conviction based on new evidence in the case. His complaint included a statement that the trial judge did not like him.

Indeed, the trial judge was familiar with the appellant's background. Bankston had a long rap sheet. The judge instructed the US Marshal's office to use whatever restraints it considered necessary in handling the prisoner, and in transporting him to and from the courtroom.

Long as Bankston's rap sheet was, the record the court focused on started on September 11, 1968, when he drove up to Citizens National Bank at Plain, Mississippi. There he took over US $23,000 at gunpoint. He crossed State lines into Louisiana with the FBI trailing him all the way.

The FBI got a lead. It brought them to Vespasian Street in New Orleans. Bankston took on a traveling companion, Toni Gentry. She had an apartment there. They arrived at the parking lot behind Ms.

Gentry's apartment building two days later, on Friday the 13th.

Bankston was outside on the lot when the FBI agents spotted him. He left an attaché case on the sidewalk as they approached. There was $14, 390 dollars in bills from the bank inside.

Bankston could be persuasive in most situations. He would try anything, grasp at any straw to slip through the net. He said that he didn't know whose attaché case that was. Who? Me? What? I dunno. Never saw it before.

Thereafter, with Ms. Gentry's consent, the FBI agents searched her apartment and found an empty leatherette case. It was later identified by bank employees as identical to the one used by the robber. That should have been that. Bankston however, was bold.

Audacity and an active criminal mind were his trademarks. The FBI transferred custody and put him in the Hinds County Jail in Jackson, Mississippi.

This was routine. There were three locals imprisoned with him, two burglars from Jackson and a rapist from nearby Bassville, Mississippi. They all wanted out and Bankston took charge.

He was a smooth talker. He quietly fashioned a replica of a pistol out of a bar of soap. He then used shoe polish to make it pass as one. It was the same trick John Dillinger used to escape from prison in March 1934.

It worked. Bankston first took the jailer captive with the fake gun, then took the jailer's pistol. Bankston left one prisoner to hold the jailer, then took the other two out of the jail and to the sheriff's office. There they overpowered the aging sheriff, sheriff Thomas, and the jail's radio operator.

They all piled into the sheriff's car. It was a tight squeeze, but the police car had one great advantage for the escapees. It had a police radio. All calls were monitored. When the police started to close in, sheriff Thomas radioed back from the car to tell the pursuers to back off.

The captives were released an hour and a half later, about 35 miles south, in Hazelhurst, Mississippi. The fugitives then fled south. Every available man the police could muster was scrambled and pressed into service, the television stations interrupted programming with alerts. It was the biggest story to hit Mississippi since the election.

The fugitives were cornered on January third near Hopewell, just a day after their escape. The three abettor-escapees were captured. Bankston got away.

It took the search parties two more days to find Bankston. It was wet weather. They found him freezing in the woods. A national spotlight focused on him as a chastened sheriff Thomas led him back to jail.

Bankston appealed, the evidence was overwhelming. On November 11, 1970, his appeals ran out. He was sent to the penitentiary at Marion, Illinois. Kidnapping and jail break convictions were added to his 25-year sentence. By the mid-1970's he was serving a 45-year term.

That should have been that. But with Bankston, nothing was ever final. He knew people in the underworld. He was a bank robber and an escapee, both high status reputations in prisons everywhere.

He was as enterprising as his reputation; and he was determined not to serve out his sentence. All of this came out as soon as the FBI ran a check. Here was the break in the Bishop case the Montgomery County Police were looking for. There was just one problem. When the FBI traced Bankston to Marion and the prison system, they discovered that Bankston had died of cancer in 1984.

Predictably, there was more. Law enforcement had missed something. With all the resources at their command: the US Department of State, the state of Maryland, and the FBI had overlooked something. It was the most glaring record the allusive prisoner left behind. Yet it was something that, like the Bankston letter, would not come out for decades. Albert Kenneth Bankston was written into the Encyclopedia of Satanism.

* * *

Bankston apprehended with Sherriff Thomas

Soap Gun

It was helicopters that kick-started the potboiler. Cattle mutilations had been simmering in the United States for decades. Large animals found dead in isolated areas with their genitals and tongues removed, and then reports of unidentified helicopters over the herd ratcheted the mutilations up to the national attentiveness.

The public interest in unexplained livestock deaths started with a horse, not a cow. On the night of September 7, 1967 in Colorado's south-central San Luisa Valley, a horse did not return for water. It was discovered two days later with all the flesh and skin removed from head and neck down to a straight cut just ahead of the shoulder. There was crushed vegetation, strange depressions in the ground, and dark 'exhaust marks' nearby. The owner, a journalist for a local newspaper, sent out press releases that were picked up by other papers. When another mutilated horse was found, rumors of unidentified flying objects (UFO's) spread and an investigation were launched.

The press dubbed the horse 'Snippy.' The three-year old mare entered the public imagination as the horse taken by UFO's. A veterinarian was consulted, but the carcass had deteriorated too much for an accurate autopsy. Later the owner of the horse and her husband were driving west when they saw three pulsating red-and-green lights pass over them.

Other witnesses corroborated this. The data was forwarded to Major Hector Quintanilla,[198] the head of Project Blue Book from 1963 to 1970. He reported that there were no satellite re-entries that day. It was also determined that none of the sighting reports were considered to be strange enough to warrant detailed investigation.

Cattle mutilation stories took on a life of their own, as they passed around the Mid-West. It was a meme, accounts spread by word of mouth. Explanations varied from flying saucers to the occult. Some explanations were even more unlikely.

In Missouri, in 1972 when no mutes were reported anywhere in the United States, another story surfaced. The FBI was probably thinking that the reports of Cattle mutes were over. There wasn't a single report that year. Instead, 1972 became the year of the Momo.

Joan Mills and Mary Ryan were driving along highway 79 in Missouri, near the Louisiana border, when they spotted a good place for a picnic. They would later report that a creature was lurking near their picnic spot. They smelled it before they saw it. "We were eating lunch," Miss Ryan recalled, "when we both wrinkled up our noses at the same time. I never smelled anything as bad in my life."

It smelled like a family of skunks. They reported that the creature was seven-foot tall, covered with hair from head to foot, had a large head, and no apparent neck. They ran and locked themselves in their Volkswagen. The creature stopped at their picnic table and helped itself to the peanut butter sandwich they

---

[198] Project Blue Book was one of a series of systematic studies of unidentified flying objects (UFOs) conducted by the United States Air Force. It started in 1952, and it was the third study of its kind (the first two were projects Sign [1947] and Grudge [1949]). A termination order was given for the study in December 1969, and all activity under its auspices ceased in January 1970.

left behind. They drove away and reported this to the Missouri State Police.[199]

The press dubbed the creature the 'Missouri Monster,' or Momo for short. Sightings erupted all over Louisiana and Missouri thereafter. One eight-year old boy reported a Momo departing the scene with a dead dog under its arm. There were later reports of sheep and other animals spirited away. Not long after there was speculation that perhaps Momos were killing off cattle and other livestock.

The comments of law enforcement and the Missouri State police are not available. One can only imagine how they handled the theft of a peanut butter sandwich. After 1972, the controversy heated up when, in May 1973, the Judy Doherty case surfaced. This time it was alien abduction. It also involved cattle.

Hers was the first alien abduction case to involve cattle. She described two little grey men, of about three and a half feet tall, with egg shaped heads. Under hypnosis she said…

> *"It's like a spotlight shining down on the back of my car. And it's like it has substance to it. I can see an animal being taken up in this. I can see it squirming and trying to get free. And it's like its being sucked up."*

These mutilations, or mutes as they came to be called, were appearing beyond America too. Brazilian sources reported similar instances of cattle abductions. A zoo in the United Kingdom reported a muted kangaroo.

All of this would have been so much exotica were it not for money. A 1500-pound Angus Bull is worth a lot of money. When it dies the insurance, companies are called on to pay up. Between the insurance companies and the ranchers' complaints, something had to be done. And so, the FBI was called in.

UFO sightings peaked in 1973. These sightings associated with Cattle Mutilations grew stronger. UFO enthusiasts were concerned as reports of Cattle Mutes were clustered by state. The

---

[199] The author extends his sympathy to the Missouri State Police who dealt with this professionally, and courteously.

preponderance of unmarked helicopters hovering over herds superheated an already alarming situation.

Farmers started to arm themselves. There were credible reports of exchanges of gunfire. There was even a credible report of gunfire directed at a farmer from the ground. The situation was getting out of hand.

At one-point law enforcement focused on a rash of pig rustling in Iowa. Although there was no evidence of a notable shootout between airborne pig rustlers and Iowans, it was something that could be quantified. At least it wasn't UFOs or Momos.

Still, the situation was unsettling. Typically, every report of pig rustling drew the same reply from hog farmers, "They stole my best pig!" That alone raised suspicion among the insurers if no one else.

Armed cowboys in pickup trucks patrolled five counties. Ranchers stopped cars on their properties with out-of-state plates. There were even high-speed chases when helicopters were sighted. Even *with* tangible culprits, someone could get hurt.

It was then that a panacea was brought forward. It came as the wave of UFO/Helicopter sightings swelled. It came in the form of an informer with a simple and purportedly elegant answer. It came from A. Kenneth Bankston, in the form of a letter, from his cell in Marion Prison.[200]

• • •

Bankston wrote letters. He corresponded with many people on the outside. An unsolicited letter from Bankston was the norm. He cast a wide net, and even wrote Kansas Senator Doyen when he heard about Doyen's belief that Satanic Cults were responsible for the cattle mutilations.

Bankston saw his opportunity. When he wrote Doyen, Bankston claimed to have inside information. He claimed to have correspondence with people in Minnesota and those in "the world of hippies."

From the outset the police presumed that the mutilations were

---

[200] Built in 1963 to replace Alcatraz prison, by 1978 Marion became America's highest security prison.

being carried out by cults. There had been rumors that hippie witches in California killed dogs and drank their blood. Starting out his pitch with Satanists killing cows and taking their blood did not come as a surprise or a revelation. In point of fact Bankston's letters did not rouse anyone until they reached Jerome Clark.

Clark published in *Fate magazine*, America's longest established magazine of the paranormal, and on the rampant Cattle mutilations. Clark was skeptical but thought there might be something to what Bankston was saying. So, he arranged to interview Bankston in Marion.

Bankston threw himself into the interview, with all the gusto and bravado he displayed in his jail break. He said that he and another inmate knew a great deal. He said that he had written Kansas State Senator Doyen to say that his own life was in jeopardy. Bankston needed protection.

That occultists were responsible was what Doyen wanted to hear. Doyen had influence too. Bankston pleaded that he and another inmate be removed to county jails for their own safety. Yellow Medicine County Jail was Bankston's specific request. It was somewhat similar to the Hinds County Jail that Bankston staged his previous escape from.

Marion prison's inmates consistently complained to any who inquired that Bankston hung around, and accessed, the prison population for whatever information he could get. Then he would massage it and repeat his own version of it. Who would believe anything he said?

By 1976 the FBI did. Although they were aware that the cattle mute scare was the best shill going; by January 1974 the mysterious mutilations were at their peak. Law enforcement was left grasping at straws.

The FBI was not blind to the prison yard consensus. Yet the Bureau reasoned that he could not have gotten all the information he had while in the isolation of Marion prison. Bankston had passed the credibility test.

As part of his plan Bankston brought another inmate, Dan Dugan, into it. Dugan subsequently claimed to be a cult member. He declared that he had been a cult member for years. The strength of his account was that it could easily be traced. While in fact, he was adapting most of the details as he went.

Dugan claimed he had joined the cult in Fort Worth, Texas. He described the killing of dogs, cats, and rabbits. He said they would be bled and the sex organs cut away. He said that cattle would be shot with tranquilizer pellets. He and other cult members would then move up to the animal and lay down large pieces of cardboard ahead of them to avoid leaving tracks. He added that if there were snow or ice a blowtorch was used to melt a circular area, so a UFO would be suspected.

Very wealthy people had been doing this since 1967. There were about 600 of them and, if their stories leaked out, Dugan and Bankston's lives would be in danger. The cult was moving on to sacrificing people too. Dugan described how four teenage drifters were sacrificed.

He went on to describe a ceremony where the cattle had to be sacrificed as sunlight starts to filter down between trees. The end of the ceremony had to be when the rays of the rising sun were on the cow. This had to be between branches of a tree and if there were no trees around, then cult members would hold up wood as a substitute for the tree branches.

This came straight out of a thesis presented at Kilgore Junior College, in Gregg County, Texas. The thesis was recent and had been destroyed by the school as obscene. It had however, entered into student folklore, as had other bits of the occult. The United Kingdom had experienced that same meme a few years earlier.

This should have been discarded by the police. Instead it further authenticated Dugan and Bankston's stories. The authorities reasoned that neither could have known any of this as they did not have access to newspapers or radio. That student folklore combined with jail yard scuttlebutt did not cross their minds.

It also attracted the attention of Donald E. Flickinger, an agent of the Bureau of Tobacco, Alcohol, and Firearms, along with a reporter from the *Fort Worth Star-Telegram*. The Texas Rangers in Kilgore, had interrogated suspects and learned that there was to be a mass meeting of Satanists in August 1975. This would mark the coming of the Age of Aquarius. It was referred to as "The Church of

Satan." To Flickinger this was another sign that Dugan and Bankston were on the level. They could not have picked this information up.

The focus was now on Anton LaVey. LaVey founded the Church of Satan in San Francisco in 1966. He also formed a group called the Order of the Trapezoid, which later evolved into the governing body of the Church of Satan.

A sensational scare rippled through San Francisco newspapers. The consequent Flickinger report summarized Bankston's and Dugan's confessions. The claim that the leader of all this mayhem had plans to 'help drive the world into another dark age, where violence and madness would rule, and the Earth would become like hell itself,' further focused the attention on LaVey.

There was another element held up as yet another proof that their story was true. The demonic leader was named by Bankston as "Howard." Nothing more. LaVey's given name – long abandoned – was Howard.[201]

About this time one of the letters Bankston sent out got a reply from the US Department of State in Washington. This time Bankston had hooked a big one. It was a Foreign Service Officer at the Department of International Conferences in Washington. His name was Bradford Bishop.

* * *

It will never be known how Bankston got Bishop's office address. What Bankston's role was in the Bradford Bishop Murders can only be surmised from the only surviving letter he wrote, the one that lay in US Department of State files for years. Ever since the letter's discovery, law enforcement has poured over it.

Given those parameters, because of the Bankston letter, two of the men that Bishop worked with to murder his family, while he was away in Northern Italy, were tracked down. Those two (both ex-convicts) were wise enough to keep the details vague. To this

---

[201] The leader of the conspiracy 'Howard,' was named in the Flickinger Report. He was not Anton LaVey. Federal Agents trailed LaVey and other persons implicated by Bankston and Dugan. The Church of Satan cooperated with the FBI to prove themselves guiltless of cattle mutilations. No evidence ever linked the mutes with occult activities.

extent, the Bankston letter shed some light on one of Bishop's plans.

Bankston ends his letter of March 15th by telling Bishop that he wouldn't be writing from Marion for a while. He and Dugan had hit pay dirt. They were to get out of Marion and sent separately to smaller jails. And so, Albert Kenneth Bankston exited the Bishop story.

* * *

Bankston escaped from his low security imprisonment on May 31st and Dugan escaped from his equally low security imprisonment in Texas on June 1st. When both were recaptured they claimed that they had escaped to get away from the vengeance of the wealthy, amateur Satanists whom they had betrayed.

Bankston was returned to Marion and to his letter writing. As an epistolarian he was prolific. He continued to pitch any story, plausible or implausible, and mail it out. That should have been the end.

Yet Bankston lingers. His letter's tantalizing references were followed-up. Nothing came of it. It is unlikely that Bankston did more than refer Bishop to the contract killers. It *is*, however, highly likely that Bishop made an offer to provide the convict with a new identity by issuing him a new passport, with a new alias.[202]

Bankston said in the letter that he was interested in Mexico or Central America. Once free, Bankston could further document his new identity. He could start by applying for a new Social Security Card using his new passport. Everything flows from a genuine US passport.

---

[202] "Needless to say, I have no way to express my heartfelt thanks," writes Bankston. It is the author's conjecture that Bishop made a false passport for Bankston and had it at the ready.

Anton LaVey, Founder of the First Church of Satan

Road sign in one of the affected areas

Gunrunning

"The secret of reaping the greatest fruitfulness and the greatest enjoyment from life is to live dangerously."

—Friedrich Nietzsche

The September 1994 Wadsworth sighting confirmed FBI suspicions that Bishop might be doing business somewhere in northern Italy and Switzerland. He knew the borders well, as illustrated by his skillful handling of his per diem while at the conference in Geneva, and during his rendezvous with the white-skinned woman on the Italian side of the Swiss border.

Switzerland has extradition treaties; yet it is one of three countries known to harbor U.S. fugitives.[203] It is very difficult to extricate a fugitive from a handful of other countries as well.[204] Further, Bishop was, and is, only a suspect. His US warrant, at the time, was for interstate flight.

Another curious report about this time came out of Britain. Scotland Yard received a credible tip that Bishop was in the United Kingdom. The extradition bureau announced to the press that they were in pursuit, making a point on how dangerous the then 56-year-old fugitive was.[205]

This occurred in October 1992; two years before the Wadsworths saw Bishop on a train in Basel. It was then about 48 degrees (9 degrees Celsius) and cloudy in East Anglia (The United Kingdom). There were showers, and some thunder. The entire country was cool and showery. No one would have thought Bishop, and his suspected confederate, would stray so far from the Mediterranean. Given Bishop's propensity to move far and fast when discovered, establishing a safe house in blustery Britain is not out of the question. Besides, war had broken out in faraway Yugoslavia. And there were guns to be smuggled.

There was a British Army Reserve system in the United Kingdom, just as Australia had its Army Reserve, the Australian Citizen Military Force. As budget cuts followed the military build-

---

[203] Sex-offender/film-maker Roman Polanski is one of the better-known examples.
[204] Iceland and France are the other two. There are six countries without extradition treaties at all.
[205] It is notable that when he was spotted in Courmayeur just prior to the murders, he was with a pale woman. The British are among the palest of Europeans.

down, military units were disbanded, their arms put in storage. Some caches of arms were neglected; some were stockpiled and forgotten to the point where no one knew who was responsible.

In light of recent developments in Europe, the British had a hunch. If and when Bishop and/or an accomplice were identified, those unattended caches could become embarrassing. The sudden appearance of British Army equipment on a Balkan battlefield would further complicate matters.

How best to handle the situation? Publicly warning a notorious smuggler that Scotland Yard is on to him, is a good way to get him out of the country.

* * *

On September 19, 1994 Croatia's war for independence was still raging. It had started in 1991 with no tanks, few artillery pieces, and fewer small arms than Croatia had volunteers. Croatian troops had fallen back on old World War Two rifles and pilfering from the Yugoslav forces fighting against them. At the start the police - the only organized force in the new country - did most of the fighting.

The UN embargo on arms shipped to any part of Yugoslavia made a difficult situation desperate. The embargo worked for the Yugoslav/Serbian cause at first. During his lifetime, Tito had armed the military to the teeth. In 1991, those arms were used against the new Croatia.

The Croatians started small shops to manufacture what small arms they could as fast as they could. This they managed, but not without great effort and whatever expertise they could get. In these desperate hours the Croatians turned to the smugglers.

They had to. They were taking heavy casualties. Any experienced smuggler – or amateur willing to run the risk – was welcome. There were deals to-be made.[206]

---

[206] Croatian officials today confirm that they had to turn to smugglers. American readers familiar with America's Civil War (1861 – 1865) may recall that blockade runners ran weapons and ammunition past the naval blockade of Southern Ports, thus supplying the confederate army. Such smugglers were considered patriots. In Croatia's case, those who got arms and ammunition to the Croatian forces would have earned the gratitude of the new nation (and possible citizenship).

It was an adventurous beginning. Nowadays the official Croatian government story says that the first arms shipments were smuggled into the country on the backs of donkeys. It is likely that this was partially true. If so, it meant a good profit for an experienced smuggler. Bradford Bishop wouldn't have passed that bit of high adventure up for the world.

In the early days of 1991, Croatia purchased 120 T-72 main battle tanks worth USD ninety-million through Swiss firms, notably Eram Bau Montage AG headquartered in Basel. As an example, the Basel firm, Baumaterial Hagendorf (BHM) with a delivery itinerary of Basel-Zurich-Gotthard-Venice-Trieste-Pula shipped two vans of small arms. (See Map)

Later more vans of small arms ammunition were shipped from Zurich via Hungary. (In the early days the Hungarian border was an important crossing point for smugglers.) Rocket launchers, mortars and US-made GD *Stinger* SAMs all arrived in Croatia from Basel. More war material followed. Demand was high. It was a windfall for the gunrunners.

With the end of the Cold War, the former Soviet Union forces pulled out of what was once East Germany. They sold equipment they would rather not take back to Russia with them. Both UN observers enforcing the embargo in Croatia and NATO, turned a blind eye.

So much equipment was diverted to Croatia that some politicians argued that turning a blind eye to it was unfair to the Serbs, who inherited their war materiel from Tito's Yugoslavia. They posited that now Serbia no longer had a superior arsenal. All of this was good business for the smugglers.

Most of the illicit arms were unloaded at ports along the Dalmatian coast by freighters, officially headed for ports in Africa, Asia, and the Middle East. Once at sea the freighters simply changed routes. Any independent petroleum smuggler knows how to do that. Arms and ammunition at this time were where the real money was.

The northern Croatian island of Krk (proper spelling, no vowels) is close to Trieste and across the water from Venice. Krk was, before the war, the main airport for charter planes carrying tourists to the Dalmatian island resorts. It became the principal drop-off point for military transport planes. There NATO surveillance looked the other way as the planes disgorged their cargo. Everything was coming up roses for arms smugglers. Even the US Department of State quietly approved.

In addition to German and Croatian exile assistance, US $1.3 billion of weapons were smuggled into Croatia during their war for independence. American advisers from a private company, the Military Professional Resources Incorporated (MPRI) arrived to aid Croatia as well. In the midst of such company, along with other soldiers of fortune, Brad Bishop, smuggler, pirate, and dastard, was now side by side with the forces that were once out to apprehend him.

Given all of this, it is no wonder that a clean-shaven and well-dressed Bradford Bishop first ducked behind a newspaper when the Wadsworths saw him in Basel. As the train pulled out of the station, he got the thrill of slipping away once again. His defiant gesture was akin to pouring gasoline on his family in Tyrell County.

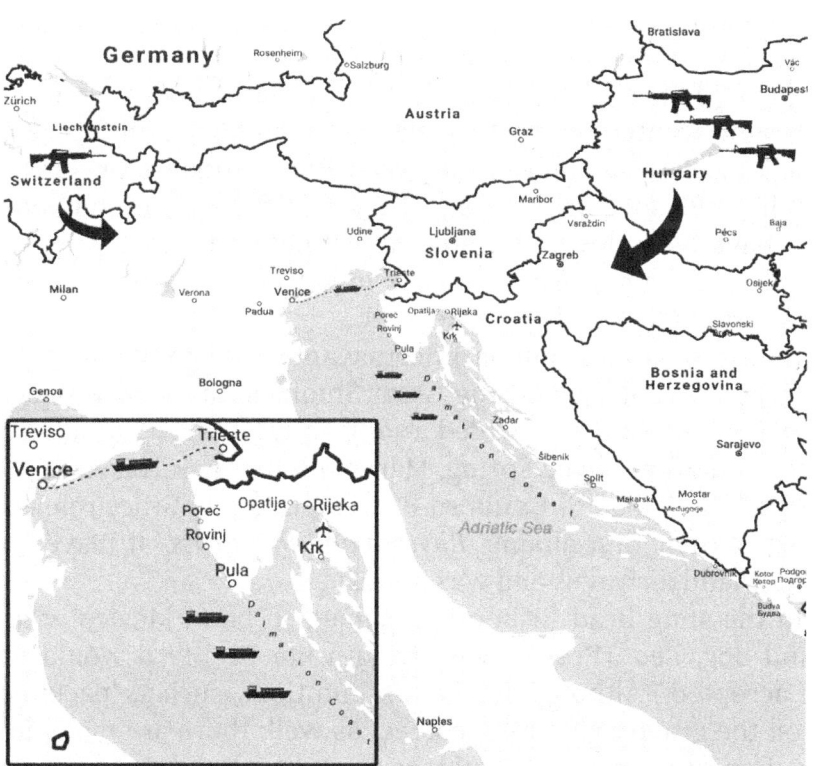

Legend, Myth, and Brief Encounter Signaling

Another self, a duplicate of every one, skulking and hiding it goes,
Formless and wordless through the streets of the cities, polite and bland in the parlors,
—Song of the Open Road, Walt Whitman

The mystery endured. The public wanted closure. If not with Bishop's capture, at least closure by explanation. The Montgomery County killings were just too horrible.

Although there was interest aplenty, there was no ending to the story. There was no closure. Bishop had simply disappeared. Any speculation about Bishop's past as a spy, or Bishop's present as a hermit living off the land in the Great Smoky Mountains National Park, lead to a dead end. The Bishop case slipped into unsettling theories and folk lore.

This is the way Bishop wanted it. Both speculative theories reek of a false trail. With all due regard to J. Edgar and Miss Randy, the two bloodhounds on the chase in 1976, speculation on Bishop's life on the run or in the mountains does not hold up. He was not going to fold up, cook over a hobo fire, and eat out of an open can.

Bishop wanted to excel. He wanted to come out on top. He saw himself as a mover and shaker. The Bitch Goddess Success was what he and so many Foreign Service Officers worshipped. He might have been down, but not out. People with those values, and that frame of mind, resurge. They might be stunned or wounded for a short while, but they strike back.

He got what most junior officers wanted. He got to be a legend. That legend went beyond the Great Smokies. In 1977 a bluegrass group, Coup de Grace, recorded a song about it for Adelphi Records in their studio at Silver Spring, Maryland. It was released in 1978, entitled "The Ballad of Bradford Bishop." Coup de Grace released it as part of their first album: *'Rhythm and Bluegrass.'* It played over the Maryland airwaves and was popular.

In the song Brad Bishop is assumed to be in Mexico with his faithful dog, Leo. (Presumably living a life Bradford would *never* have accepted.) Although further assumptions, such as 'packing the dirt on the grave tight' are incorrect as well; there are many in the State Department who would agree with the verse about 'not taking [the State Department's Higher Up's] guff.'

Perhaps the most notable of the writers, publishing in the wake of the stalled investigation, was Carolyn Banks. Like so many she was fascinated by the case. A successful fiction writer, she wanted to write a non-fiction book about the Bradford Bishop murders. Had she done so it would have been her first non-fiction. She approached her publisher, Viking Press about it. Viking Press would not support her by saying that, there were too many loose ends; nor was there an ending.

Both were true. Although it must be pointed out that the State Department was noticeably avoiding the investigation. Further, the Montgomery County Police, though themselves determined, were often frustrated by what they saw as the non-cooperation of other law enforcement agencies (The CIA in particular). What was a writer to do?

Viking suggested Ms. Banks' forte: fiction. This she went at with gusto. Her book *Darkroom* got good reviews. The 1982 edition's cover featured a sketch of the broken bathroom door that Lobelia hid behind.

The plot line was that Bradford Bishop was part of a CIA drug-induced experiment gone wrong. She writes about Bishop as someone who retreated into isolation. Carolyn knew how to write suspense; but she could only base it on those newspaper clippings she could gather before 1979. She made the rest up.

Sometime shortly after *Darkroom's* publication a man came to her house in a wooded area of Virginia. Her property included a small, finished building. It was a guest house. The man was willing to work if, in return, he could stay in the guest house. They came to an agreement.

The man chopped wood and did other chores. He became friendly with Ms. Bank's son. After some days he told Ms. Banks that he would have to move on, and he asked for a lift into town. This Carolyn did. At his request, she dropped him off at the gates of Langley, Virginia. (Home of the CIA, the US Central Intelligence Agency)

Bradford Bishop's age-progressed bust (with hair on top of his head)

Her story retained a presence in North Carolina. In 1983 Frank Stephenson, a Chowan University professor in North Carolina, wrote a screenplay titled, *'Bradford Bishop, Where Are You?'*

His story presented Bishop as an intelligence agent trained at Harvey Point in Perquimans County. The plot presented the possibility that Bishop was a double agent and faced exposure. The theory presented was that Bishop knew the area where the bodies were discovered; and he had to run. It follows the storyline conjecture of Bishop as a victim.

Bishop's former roommate at Yale and now a museum curator, Dayton Lummis, came out with a slim volume as well. Dayton was concerned, as were all his fellow 'Houn residents. Over the years they spoke with each other about it. They agreed that good ole Brad could not have done such a heinous thing. Ultimately Mr. Lummis came out with the theory of what he calls, "Balkan Revenge." He published his recollection, along with his theory, in 2010 entitled *Not Wanted*.

Lummis puts forward that his old college friend could not have committed this crime, but that Brad was, himself, a victim. The contention is that forces of revenge from Yugoslavia located Bradford, bided their time, and struck when the middle-aged FSO was at his weakest. The theory is based on long Balkan memories, and on Bradford's indiscretions before or during his visit to Yugoslavia with his wife after his military service.

Lummis' contends that his old college roommate was awarded a 'jockstrap medal.' That is when the CIA or a secret organ of the US government awards a medal for bravery or meritorious service. Such a medal cannot be worn in public. The inside joke is that a man can only wear the medal on a hidden place, his jockstrap, thus the term jockstrap medal.

Brad's ever-loyal (and notably crusty) roommate says that such medals are 'not given out lightly.' He believes that then Staff Sergeant Bishop was under fire during a secret mission, and that Bradford acquitted himself admirably. Other 'Houn alumni tend to agree.

There is a certain shade of CIA validity to this. It bears repeating that the intense bludgeoning of the Bishop family with a hammer could only remind the CIA of the UDBA. (Only the UDBA kills like that.)

In 1976 there was a secret, low-level war sputtering between Croatian émigré forces and the UDBA. Were Dayton Lummis in his book *Not Wanted* correct, then a UDBA strike would not be out of the question.

This has led to much speculation over Bishop's whereabouts. The reason offered for *not* killing Bishop immediately, is that it would be more painful for him to live and so suffer the pain of the loss of his family. Recalling their excruciating deaths thereafter would be continuous punishment. Later, it was posited by some, that Bishop was disposed of. They further suggest that he is in an unmarked grave, perhaps in Paraguay.[207]

Brad's high school friends could not believe that their old classmate was capable of such violence either. They point out that Brad was always highly competitive, and that his mother pushed

---

[207] Although law enforcement confided to the author that Mr. Lummis' book is 'silly,' the author does not think that the book is without merit.

him to the point of resentment. Yet they could not imagine that he was capable of family annihilation.[208]

Bishop was spotted at least twice in South Pasadena in 2009. Both of these sightings were by the US Post Office in South Pasadena. Both sightings reported that Bishop had retained his beard. The sightings spread by word-of-mouth and horrified everyone.

In 2009 the class of 1954 was due for their 45th reunion at the Newport Harbor Yacht Club, the same place where Brad and Annette attended for the 20th anniversary reunion. The FBI was contacted. The class president expressed class fears that Bishop might return to machinegun the entire class, and 'go out in a blaze of glory.'

The FBI sent two armed plainclothesmen. The reunion went off without a hitch. Most of those who knew both Brad and Annette had put it behind them. Yet the specter of Bradford Bishop loomed over the reunion. Who would dredge all that up again?

Even the Yale alumni dropped the matter, listing Bishop in their class roll as 'whereabouts unknown.' His many roommates had, for decades, been asked about Brad. They have grown weary of it. For Bishop's successful Yale graduating class it was, and still is, unsettling. In retrospection it is awkward that, when weighting the comprehensive sum of all of his classmates' accomplishments and stellar careers, the salient event in their lives is their recollection of this one C student.[209]

On a certain level the specter is tolerable. On the other hand, Brad was, and still is, thumbing his nose at everyone. For all their honors and athletic glory at Yale, at the end of the day Brad is the most notable, and the most sought after, graduate of the class of 1958. To their sleazy, rakish colleague, that's winning.

Yale and South Pasadena High graduates turned that page. All of that was a dismal episode in the past. And that should have been that.

---

[208] This was prior to Bradford's years at Yale and State. The author posits that his high school classmates knew a different Brad Bishop.
[209] In light of this it is notable that he gloated at his squash victories over his Yale friend, Dayton Lumis, saying, "You have to face it man – I am just better than you are."

After decades of inactivity, and doubts surrounding the sightings in Sweden and Sorrento, the FBI was ready to call it a day on the Bishop murders. There were still many unanswered questions. Like the Swedes decades before, the 21st century FBI could close the book, and even cite to the Trenny Lynn Gibson case. As with Miss Gibson, the Bishop disappearance could be set aside as just another legend, or another secret, of the Great Smoky Mountains National Park.

It is no wonder the long-time fugitive felt safe enough, to return to South Pasadena in time for his 45th High School reunion. The authorities were no longer actively looking for him. His past was old news. He had 'aged out' of crime.

Furthermore, he had moved on from the position he found himself in during the 20th reunion. By 2009 he was 73 years old. It is likely that he was successful and wanted to say so.

To many it had to come as a surprise when the FBI put the 77-year old specter on the ten most wanted list in April 2014. Law enforcement, except the Montgomery County Sheriff's Office, had put it away. The dwindling number his of friends, and distant relatives, would rather not have old wounds reopened. Indeed, many commentators and journalists had come to closure by believing that he was dead.

Blended with Bradford's personality, his appearance in South Pasadena pointed to what covert operations call a 'Brief Encounter,' or BE. That is to say that, now retired, Bishop was 'signaling' that he was alive and smarter than all of them: the police, his Yale class, the State Department. Applying non-espionage language, it was a 'summing-up.' Bradford Bishop was simply saying, 'I can go wherever I like,' and I am 'smarter and better than you.'

It was all very Foreign Service.

The South Pasadena Post Office (Circa 1960)

Of the two known 2009 sightings, Bishop is described as shabbily dressed. He was reported to have come up to one witness from behind saying, "Brad Bishop is back! Brad Bishop is back!"[210]

The scope of the search and the world-wide alerts left Tyrell County, and the town of Columbia, North Carolina, bewildered. The Bishop murders became a part of Tyrell County's history. The horror and haunting, that followed the discovery of the five bodies, left a chill in the county that imbedded itself in the county's collective consciousness.

The State of Maryland got caught up in the aftermath as well. Cars still pause by 8103 Lilly Stone Drive to have a peek at the 'murder house.' Selling the property was taking on proportions never dreamed of prior to the murders.

---

[210] There is an 'old saw' about people and clothing. "Poor people dress up and rich people dress down."

Even if a real estate agent didn't elaborate on the 8103 Lilly Stone Drive's history, an appraiser would. Neighbors often volunteer news that lenders would rather leave out. The stigma of a heinous crime, it was thought, would take 10 to 15 years in order for it not to be a factor in the sale of the house. The Bishop case, thus far, has pushed the boundaries beyond that.

Consequently, the State of Maryland passed a law requiring real estate agents to disclose a residence's history. The agent has to be upfront about any bad reputation, or dark side of the property. In Maryland it is commonly referred to as 'the Bishop Law.'

John Doe

"The finest trick of the devil is to persuade you that he does not exist"
—Charles Baudelaire

Just because the devil isn't under *every* bushel basket, does not mean that he isn't under *a* bushel basket
—Dr. Timothy Keller

On October 18, 1981, about 200 miles southwest of the Elkmont entrance to the Great Smoky Mountains National Park, a man was hitch-hiking. He was killed when a vehicle hit him. His legs were badly mangled and he had nothing in his pockets.

The body was sent to the Jackson County coroner. It was assumed that he was homeless and had been 'living on the streets' for some time. The coroner listed him as 155 pounds, 5 feet 9 inches [or 1.753 meters or 69 inches] with blue eyes. The estimate at the time was that he was 55 years old when he died.

That was all. The coroner took a headshot photo and sent the body to Cedar Hill Cemetery, a municipally owned cemetery in Scottsboro. The gravestone simply read, "White Male, Died October 18, 1981/ Due to Accident on Hwy 72 E, Scottsboro, Alabama / Buried on Nov. 11, 1981/Without Being Identified."

In 2014, a special on the Bishop case aired on television. Jeremy Collins, a salesperson for a family-run sign company and his wife saw the show. Jeremy was struck by the brutality of the murders, and that the picture of Bradford Bishop was a photo from the 1970's. He recalled a photo run in the *Daily Sentinel*, Jackson County's oldest continually running newspaper. That 1981 photo was taken not long after.

He considered similarities in the hairline, nose, chin, and later some growth above the eye and earlobe. He and the Scottsboro police chief compared the two pictures. The height difference could be due to the horribly mangled legs on John Doe when he was found. Bishop was nearly 40 when he disappeared. Living on the streets or in the Park however, could have aged John Doe to where he could have been 45 when killed.

Bishop's eyes were brown. This could have been a routine mistake from 1981, or so the eager pursuers of the FBI and the

Montgomery Sheriff's Office hoped. If John Doe was Bishop, it would have been a spectacular find. *The Daily Sentinel* sent a photographer to Cedar Hill to take a photo of the exhumation.[211]

Among Bishop's pursuers, there was a distinct atmosphere of elation. Here was a neat wrapping up of the Bishop case. It fit in with the initial theory that Bishop wandered off into the Park and perished.

Here Bishop's pilot license could have come into play. Over the six years (1976 – 1981) since the last known photo of Bishop, the alleged family annihilator could have left the country for points south. In South America he could have been flying drugs into the US in a small plane. Pilots engaged in those operations do not carry identification. Hitch-hiking to a small airport to make the illicit return journey fit the hypothesis.

There had been a technical change that gave the FBI a further edge. The fugitive of 1976 could not have known that a DNA profile would be part of most crime detection kits in the 21st century. The police were able to assemble a DNA profile from the shaving kit and razor they found in Bishop's station wagon parked at Jake's Creek Trail. They also had a sample from the cigarette he cast aside when he left the Columbia, North Carolina burial site.

It was time for summation and closure. If there was a match, then Bishop had lived a hard life and died without a dollar in his pocket.[212] One investigator commented that if John Doe was Bishop, then death on the highway was "too quick and too easy."

The Montgomery County police had kept the case open over the years. It was the County Sheriff and others who followed up the occasional lead and continued to run Bishop's Social Security number.[213] To this date, every new officer in the county's police force covers this case as part of his or her initial training. Now, it seemed, there was a final chapter to the decades-long chase.

---

[211] DeWayne Patterson, Daily Sentinel

[212] This fits in into the almost universal assumption, at the time, that the fugitive was living like a hobo. This idea and image is hard to purge from police theories. Considering that Bishop could have been hired on to fly drugs into the United States from South America, is a step forward in police thinking. The plane might have crashed, and the suspect might have been making his way to a drug smuggler's airport, to return to the drug route's point of origin. No inquiry of a small plane crash in 1981 in the area was made.

[213] 556-48-3489

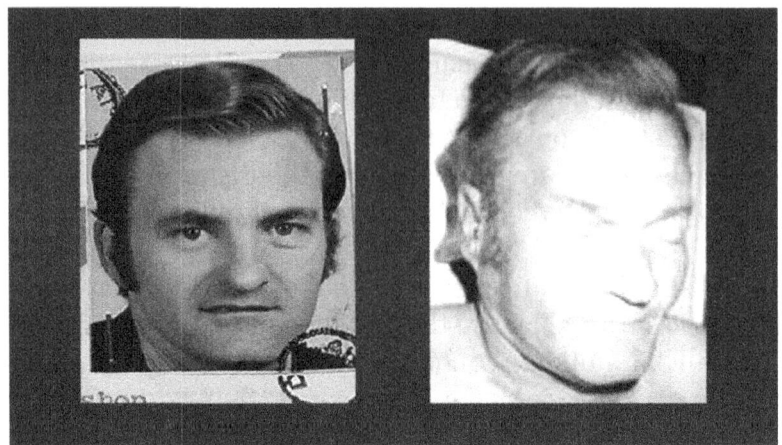
FBI Comparison headshot: Bishop on the left, John Doe on the right

The DNA profile did not match. Anticipation turned to ashes. The specter, Bishop's brutality couched in worldly FSO sophistication, hovered over his pursuers. Surely, it was thought when John Doe was exhumed, Bishop's apparition would no longer smirk at the authorities. Instead, he may have broken into laughter, a dark laughter. If he did, there was more to his snicker than one mistaken disinterment.

There was another upshot of the television special Jeremy Collins viewed, *"The Hunt." The Hunt* featured two cases in two fifteen-minute segments. The Bishop case was the second segment. The first segment exploded the next day.

Charles Mozdir, aged 32, was the fugitive featured in the first segment. He had been arrested in 2012 and accused of child molestation in California. He stood at six feet two inches and weighed 280 pounds. He disappeared before his trial; and ever since, he was thought to be armed and dangerous.

When *the Hunt* aired, several people called the police. A viewer recognized the child molester. He was working in a tiny shop, Smoking Culture, at 177 West Fourth Street, in New York's Greenwich Village. It was in a neighborhood featuring retail outlets like the nearby Pink Pussycat, an erotic sales store.

New York City's police force includes a federal fugitive task force. The force coordinates federal, state, and local authorities in pursuit of dangerous fugitives. They assist in investigations of people like Bishop. That July day three members of the force walked up the steep steps to Smoking Culture and entered a surprisingly open space in the middle of the tiny shop. Mozdir was behind the counter.

Mozdir pulled out a .32 caliber handgun and fired. He hit the lead detective in the chest and the stomach. His next two shots hit each of the two deputy United States marshals. Despite their wounds the three drew their police weapons and returned fire. Mozdir was shot dead. The surviving police recovered twenty rounds of live ammunition from Mozdir's tattooed corpse before medics wheeled him out of the Greenwich Village shop on a gurney.

First responders gathered. The Federal Fugitive task force injured were bandaged and taken to a nearby hospital. And the girls at the Pink Pussycat were interviewed by the press.

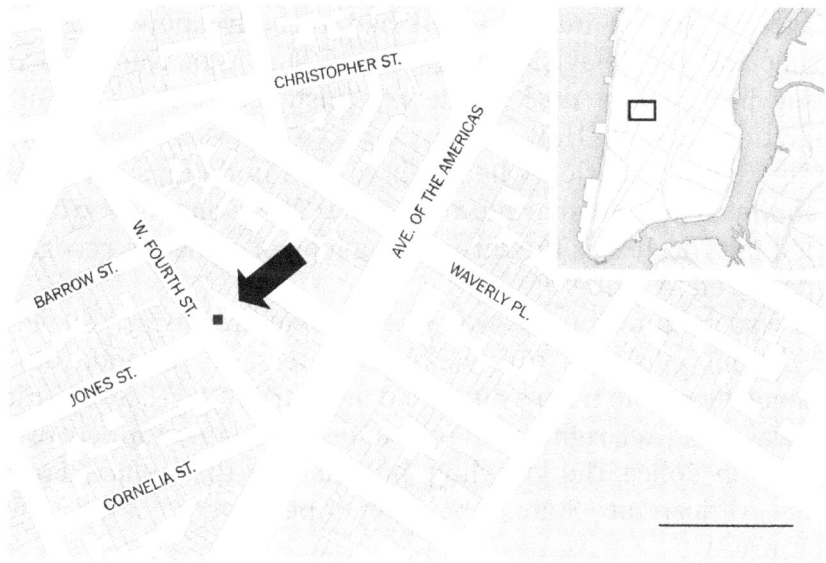

Smoking Culture in Greenwich Village, Manhattan

For the decades-long fugitive this was an abrupt reminder. When the ex-Foreign Service Officer suddenly appeared on the Ten Most Wanted list, the FBI considered that the class of 1954 might have been right about Bishop's being in the United States after all.

A lifetime of philandering, and the very meanness of the

murders shocked a now media-savvy world into a buzz of action. Bishop, the thrill-seeker, may have been right under their noses all along. The FBI immediately focused on southern California, as a place Bishop may have gone to retire. They were wrong.

The FBI had underestimated Bishop's audaciousness, and complete disregard of the combined forces of the federal fugitive task force. The next sighting placed Bradford Bishop right under their noses. That sighting was just ten days after the announcement that he was now one of America's ten most wanted. He was sighted in Annapolis, Maryland.

There he was, taking a turn on Chandler dock with a woman. The woman was a brown-haired person, not unlike Annette. The FBI estimated her age to be just over half of his.

Bradford was neatly dressed. He could have come out of a country club or from shopping for a local condominium.[214] He kept the goatee covering his prominent chin. He looked precisely like the age-progressed bust the FBI had recently spewed over the internet and the television airwaves.[215] That was when the man passing him on the dock made his mistake. At the moment of recognition, he said, "Holy shit."

The fugitive snarled when sighted, and in doing so gave away yet another clue. He snarled a lip snarl. The woman he was with snarled in sync. It was the threatening look of someone recognized and prepared to strike.[216]

It was spontaneous. It was just as spontaneous as the gleeful and defiant gesture, thrown with intent to offend, at the Wadsworths on the train as it pulled away from Basel, Switzerland. That was Brad all right: the Yale undergraduate stopped by the New Haven Police, the growling 'put them in their place' Foreign Service Officer at State, the ASA operative seeking covert adventure.[217]

---

[214] The author has come across cases where a wealthy, older man has parted with a long-time companion by purchasing a condominium for her use, far from his sphere of operations. In the author's experience, these had to do with divorces.
[215] The woman had a concealed carry purse. At this moment she reached for her gun.
[216] The lip snarl on the right side was another known Brad Bishop characteristic, and a dead giveaway.
[217] The man who sighted Bishop noted that Chandler Dock is narrow and that Bishop stared at the man with a, "I want to kill you look."

At the moment, they passed each other Bishop 'went robot' on the man and walked on with a blank stare. The man saw Bishop and the brown-haired woman get into a parked car. They sped away before he could do more.

It took a week for the man to report the sighting to the FBI. It is disturbing that it took the FBI another two to three weeks to respond to the sighting. Perhaps the FBI can be forgiven as it was overwhelmed by all the hoopla following Bishop's placement on the FBI's Ten Most Wanted List.

Their operation center was inundated with phone calls, including actual first-hand accounts from Bishop's many female liaisons over the years. Some of them went back to his time at Yale. Given the avalanche of calls and sightings, it must not have occurred to the FBI that Bradford Bishop would return to the same state where he committed the murders.

These, along with the class of 1954 sightings of 2009, were the first solid sightings since 1994.[218] Bishop had to notice the sudden FBI campaign on the airwaves. He had to be impressed with his accurate likeness in an age-progressed bust on the news ten days before. It may be why he had an armed escort with him.

After making threatening faces, as if he would kill the eyewitness, he slipped away. All three, the suspect, his escort, and the witness, were out in the open in broad daylight. Then he vanished.

---

[218] The 2009 sightings were originally not treated as pertinent sightings until 2014

A sketch of the April 2014 sighting of a man reputed to be W. Bradford Bishop Jr. with an unknown woman, and a concealed carry purse, as they came around a blind corner at the far end of Chandler Dock in Annapolis, Maryland

The End Game

> The best author will be the one who is ashamed to become a writer.
> —Friedrich Nietzsche

For over forty years Bradford Bishop has eluded the authorities. He took advantage of State Department privilege and laxity. He evaded police by crossing interstate and international boundaries. He lived a secret life apart from his family. About this, the US Department of State and other government agencies kept silent.

At this point, the author does not think Bishop will be caught and brought to justice. In part this is because the actuarially charts are against it. He is now past eighty. He has outlived half his generation. He has eight more years to live according to the actuarial charts and has a six percent chance of dying at any given point in what life he has left to him.

His father died at age 69 of a lingering illness (heart disease). Bradford Jr. himself smoked cigarettes, as did many of the silent generation. That may further shorten his life.[219]

Yet his father's father lived to be 83, and his paternal grandmother lived to be 96. This was at a time without 21st century medicine. Although his maternal grandmother, an immigrant from Germany, passed away at 33, his maternal grandfather reached the age of 83.[220]

Of the traits, he has exhibited throughout his life, the tendency to react quickly when detected, to slip away when pursued, and to muddle bureaucracy stands out. Complex planning (thwarting would-be pursuers by misleading them) is another trait born of his years at State. He plainly enjoys this.

His secretive 'other life' features bolt-holes. Making an escape with - to our knowledge – only US $400 suggests that the withdrawal was an afterthought; and that he had a bolt-hole to run

---

[219] A major hospital, Anne Arundel Medical Center, is a five-minute drive from Chandler Dock. Condominiums are a minute or so away. It is noteworthy that, while there are beautiful faraway places to retire to, a senior citizen's life can be saved if he or she can get to a hospital within minutes.

[220] Bradford Bishop Jr. had a hereditary heart murmur. Anne Arundel hospital offers a lengthy recovery treatment after heart valve surgery. It is notable that the witness recalls of this sighting that "Bishop was as white as a sheet."

to. (Perhaps multiple plans and multiple bolt-holes) With enough money he could have funded several 'safe houses.'[221]

There are three consistent traits beyond the complexity of Bishop's crimes. The first is distance. When sighted he consistently and rapidly puts huge distances between himself, and any would-be pursuers. This was true from the night of the murder, the disposal of the bodies, and the disposition of his station wagon. It is probable that he put a lot of distance between himself and Chandler Dock in Annapolis when he was sighted in April, 2014[222] as well.

The second is thrill-seeking behavior. To flit close to the flame and get away with it is validating for him. For Bishop, this is continuous proof that he is smarter and better than his peers are at Yale, the ASA, and State (Especially State). Bishop never was a 'desk-jockey' who anticipated the quiet enjoyment of coffee breaks.

The third is Coastal. Lobelia used to drive young Bradford to the beach after polytechnic school. A day at the beach in a Mediterranean climate is in his blood. Anywhere by water, that is neither too hot nor too cold, is his natural environment.

To this, the author adds an aversion to humidity. No one who spent the formative years of his or her life in California does not like hot, humid days. To water, wind, and beach, an aversion to humidity should be added.[223]

After years of research, the author will venture a guess. William Bradford Bishop Jr. planned to mislead the authorities by leaving his car at the Great Smoky Mountains National Park. He knew that people had disappeared in the Park. It was not just the perfect lure, it was a way to disappear and become a legend.

He had long since left his College friends with a burden. They have had to deal with the continuing search for any clues germane to the character, of the most noteworthy graduate of the class of 1958. The monster in Bradford Bishop resonates long after 1950's monster movies faded.

---

[221] The cost of gasoline he expended for his flight was 60 to 66¢ per gallon. He traveled an estimated 767 miles. His 1974 station wagon averaged 7 to 15 miles per gallon.
[222] He assumes the police are slow to react.
[223] Annapolis is surrounded by water and notably humid during the summer.

In the early 21st century, he will have yet another chance at fame (infamy). An anonymous death under a false identity, followed by cremation, would perpetuate and preserve his legend. The author posits that he returned to California, around 2009, as a senior citizen and under a long-held false identity. This was, in part, to have one last sneer at the herd that outstripped him.

To denigrate and belittle State Department hirelings, as well as the police who pursued him is not enough.[224] He has to flout it to 'put them all in their places.' To do this he needed to write a brief account on how he got away. It is likely that he would tout his successes and escapades as well. All of that could be contained in a notebook, not unlike the "Nicholson" diary.

The 2009 sighting was by the South Pasadena Post office. Post office boxes held for decades can be unwieldy. Junk mail can accumulate in unopened boxes. It is more likely that Bishop took the tried-and-true Foreign Service Officer method of concealing money acquired from illegal visa sales. He would have used a bank safety deposit box. Taking one out in his hometown would be just one, last, clever 'cock a snoot' at everyone.[225]

Paying for the box years in advance is something any experienced Foreign Service Officer would know about. Simple arrangements for a fiduciary, to hold the key, would likely include instructions to distribute the notebook. *The Washington Post* would be the logical recipient.[226]

But why the post office? Was Bishop rooming around there? Probably not. It is likely that Bishop was using 'General Delivery,' a procedure where the receiving post office holds a parcel for ten days. If not claimed, it is sent back.

If Bishop follows the pattern of retired, disgruntled FSOs, he would have taken the time to write some sort of memoir. It would not be short and sweet either. It is unlikely that he carried it on him as he traveled. Therefore, mailing a package to himself 'General

---

[224] Casually returning to the state of Maryland is a clear, if familiar, message: "I'm smarter than you."
[225] There are three banks close by the South Pasadena Post Office. All three are on Fair Oaks Avenue. Of those three, the former First Savings and Loan Association of South Pasadena at 1000 Fair Oaks Avenue, in operation since 1936, would have been known to Bishop.
[226] To do this neatly, forming a shell company in states like Delaware, Nevada, or Wyoming and representing oneself as a board member would prevent discovery. Using the Isle of Mann or other European vehicles to transfer funds to other shell companies in the United States is also likely.

Delivery' would provide secrecy and safety.

* * *

The quality of medical care in the United States is notable. Wealthy foreigners come to the US for treatments they cannot easily get elsewhere.[227] The senior Mr. Bishop was in declining health when he passed away one month short of age 70. It is entirely possible that the junior Mr. Bishop might prefer access to advanced medical attention should a similar condition arise.[228]

There is also the question of how he got away after he left his station wagon by the Kuhlman Cabin and Jake's Creek trail. The author believes that an accomplice drove him back to the Camp Lejeune area.[229] There he could have boarded a military plane bound for Italy. There were such flights departing from the Camp Le June training area; and someone with the proper credentials could have taken advantage of those flights.[230]

One sighting brought to the author's attention via the US Department of State's Ralph Bunch Library. The Library has been a helpful research asset for years. One presumed retiree reported that she heard about the author's research while in the library. That person said to the page at the desk that she had seen Bishop in southern Spain in 1978. She said she never reported it and left the library without the page gathering any contact information.[231]

State Department culture is so obsessed with promotion that little of note gets reported. This is consistent with what evidence we have concerning Bishop's flight. The theory that he made a beeline for the Mediterranean, and later to the south of Spain, fits neatly into the author's theories. This cannot, however, be held up

---

[227] Most notable are interventional cardiology procedures and rehabilitation.
[228] This is why it is notable that the April, 2014 sighting commented on how pale Bishop looked.
[229] The author proposes that the accomplice was an Ethiopian woman of Bishop's age, and probably of his acquaintance during his tour of Addis Ababa. It is also proposed that she kept Leo, the Bishop family dog.
[230] The assumption here is that Bishop made meticulous plans that included his escape route. If he had an accomplice with a vehicle to speed him away from where he left his car, he would have had some certainty that he could board a convenient carrier on the subsequent leg of his escape. Thus, he had to have a passage to a port of departure where he could 'blend in' (i.e. a military base with flights to Europe).
[231] This is so typical of the US Department of State on so many levels that, in and of itself, the report becomes credible.

as valid until the elusive Foreign Service retiree who was at the Ralph Bunche Library comes forward.

There is a logic to this. Brad Bishop Jr. always wanted to take to the open road. He looked to himself for strength, as did Nietzsche. It is rational to see Bishop - finally rid of status anxiety and serax, free of the 'mother complex,' and finally becoming 'afoot and light-hearted' - taking to the open road at last. With no impediments and a presumed network of associates, he indeed had the world before him.

He was doing what he, and many Foreign Service Officers, daydream of doing. With a new identity, and enough money from illicit passport sales to finance his rambling, he could say, 'Strong and content I travel the open road.' He was 23 years old again.

In the interim years, between 1976 and the 21st century, it is likely that he lived a libertine lifestyle. Like most Foreign Service officers, it is likely that he went on to see places of personal interest: Sweden, Australia, the beaches of the Mediterranean and the Adriatic. It is likely that, for a time, he called Italy 'home' and – if he had to run - had at least one bolt-hole hiding place in northern Italy, and perhaps a second along the Croatian coast.[232]

It is impossible to imagine that Bishop would have been content to settle down as a recluse. Nothing in his history or character supports that. He is all about winning. To win, he has to have a person or persons he can be better than.

Once Interpol had a red notice to act on, any legitimate employment, with or without a false identity, could be a threat. He had only one option: to turn to a life of crime in an environment he felt comfortable in. The author's reasoned opinion is that this was part of Bishop's plan after the contract killers walked away from the job in early 1976. Typical of so many Foreign Service officers the author interviewed, the 'gray economy' of smuggling is an enticement.[233]

---

[232] The Dalmatian coast is notably beautiful. If Bishop has to scrap any plans he might have of retiring to the United States, settling there (possibly with dual nationality) is similar to settling in a 1960's version of Southern California.

[233] Speculation has it that Bishop taught English as a foreign language while in Italy. With no red notice issued, the author acknowledges that, for the first few years after Bradford Bishop disappeared, this was possible.

It is in the author's academic experience that 'C' students are the ablest businessmen. It is likely that, with two or more shipments of smuggled oil on a small tanker, Bishop would have pocketed more than a skilled physician in the United States clears in a year. After the oil shock years of the nineteen-seventies and early nineteen-eighties, Bishop could have moved on to smuggling migrants. It is a business with huge rewards, little startup capital costs, and few risks. Just leave your heart at home; and Bishop came with that reputation.

He had the experience, and most likely the contacts, to set up operations in gray markets. He may even have contracted as a freelance operative for a Balkan country to do some information gathering. This could further explain the message to Main State about the purported sighting of Bishop residing at or near a foreign mission in the United States on July 5th 1978.

So, who is Brad Bishop? He is predictable. In the final analysis failure to keep pace with what was expected of him at Yale, and turning to medication, made him a 'C' student. Like most 'C' students, he succeeded far beyond 'A' students on life's huge stage.

He was also, first and foremost, a Foreign Service officer. He did not have to fit himself into that mold. He already embodied it: ambition, wanderlust, and narcissism. What he did not know was that in a system of timid sycophants, any irregularity without the protection of an even greater sycophant, spells catastrophe.

He was as devastated as any other FSO would be at the moment of career catastrophe. He had put his every effort, every waking thought into this. And, if enough of one's self, one's persona, one's essence is poured into a thing, and that thing dissolves, then all power is lost. There is a meltdown. Indeed, in extreme cases, there is no 'self' left. [234]

---

[234] The notion of a power too great for humans to safely possess is an evocative one. For those who have read JRR Tolkien's books, *The Lord of the Rings*, the one ring of power explains why Brad Bishop didn't just abandon his family. When the one ring is destroyed, all of what the evil lord put of himself into it was also destroyed. Those who carried the ring had physical and spiritual after-effects. This may explain why FSOs do not improve with age.

This is felt by the Officer Corps at State, but not grasped. Like so many others at the moment of career catastrophe, Bishop saw himself tossed out of the elite. The totality of ASA reprimands, Yale shortcomings, his mother's taking control of his household, and the agonizing years waiting for promotion, his career disappointment presented his efforts as nothing; and consequently, he was nothing. For anyone who wanted the spotlight - 'top billing' in any endeavor - this is devastating.

Something vital was taken away from the mid-level officer. He had done everything the Foreign Service way. He saw the 'stretch' he bid on taken away. Further, he saw that stretch as something he earned.

He felt cheated. He had to 'get even.' He was better than the people he worked with. To his way of thinking, he was the 'comer' thwarted. He would go rogue, because he, himself, saw no other place to go.

He was going to prove that he was better. He was the smarter FSO. For all his adult life, he sought to validate himself. Indeed, if you count his getting elected Vice President of the class of 1954 and not President, one could add adolescence to adulthood.[235] This fury, amplified to a heated pitch by the Foreign Service itself, is the answer to the oft asked question, "Why such rage?"

In Bradford Jr.'s thinking, his family and his life at Main State as a bureaucrat were one piece. His mother was the head of household, to the point where he resorted to demanding a spotless home in order to assert his dominion. His wife, who was now exploring a career and the possibility of a job, was the enemy.

When he said to his secretary, "After 35 a man is no more [sic] good." That had to do with his career at State as well as his home situation. Here lies the answer to the oft-asked questions, "Why didn't he just abandon his family? Why kill them?"

They had become one. In his reckoning, they brought him to where he was: a failure. They misdirected his life. He did not lead the family anymore. The heat of passion, triggered by State's shame and honor culture, was about revenge. It was time to settle scores.

The answers the police sought have always been simple.

---

[235] His mother wanted to know why 'her Brad' was Vice President and not President.

Scientists consistently say, of the unraveling of any riddle, that anything that is true is simple and neat. For Bishop the potential 'comer,' it was not just about running away *from* something. It was about running *to* something. Putting the pieces together for the first forty years of his life, points to where and how he spent the next forty years of his life.

The key to locating Bishop is knowing where to look. It is a Foreign Service officer trait to think that the second forty years of life, will be more interesting than the officer's first forty years. Once Bishop's first forty years are sorted out, it dictates the course of the next forty years.

Yearning to leave a legend behind in one's wake has always been very Foreign Service. Failure was not in his mother's plans for him nor (bitch goddess worship aside) was it becoming of a Yale graduate. It was the steep hierarchal system, and petty elitism, of the US Foreign Service that sharpened, what should have been a dull resentment, into a lethal weapon.

Indeed, William Bradford Bishop Jr. had far more in common with his fellow Foreign Service Officers, past or present, than any at the US Department of State would care to admit.

Epilogue

The US Department of State

 The murder of the Bishop family by an active duty Foreign Service Officer precipitated a change in the personnel evaluation system. The way the system ran afterward was to have junior officers go through a tenure process. Some would be eliminated early. After that, if the FSO gets to mid-rank, there would emerge an unspoken lifetime guarantee (except for issues of cause). That way a Foreign Service Officer would not be 'out on the street' without a minimal pension or any visible means of support.

The Biographical Register

 The Last Biographical Register was issued in 1974. Only "real" Foreign Service officers were listed. It was therefore a simple matter for foreign agents to pick out American agents undercover at embassies and consulates abroad. The damage to America's efforts at espionage overseas was such that elitism had to be put aside, at least in this case.

The Army Security Agency

 ...was reorganized in 1976. It was folded into the US Intelligence and Security Command. In the process the new command lost its characteristic, vertical organizational structure. Consequently, the CIA could honestly say that Bishop did not work for them.

Montgomery County

 ...passed a law in the 1980s that realtors must disclose to potential buyers that a heinous crime had occurred in a home. The Bishop murders are cited as the example. This is referred to as the "Bishop disclosure."

Fort Holabird

 Ft. Holabird was used to guard witnesses in major federal cases, such as those witnesses in the Watergate hearings. E.

Howard Hunt, Charles Colson and John Dean were among the Watergate witnesses held there. Fort Holabird closed in 1973. The City of Baltimore redeveloped it as an industrial park.

Hailie Selassie

Land reform eluded Haile Selassie. A notable famine struck parts of Ethiopia from 1972 to 1974. The exposure of attempts, by corrupt local officials, to cover up the famine from the imperial government resulted in general outrage. The Soviet Union's depiction of Haile Selassie's Ethiopia as backwards and inept (relative to the purported utopia of Marxism-Leninism) contributed to the popular uprising that led to Halie Selassie's downfall. The Derg (revolutionary forces) imprisoned him and announced the end of the Solomonic Dynasty. A reign of terror followed. Haile Selassie died in custody in 1975 at age 83.

The Derg

The Derg, or Dergue (Ge'ez: ደርግ, meaning "committee" or "council") is the short name of the Coordinating Committee of the Armed Forces, Police, and Territorial Army that ruled Ethiopia from 1974 to 1987. It took power following the ousting of Emperor Haile Selassie I. Between 1975 and 1987, the Derg executed and imprisoned tens of thousands of its opponents without trial.

Kagnew Station

The US government supported Ethiopia in its claim to Eritrea. When the Derg ousted Emperor Haile Selassie, tensions rose and the US started phasing out operations. The Derg abrogated the 1953 United States Ethiopian Mutual Defense Assistance Agreement, terminated the lease on Kagnew Station, and gave US military personnel a week to leave. On April 29, 1977, the last Americans left Kagnew Station.

Halie Selassie's Lions

The descendants of the imperial court's lions are in the Addis Ababa Zoo. In 2012 tests showed that they were genetically distinct. Captivity maintained the lineage, while showing little effect of inbreeding.

Edward Korry

Ambassador Korry remained as American Ambassador to Ethiopia until 1971. He went on to another ambassadorial assignment this time, to Chile, from 1967 to 1971. He was accused in the press of contributing to the 1973 coup that brought Augusto Pinochet to power. This he denied. When he passed away a clipping of a newspaper report, on the Bradford Bishop murders, was found in his files.

Gaborone

Gaborone grew to a city of over 400,000. Botswana is often put forward as one of the successful countries of post-independence Africa. The State Department pitches it now as a 'reward assignment.' State calls it the 'Paris of Africa.' Although it has changed over the years, when compared with other African posts, it is widely considered 'easy living.'

Tanzam Railway

...was built in five years, from 1970 to 1975. It was the largest foreign aid project China had ever undertaken. More track was added on, and it is now known as the TAZARA railway. The Tanzam railway did not make its goal of two million tons of freight shipped per annum. The railway fell into disrepair in recent decades due to lack of parts and maintenance. At this writing the governing rail authority was on the verge of collapse with debts estimated to be as high as US $700 million. The Chinese have generously agreed to come to its aid.

Kazungula Bridge

The Kazungula pontoon ferry still plies the waters of the Zambezi River. In the 21st century construction got underway to build the long-anticipated bridge. As of this writing it is yet to be completed.

The Caprivi Strip

The boundaries of the Caprivi Strip continued to be disputed. In 1999 Namibia and Botswana went to the International Court of Justice over its southernmost boundary. Botswana won the territorial dispute.

In a side note, the islands in the North Sea that Leo von Caprivi negotiated for Germany in the Heligoland–Zanzibar Treaty were vital to Germany's growing navy. They became important German military assets in the First and Second World Wars.

Roy Harrell Jr.

The police authorities now discount Roy Harrell's siting of Bishop in a men's lavatory in Sorrento Italy on January 11, 1979. Under questioning his story varied over time. Roy insists that he was telling the truth. As of this writing he still believes that Bishop was hiding in plain sight in southern Italy.

Albert Kenneth Bankston

In recent years, it has come to light that Bankston tried to get the attention of the authorities after his jailbreak from the Yellow Medicine County Jail. He vigorously claimed that he had been in contact with Bradford Bishop. His claims were dismissed.

Mary Daly

Daly's work continues to influence feminists to this day. She is best known for refusing to allow male students into her advanced classes at Boston College. In 1998 a discrimination claim was filed against her by two male students.

She is often quoted from a 2002 interview as having said, "If life is to survive on this planet, there must be a decontamination of the Earth. I think this will be accompanied by an evolutionary process that will result in a drastic reduction of the population of males." Ms. Daly passed away in 2010.

Francis Gary Powers

Francis Gary Powers left the CIA and flew a Bell 206 Jet Ranger helicopter for KNBC. He was covering brush fires when the helicopter ran out of fuel and crashed at the Sepulveda Dam recreational area in nearby Encino, several miles short of its intended landing site at Burbank Airport. He was killed on August 1, 1977, Bradford Bishop's 41st birthday.

Reinhard Gehlen

Reinhard Gehlen was one of the legendary Cold War spymasters. He eventually became head of the West German intelligence apparatus. He served as the first president of the Federal Intelligence Service until 1968. As president of the Federal Intelligence Service, itself a civilian office, he was promoted to lieutenant general of the Reserve in the West German Bundeswehr, and thus became the country's highest-ranking reserve officer. In some quarters, he is regarded as a lifelong German patriot.

Ante Pavelić

At the close of the Second World War in 1945, Pavelić ordered his troops to keep on fighting even after the German surrender. He, himself, fled to Austria and detailed Vjekoslav Luburić to lead the remaining fighters in the ongoing war. He made his way to Argentina where he remained politically active. In 1957, he was wounded in an assassination attempt, after which he went to Spain. There he died from his wounds on December 28, 1959.

Friedrich Wilhelm Nietzsche

Nietzsche rejected traditional morality yet could not replace it with an alternative morality. He went mad and spent the last 11 years of his life in a vegetative state.

Albert Camus

Albert Camus died on January 4, 1960 in a car crash. He was in a rare French sports car, a Facel-Vega HK500. The car was driven by his publisher. He was traveling to Paris and, at the last minute, had decided to join his publisher and travel by car instead of by train. The unused train ticket was found in his bag along with a French translation of Nietzsche's Die fröhliche Wissenschaft.[236]

Snippy the Horse

After an attempted autopsy the articulated bones of Snippy were cleaned and mounted. The skeleton went missing in the 1970's and resurfaced in 2005. The skeleton was put up for sale on Ebay, but the reserve price was not met. As of this writing the bones are still for sale.

The Roy Rogers Killings

Thirty-nine-year-old James Leroy Breedon was convicted of the killings at the Roy Rogers Restaurant on Little River Turnpike. His rap sheet was long. In 1954 (The same year Bishop was elected vice-president of his high school class.) he was found to have a sociopathic personality.

Riverside Alpine Hotel

...in Truckee, California was a popular resort destination for the upcoming 1960 Winter Olympic Games. It is better known as one of the most haunted hotels in California. Most

---

[236] This is a book Bishop would have learned about in his studies at Yale. In it Nietzsche first considered the idea of eternal recurrence. He explains it this way... 'What if some day or night a demon was to steal after you into your loneliest loneliness and say to you: 'This life as you now live and have lived it, you will have to live once more and innumerable times more' [...] 'Would you not throw yourself down and gnash your teeth and curse the demon who spoke thus? Or have you once experienced a tremendous moment when you would have answered him: 'You are a god and never have I heard anything more divine.'

The Gay Science, s. 341, Walter Kaufmann translation

notable among the spirits is purported to be a little girl who drowned in a bathtub in Room 403. A man who is said to have shot his wife dead in one of the rooms, and then went out to buy drinks and to brag about it and was promptly arrested. Since then, the apparition of a young woman has been seen in the Hotel, and there is a distinct feeling of negativity in the basement.

John List

John List hid in plain sight in Colorado for 17 years. Before he was discovered he was sometimes described as 'the bogeyman of Westfield,' (New Jersey). He was apprehended when the FBI had an age-progressed bust of List made. It was shown on television and a neighbor recognized her church-going neighbor, 'Robert Clark.' List was apprehended by the FBI, tried, and later sentenced to five life terms in prison. When sentenced, the courtroom broke out in applause.

Frank Caprio

...the psychiatrist, who prescribed antidepressants for Bishop, refused to speak with investigators after the killings. He cited patient-physician confidentiality. He was so shaken by the Bradford Bishop murders that he abandoned his practice. He died in New Jersey in 1995.

The Class of 1954

The South Pasadena Class of 1954 still holds their annual reunion. Some husbands of graduates also attend. In 2009 one of those husbands, not himself a class graduate, told a story of three and half months earlier. An old man shuttled up to him by the post office while he was waiting to cross at the corner. The old man was shabbily dressed. He said, "Did you hear? Brad Bishop is back in town."

It is notable that when the FBI placed Bradford Bishop on the ten most wanted list, and commenced the search in 2014, that the focus was on Southern California.

Ron Currie

Bradford Bishop's best friend traveled to Bethesda in the immediate aftermath of the murders. He was not let into 8103 Lilly Stone Drive by the police. He later was beset by so many inquiries from the media that he left for the desert to escape them.

The Class of 1958

The Yale Class listing for Bradford Bishop simply reads, "Whereabouts Unknown."

Afterword

Mea Culpa. I have opened a can of worms. It is with humility that the author reports that the Bishop case was reopened on a huge scale due to an archival quirk. While researching the case for a series on 'Crimes at American Embassies Abroad,' the author uncovered some hitherto undisturbed information. Recovering rare archival material and digging out obscure and verifiable facts is what college professors do.

A forty plus year crime is no longer a current event. It isn't even a cold case. It is history. Only academic research could have moved this sort of 'cold case' forward.

As previously stated, the author anticipates the receipt of Bishop's last will and testament, in long form, after his demise. If not, the FBI will not remove Bishop from the fugitive category until 2056, when Bishop would have turned 120 years old.

Until then, this manuscript closes the book on the Bradford Bishop murders. In the process, my efforts were such that the FBI placed Bradford Bishop Jr. on its ten most wanted list. They placed a reward of US $100,000 on his head.[237]

The fugitive made mistakes. Had Bradford Bishop not been a Foreign Service officer, the author would not have done the research. Had the Bankston letter not been discovered, Bishop's plot to hire contract killers to murder his entire family and rise to prominence at the US Department of State on sympathy, might not have been known. He might even have risen in the ranks to a leadership position at State.

Had Bishop not used gasoline at the grave site in Tyrell county, the discovery of the bloody Bishop station wagon would have led to the assumption that the entire family - including Bradford Jr. himself - were victims whose bodies were disposed of somewhere in the Great Smoky Mountains National Park.[238] Had Bishop not been so lax, he would not have absent-mindedly used his credit card at Outdoor Sports in Jacksonville to purchase a pair of tennis shoes. It was an act consistent with his observed adult behavior.

---

[237] How much is your life worth? It is the author's contention that no one would turn Bishop in for US $100,000.

[238] Purchasing the gas can was a second thought. It was likely a snap decision in a fit of rage.

As Bishop's life span nears its close, the author wishes to make one more observation. Bishop has bested his Yale classmates, and the jelly bean counters at State. Bishop shares a common thread with Foreign Service officers throughout the years. That is the shared aspiration to become an enduring legend and an ambassador by age 50.

Bishop worshiped his career. He rested his heart in his career, and that ate him alive. Becoming a leader at State is a good thing, but he turned it into the ultimate thing.

He sacrificed his family for his career. Like so many Foreign Service officers at State, he turned his career into his idol. Indeed, had the contract killers succeeded in murdering little Geoffrey just prior to his fifth birthday, it would have been child sacrifice.

David Casavis
New York University

Notes

Abbreviations in use

AFSA American Foreign Service Association
APB All Points Bulletin
ASA Army Security Agency
CIA Central Intelligence Agency
CIC Counter Intelligence Corps (Army)
CLO Community Liaison Office
CMF Citizen Military Forces, Australia – or the Australian Reserve
CPI Consumer Price Index
DIA Defense Intelligence Agency
DCM Deputy Chief of Mission
DNA Deoxyribonucleic acid
EER Employee Evaluation and Review
FSI Foreign Service Institute
FSO Foreign Service Officer
G2 In the US, it refers mostly to Army intelligence (with N-2 for Naval Intelligence)
HOP Hrvatski Oslobodilacki Pokret – Croatian Liberation Movement
HRB Hrvatsko Revolucionarno Bratstvo - Croatian Revolutionary Brotherhood (CRB)
IRS Internal Revenue Service
KGB An initialism for *Komitet gosudarstvennoy bezopasnosti* (Soviet Security Agency)
KJRM *Kraljevska Jugoslavenska Ratna Mornarica*, Краљевска Југословенска Ратна Морнарица (Royal Yugoslav Navy)
NATO North Atlantic Treaty Organization
NDH *Nezavisna Država Hrvatska* - Independent State of Croatia (1941 – 1945)
NSA National Security Agency (Also known as "No Such Agency.")
OPEC Organization of Petroleum Exporting Countries: A union of oil producing countries that regulate the amount of oil each country is able to produce.
PAO Public Affairs Officer

PNG Persona non-grata
PX Post Exchange (US Army)
SBI State Bureau of Investigation
SFRY Socialist Federal Republic of Yugoslavia
SIGINT Signals intelligence; the amalgamation of COMINT and ELINT into one unit of intelligence gathering dealing with all electronic emanations and transmissions
SS Schutzstaffel was a major paramilitary organization under Adolf Hitler
SWAPO South-West African People's Organization
TDY Temporary Duty
UDBA Uprava državne sigurnosti. Yugoslavian State Security Service
UDI Unilateral Declaration of Independence
UN United Nations
USIA US Information Agency
USAID US Agency for International Development
USIS US Information Service
WAO Women's Action Organization
WFP World Food Program

Pictorial and Graphic Materials

Alpine Truckee Hotel courtesy of the Truckee Hotel, California

Anton LaVey: Church of Satan

Basic Road Map, 1941, National Park Service

Bishop Sighting with Unknown Woman: Police Sketch

Bloody Hand, 2009 Murder by XPeaceXLoveXRawrX Cover by Rebecca Arthur

Botswana pilot license photo, Government of Botswana

Calhoun College Coat of Arms, Yale University

Cedar Hill Cemetery: Daily Sentinel

Cheetah with RFK courtesy of @SMGebru: #tbt 1966

Distrikt brčko – "sigurnosna kočnica" osamostaljenju RS: Ivan Ristić

Eastern North Carolina 1808, Cummings 1966

Execution Victim: Jasenovac Memorial Site Memorial Museum

FBI Sketches – End picture, Bishop in Annapolis, Bishop Age-Progressed by Karen T. Taylor

Great Smoky National Park 1941, US Department of Interior

Great Smoky Mountains National Park Map, National Park Service

Gun Running Map by Michael Hallan

Hammeryr4 @handschar division

Horn of Africa: Courtesy of Google Maps

Kazungula Bridge 2015, NYU Digital Studio (Rebecca Arthur)

Main State: Courtesy of the US Department of State, Washington, DC

Lion and Emperor – courtesy of Ethiopian Review

KJRM Dubrovnik, *British Pathe Gazette. [Universal Newsreel] Retrieved 15 July 2016.*

Map of Caderock Springs Rebecca Arthur, Elliot Brown, Jr.

Maps of Ethiopia. July 25, 2015 modified by Rebecca Arthur

Multiple Listing Service: 8103 Lilly Stone Drive

Momo: Thought to be originally a police sketch, credited to Heartland.ehclients.com

Montgomery County: Chief Engineers Office N.D.V. (Maj. Gen. J. F. Gilmer) Circa 1850

Montgomery County Flag - Public Domain via Commons

Passport Photos by US Department of State

Passport Photo, Albert Camus, by the Republic of France

Peace Corps Ethiopia: Norman Rockwell

Polytechnic School Emblem: Polytechnic, South Pasadena, California

Rialto Theatre: South Pasadena Local History Images Collection

Robbin Island Prisoners: Republic of South African, Department of Correctional Services, Robben Island Museum

Rondavel Koedoesrant, National Cultural History Museum, Pretoria

Sheriff Thomas and Bankston – Tuscaloosa News, Tuscaloosa Alabama

South Pasadena High School Emblem: Tigers South Pasadena, California

South Pasadena Post Office: South Pasadena Local History Images Collection

Tract C, Navy Cruise Book 1973 courtesy of Dan Carr and Randy Harris

Tree: Polytechnic School

Untitled Police Sketch: FBI

War Department, US Government 1945 photo

Wodonga Military Region – Pryce Mandel

Glossary of Terms

Aha Moment: A moment of sudden insight or discovery.

All Bases Covered: An idiom ...to deal with every part of a situation or activity

Amembassy: American Embassy

Analeptic: Restoring; invigorating; giving strength after disease.

Apartheid: A ridged policy of segregating and economically and politically oppressing the non-white population

Avuncular: An adjective: of, relating to, or characteristic of an uncle

Balletomane: A ballet enthusiast

Bear Market: A market, especially a stock market, characterized by falling prices; the opposite of a bull market.

Bedroom Community: A suburban area or town where many commuters live, often quite a distance from the place of employment

Big Box: Pertaining to or describing a very large retail store that does a high volume of business and usually has low prices.

Bill of Lading: "Lading" specifically refers to the loading of cargo aboard a ship. It is a document or script signed on behalf of the owner of a ship in which goods are embarked, acknowledging the receipt of the Goods, and undertaking to deliver them at the end of the voyage, subject to such conditions as may be mentioned in said bill of lading

Bitch goddess: Worldly or material success personified as a goddess, especially one requiring sacrifice and being essentially destructive: He went to New York to worship the bitch goddess success.

Boon Docks: A remote rural area (a term usually preceded by the word 'the')

Bootlegging: A verb used with an object: to deal in (liquor or other goods) unlawfully.

Brinksmanship: The technique or practice of maneuvering a dangerous situation to the limits of tolerance or safety in order to secure the greatest advantage, especially by creating diplomatic crises

Burn One's Bridges: To cutoff the way back to where you came from, making it impossible to retreat.

Bushwhack: To make one's way through woods, forest.

Cagey: Cautious, wary, or shrewd.

Caliginous: Misty; dim; dark.

Cat Nap: A short, light nap or doze.

Chargé d'affaires: A diplomat inferior in rank to an ambassador or minister who heads a mission when no ambassador or minister is assigned

Chief Cook and Bottle Washer: A person who does a wide variety of routine, sometimes menial, tasks.

Chopper: Informal, a helicopter.

Cinemascope: A wide-screen process using anamorphic lenses in photographing and projecting the film.

Clientitis: The tendency of resident in-country staff of an organization to regard the officials and people of the host country as "clients"... This condition can be found in business or government. The term clientitis is somewhat similar to the phrases "gone native" or "going native" (Or in British English "gone bush.")

Cock a Snoot: A gesture of defiance, disrespect, or derision; also *cock a /one's snook*

Comer, A: A person or thing likely to succeed, a person who arrives somewhere.

Communist Bloc: Communist countries considered collectively, especially during the existence of the Soviet Union.

Coonskin hat: A hat made out of an animal skin. The hat is made out of the fur of the raccoon, an animal common in America, and usually sports a tail.

Doolally: "Insane, eccentric, feeble minded" from British English slang, by 1917 the slang term was prevalent among the armed services. Also, in 'full doolally tap' combined with the Urdu word for "fever", from Deolali, near Bombay, India, which was a military camp (established 1861) with a large barracks and a chief staging point for British troops on their way to or from India; the reference is to men whose enlistments had expired who waited there impatiently for transport home.

Dovetail: To join or fit together compactly or harmoniously.

Downers: An old or diseased animal, especially one that cannot stand up.

Endorheic: Of or relating to interior drainage basins.

Epigram: Any witty, ingenious, or pointed saying tersely expressed.

Epistolarian: One who writes letters

Euphony: Agreeableness of sound; pleasing effect to the ear, especially a pleasant sounding or harmonious combination or succession of words.

Existential Angst: Existential angst is the anxiety of the possible meaninglessness of existence.

Fair-Haired Boy: A person, especially a young one, treated as a favorite or considered especially promising by a superior or the members of a group.

Faux Pas: A slip or blunder in etiquette, manners, or conduct; an embarrassing social blunder or indiscretion.

Fence Mending: The practice of reestablishing or strengthening personal, business, or political contacts and relationships by conciliation or negotiation, as after a dispute, disagreement, or period of inactivity

FHO: Foreign Armies East (Fremde Heere Ost) a German military intelligence organization that focused on analyzing the Soviet Union and other East European countries before and during the Second World War.

Fifth Wheel: An extra wheel for a four-wheeled vehicle. A superfluous, unneeded, or unwanted person or thing.

Fix is in, the: A process (for example, a court case) has been rigged behind the scenes and its outcome will not reflect true justice.

Flash in the pan: A brief success

Folkways: The ways of living, thinking, and acting in a human group, built up without conscious design but serving as compelling guides of conduct.

Foreign Service Brat: A person whose parent(s) served full-time in a Foreign Service posting abroad during that person's childhood... A Foreign Service brat may spend the majority of his or her childhood outside his or her parents' home country.

Free-For-All: A fight, argument, contest, etc., open to everyone and usually without rules.

Gang-up: An act of uniting in opposition to someone or something.

Gentleman's C's: A grade given to a student (traditionally with wealthy parents) instead of a failing grade.

Getting in on the Ground Floor: To be involved at the very beginning of something. This alludes to riding in an elevator that will become increasingly crowded as it ascends. You will be able to get in most easily at the lowest level.

Go for broke: To exert oneself or employ one's resources to the utmost.

Go with the flow: To be relaxed and accept a situation, rather than trying to alter or control it.

Gold ring, reaching for the: While kids rode on a merry-go-round, those on the outside had a chance to reach for a gold (or brass) ring hanging outside the carrousel. If he or she managed to grab it, s/he received some prize.

Grasping at straws: When you're on the spot and you're looking to say something concrete but you have nothing to say.

Gray Economy: A system involving the secret but not illegal sale of goods at excessive prices.

Gray Markets: An unofficial market or trade in something, especially unissued shares or controlled or scarce goods.

Guff: Empty or foolish talk; nonsense. Insolent talk.

Gunrunning: The smuggling of guns or other ammunition into a country.

Hardscrabble: Having harsh and difficult conditions because of poverty.

Hello Number: If a spy is dialing a hello number, it usually means he or she is in trouble. This trade craft term refers to a phone call in which the person on the other end doesn't identify who or where he or she is, giving only a code-word or some other signal the spy would know the meaning to.

Random example: Spy calls the hello number and the person on the other end says "it's raining in Florida right now." To anyone else listening, it could mean the weather is terrible in the Sunshine State, but the real meaning could be that the spy needs to get on a plane and get out of the country immediately.

High Flyer: A person who is extravagant or goes to extremes in aims, pretensions, opinions, etc.

Host Country: A nation in which representatives or organizations of another state are present because of government invitation and/or international agreement.

In a nutshell: …in very brief form; in a few words

Interpol: International Criminal Police Organization (French: *Organisation internationale de police criminelle*, **OIPC - ICPO**) is an intergovernmental organization facilitating international police cooperation.

Ivy League Colleges: A group of colleges and universities in the northeastern U.S., consisting of Yale, Harvard, Princeton, Columbia, Dartmouth, Cornell, the University of Pennsylvania, and Brown, having a reputation for high scholastic achievement and social prestige.

Jersey: A close-fitting, knitted sweater or shirt.

Jockstrap: An elasticized belt, a men's undergarment, with a pouch for supporting and protecting the genitals, worn especially while participating in athletics.

Jot and Tittle: *Jot* and *tittle* refer to tiny quantities. A *jot* is the name of the least letter of an alphabet or the smallest part of a piece of writing. A *tittle* refers to a small stroke or point in writing or printing. In classical Latin this is applied to any accent over a letter, but is now most commonly used as the name for the dot over the letter 'i.' It is also the name of the dots on dice.

Kosovar: A native or inhabitant of Kosovo.

Lamina: A layer or coat lying over another, as the plates of minerals or bones.

Letterman: A person who has earned a letter in an interscholastic or intercollegiate activity, especially a sport.

Live off the Grid: (adj.) Unrecorded, untraceable through normal means.

Mea Culpa: A Latin phrase that means "through my fault." The phrase comes from a prayer of confession of sinfulness.

Meme: A cultural item that is transmitted by repetition and replication.

Mielie Meal: Mealie-meal is a relatively coarse flour made from maize which is known as mielies, or mealies, in southern Africa, from the Portuguese milho. The Portuguese had originally brought corn (maize) from the Americas to Africa.

Modus Operandi: A particular way or method of doing something.

Mopani: The Mopani, or Mopane, worm is a large edible caterpillar. It is an important source of protein for millions of indigenous people of Botswana

Nay Theist: A Nay Theist is *not* an atheist or agnostic. The Nay theist is well aware of the existence of the gods (or God) and freely admits it; he just refuses to worship them, or to "believe" in them in any strong Spiritual sense beyond merely acknowledging the fact of their existence.

Nihilism: The rejection of all religious and moral principles, often in the belief that life is meaningless.

Persona Non-Grata: A person who is not welcome.

Photo Op: Short for Photo Opportunity

Ply your Trade: To do your usual work or business.

Postulate: To claim or assume the existence of or truth of something, especially as a basis for reasoning or arguing.

Potboiler: A mediocre work of literature or art produced merely for financial gain.

Prove Out: To turn out well, to succeed

Prep Work: "Preparation Work" or work done to make ready for something.

Proustian Moment: An involuntary memory usually brought on by a smell or taste.

Quiet Move: (Chess) A quiet move is not a capture, check or immediate threat to the opposition. This includes subtle developmental moves or moves that improve a piece's position (placing it on a more active square).

Rap Sheet: A record kept by law-enforcement authorities of a person's arrest and convictions

Recluse: Characterized by seclusion; solitary.

Red Flag: To provoke the attention of; alert; arouse.

Red Notice: An Interpol Red Notice is the closest instrument to an international arrest warrant in use today. Interpol (the International Criminal Police Organization) circulates notices to member countries listing persons who are wanted for extradition.

Rondavel: (South African) a circular often thatched building with a conical roof.

Screw-up: Slang. To ruin through bungling or stupidity.

Scupper: Nautical… A drain at the edge of a deck exposed to the weather, for allowing accumulated water to drain away into the sea or into the bilges. Any opening in the side of a building, as in a parapet, for draining off rain water.

Scuttlebutt: Rumor or gossip: A nautical term derived from a drinking fountain for use by the crew of a vessel.

Self-Starter: A person who begins work or undertakes a project on his or her own initiative, without needing to be told or encouraged to do so.

Seven Sisters Colleges: The Seven Sisters are a loose association of seven liberal arts colleges in the Northeastern United States that are historically women's colleges. They are Barnard

College, Bryn Mawr College, Mount Holyoke College, Radcliffe College, Smith College, Vassar College, and Wellesley College.

Shill: A person who poses as a customer in order to decoy others into participating, as at a gambling house, auction, confidence game, etc.

Short Timer: a person, as a soldier, who has a short period of time left to serve on a tour of duty.

Shot Across the Bow: A warning to stop doing something.

Signaled Out: When a single individual or thing is separated out from a larger group, usually by being especially noticed or treated differently, that individual or thing is being "singled out."

Sleazy: Contemptibly low, disreputable, squalid; sordid; filthy, dilapidated.

Snob: A person who imitates, cultivates, or slavishly admires social superiors and is condescending or overbearing to others.

Snooty: Showing disapproval or contempt toward others, especially those considered to belong to a lower social class.

Spigot: A faucet for controlling the flow of liquid from a pipe or the like.

Spring Break: A vacation from school or college during the spring term.

Status Anxiety: An anxiety about what others think of us; about whether we're judged a success or a failure, a winner or a loser.

Stratovolcano: A large, steep volcano built up of alternating layers of lava and ash, or cinders.

Strike a chord: To trigger a feeling or memory.

Suck it up: To become serious; stop dallying or loafing.

Swanning about: This term made its way into mainstream English to mean anyone moving about in an irresponsibly carefree or aimless pattern. *Swanning around* and *swanning about* are primarily British terms, they are rarely seen in the United States.

Talking Shop: (informal) A group or committee that has discussions that never result in action.

Tie-Line: A line that connects two or more extensions in a PBX telephone system.

Town and Gown Riots: ...in a college town, the relations between "town and gown" are those between the residents of the town and the students and faculty associated with the school, who in the past wore academic gowns. Such relations are often not friendly or pleasant.

Townies: A non-student resident of a college town.

Transposition: A transposition in chess is a sequence of moves that results in a position which may also be reached by another, more common sequence of moves.

Turn a blind eye: An idiom describing the 'ignoring of undesirable information.'

Twisting in the Wind: To suffer the agony of some humiliation or punishment. (Alludes to an execution by hanging.) To be abandoned to a bad situation, especially to be left behind to incur blame.

UBDA: Serbo-Croatian acronym (UDBA), Uprava državne sigurnosti, abbreviation UDB (simplified: Udba or UDBA), was the Yugoslav security service and thus the secret police of Yugoslavia. The UDBA was founded in 1946 and disbanded with the collapse of Yugoslavia in the early 1990s.

Übermensch: German... The concept of the Übermensch is in contrast to the other-worldliness of Christianity. The Übermensch is not driven into other worlds away from this one. 'God is dead' means that the idea of God can no longer provide values.

Uptight: Tense, nervous, jittery, or annoyed or angry... stiffly; Conventional in manner or attitudes.

Vaudeville: A theatrical piece of light or amusing character, interspersed with songs and dances.

Viscous: Of a glutinous nature or consistency; sticky; thick; adhesive.

Waiting move: A passive but harmless move played while waiting for initiative from the opponent (Chess term).

Wally the Spook: Sometimes referred to as 'The Spook' or 'Sneaky Pete,' he was the logo of the Army Security Agency in Korea during the 1950's and 1960's. He is depicted as a small figure with dagger in hand.

Wassail: A salutation wishing health to a person, used in England in early times when presenting a cup of drink or when drinking to the person.

Wetwork: Assassinations and related dirty tricks... The UDBA used the term "Black Actions" (*crne akcije*). Many of these were sensational, needlessly brutal, and also involved the murder of children, including acts committed in the United States.

What Gives? What happened? What went wrong? What's the problem?

Wheels Up: The time or point when a plan or operation is executed... it comes from the military to describe when a plane lifts off to start a deployment, at that point an operation is considered hot (officially started). For the Foreign Service, it is the inverse. It is when an operation is finished.

Wildcatter: A oil prospector.

Yalie: A Person who attends Yale

Addenda

Bradford Bishop has been analyzed, by some professionals, as suffering from the syndromes listed as follows. (Similar analyses are not unknown among other members of the Foreign Service Officer Corps.)

Narcissistic Personality Disorder

1. An exaggerated sense of self-importance (e.g., exaggerates achievements and talents, expects to be recognized as superior without commensurate achievements)
2. Preoccupation with fantasies of unlimited success, power, brilliance, beauty, or ideal love
3. Believes he is "special" and can only be understood by, or should associate with, other special or high-status people (or institutions)
4. Requires excessive admiration
5. Has a sense of entitlement?
6. Selfishly takes advantage of others to achieve his own ends
7. Lacks empathy
8. Is often envious of others or believes that others are envious of him
9. Shows arrogant, haughty, patronizing, or contemptuous behaviors or attitudes

Source: *The Diagnostic and Statistical Manual of Mental Disorders (DSM) IV*

The Mother Complex

The mother complex is a potentially active component of everyone's psyche, informed first of all by the experience of the personal mother, then by significant contact with other women, and by collective assumptions. The constellation of a mother complex has differing effects according to whether it appears in a son or a daughter.

> Typical effects on the son are homosexuality and/or Don Juanism, and sometimes also impotence [though here the father complex also plays a part]. In homosexuality, the son's entire heterosexuality is tied to the mother in an unconscious form; in Don Juanism, he unconsciously seeks his mother in every woman he meets.

["Psychological Aspects of the Mother Archetype," CW 9i, par. 162.]

Annette Bishop's Senior High School graduation picture (1955)

Don Juan Complex

The Don Juan complex derives from constant personal frustrations incurred in intimate relations with women. A sad love story with a broken-heart-end, or sexually traumatic experience might also be in the roots of this masculine complex.

The complex's manifestations vary from case to case, whereas, the common aspects are as follows:

- Psychological perception of a woman as a source of pleasure, which can and should bring satisfaction to a man;
- Ignorance about women;
- Easy-going and superficial attitude towards all women without exception;
- Tendency to change the intimate partners frequently, without concentration on someone in particular;
- Dramatization of the relations with women, i.e. leaving without saying 'good-bye' etc.;
- Habit to live at woman's cost;
- Incapacity to truly love a woman and to build the long-term and stable relations with her.

Unfortunately, such people are not capable of creating a family, and in a case when the person aims at changing his life, the psychoanalysis and personal-relations therapy shall be applied.

Source: *Analytical Psychology and Psychoanalysis. April 8, 2011*

Insomnia

Causes of **acute insomnia** can include:

- Significant life stress (job loss or change, death of a loved one, divorce, moving)
- Illness

- Emotional or physical discomfort
- Environmental factors like noise, light, or extreme temperatures (hot or cold) that interfere with sleep
- Some medications (for example those used to treat colds, allergies, depression, high blood pressure, and asthma) may interfere with sleep
- Interferences in normal sleep schedule (jet lag or switching from a day to night shift, for example)

Causes of **chronic insomnia** include:

- Depression and/or anxiety
- Chronic stress
- Pain or discomfort at night

©2005-2016 WebMD, LLC.

Involutional Megalomania

...The sad phenomenon of scientists whose outlook seemed to have become poisoned by discovery, pseudo-discovery or hope for discovery. As individuals, they seemed to have become impervious to contrary evidence, resentful of criticism and to have exaggerated expectations of rewards and recognition. Their findings, when they had any, they often elaborated in a grandiose way; their data became woven into a system of almost delusional proportions. Such behavior is not infrequently a besetting sin of late middle life: at a time when men begin to write definitive books and, if never before, to show that they think big. The writer has, in an impertinent moment, called this phenomenon involutional megalomania, but the syndrome at times afflicts men in their youth, too, so there is no age exempt from the dangers of thinking big. Megalomania seems to be an appropriate word for epitomizing the phenomenon of the exaggerated thought, the too-aspiring action and the excessive eagerness for eminence, acclaim and power. In psychiatry it is a word not much used and appears but rarely in textbooks, although there are several references under this heading in Freud's *interpretation of Dreams,* published in 1900. *The Oxford*

University Dictionary indicates that the first known occurrence of this word, i~ English, was in 1890. It is not frequently found in non-psychiatric writings and is not listed in the 1898 Edition of Skeat, ~ nor does it occur i~ the *Encyclopedia Britannica, 4* 1928 edition, or even in the 1963 edition of the *Columbia Encyclopedia.* It is defined in the *Oxford Universal Dictionary* ~as "insanity of self-exaltation, or a passion for big things." *Dorland's Illustrated Medical Dictionary* ~ of 1951 describes megalomania as "delusions of *grandeur;* unreasonable conviction of one's own extreme greatness, goodness, or power."

B. A. CLEGHORN~, M.D. *Address to the "Interdisciplinary Group," ~ Montreal, March 18, 1964.*[239]

Possible side effects of oxazepam (serax).

- confusion;
- unusual risk-taking behavior, decreased inhibitions, no fear of danger;
- hyperactivity, agitation, hostility;
- hallucinations;
- feeling lightheaded, fainting;
- jaundice (yellowing of the skin or eyes); or
- problems with urination.

---

[239] It is almost certain that Dr. Frank Caprio attended this conference. He told Brad Bishop Jr. about this in one of his psychotherapy appointments. Like Yale's admonishment of the 'Bitch Goddess Success,' it was upsetting and was contrary to his self-image, self-esteem, and world view.

Addenda

Foreign Service Officer Culture at State

Department-wide dysfunctions

Status Anxiety

We care about our status for a simple reason: because most people tend to be nice to us according to the amount of status we have. It is no coincidence that the first question we tend to be asked by new acquaintances is, 'Where were you posted and what do you do?' The origins of status anxiety range from the consequences of the promotional system, to the secret dismay at the success of friends.

Alain de Botton

Existentialism

A philosophical theory or approach that emphasizes the existence of the individual person as a free and responsible agent determining his or her own development through acts of the will.

Existential Angst

Existential Angst is when one relates to being aware of the possibility that life lacks meaning, causing an extreme form of anxiety, and a feeling of despair or hopelessness.

Mid-Life Crisis

"Midlife transition" is a natural stage that happens to many of us at some point (usually at about age 40, give or take 20 years).

Midlife transition can include:

- Discontentment or boredom with life or with the lifestyle

(including people and things) that have provided fulfillment for a long time
- Feeling restless and wanting to do something completely different
- Questioning decisions made years earlier and the meaning of life
- Confusion about who you are or where your life is going
- Daydreaming
- Irritability, unexpected anger
- Persistent sadness
- Acting on alcohol, drug, food, or other compulsions
- Greatly decreased or increased sexual desire
- Sexual affairs, especially with someone much younger
- Greatly decreased or increased ambition.

Middle age is a time in which adults take on new job responsibilities and therefore often feel a need to reassess where they are and make changes while they feel they still have time. In his 1965 article "Death and the Midlife Crisis" for the *International Journal of Psychoanalysis*, psychologist Elliot Jaques coined the term "midlife crisis," referring to a time when adults realize their own mortality and how much time they may have left in their lives.

The midlife transition (or crisis) can also be understood using a Myers-Briggs personality model stemming from the works of Carl Jung. The stages are as follows:

- Accommodation—presenting ourselves as different people ("personae") based on our situation
- Separation—removing the personae we wear in different situations and assessing who we are underneath; rejecting your personae, even if only temporarily
- Reintegration—feeling more certain of your true identity and adopting more appropriate personae
- Individuation—recognizing and integrating the conflicts that exist within us, and achieving a balance between them

Sources

- Death and the Mid-life Crisis. Jaques E, *Inter. Journal of Psychoanalysis.* 1965 Oct;46(4):502-14.
- *Psychological Types* (Collected Works of C.G. Jung, Volume 6)
- *MBTI Manual (A Guide to the Development and Use of the Myers Briggs Type Indicator)*
- *Handbook of Midlife Development.* Lachman, Margie E.
- National Institute of Mental Health
- U.S. Department of Health & Human Services - The President's Council on Physical Fitness and Sports.

Categorizing the Killers: Four Types of Family Annihilator

Self-righteous: The killer seeks to locate blame for his crimes upon the mother who he holds responsible for the breakdown of the family. This may involve the killer phoning his partner before the murder to explain what he is about to do. For these men, their breadwinner status is central to their idea of the ideal family.

Disappointed: This killer believes his family has let him down or has acted in ways to undermine or destroy his vision of ideal family life. An example may be disappointment that children are not following the traditional religious or cultural customs of the father.

Anomic: In these cases, the family has become firmly linked in the mind of the killer to the economy. The father sees family as the result of his economic success, allowing him to display his achievements. However, if the father becomes an economic failure, he sees the family as no longer serving this function.

Paranoid: Those who perceive an external threat to the family. This is often social services or the legal system, which the father fears will side against him and take away the children. Here the murder is motivated by a twisted desire to protect the family.

In all of these cases masculinity and perceptions of power sets the background for the crimes. The family role of the father is central to their ideas of masculinity and the murders represent a last-ditch attempt to perform a masculine role.

Characteristics of family killers revealed by first taxonomy study: August 14, 2013
Yardley. E, Wilson. D, Lynes. A, 'A taxonomy of male British family annihilators, 1980-2013,' *The Howard Journal of Criminal Justice*, August 2013

The Bankston Letter

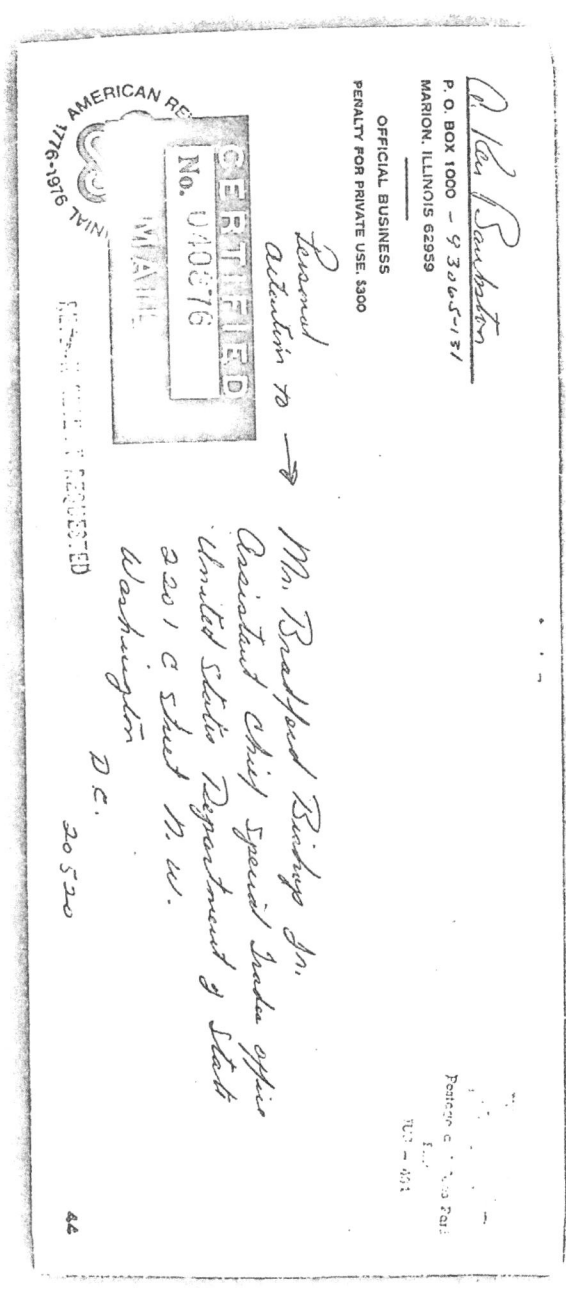

March 15, 1976
A. Ken Bankston
Box 1000 PMB 93065-131
Marion Federal Penitentiary
Marion, Illinois 62959

Mr. Bradford Bishop Jr.
United States Department
Washington, D.C.

Mr. Bishop After reviewing everything I set forth and your suggestions I can see that you would be in a Better seat to see the facts. Needless to say I have no way to express my heart felt thanks. As I stated in my February letter, #4, David Paul Aiken knew the route this was taking and since then we have contacted Mrs. K. Graham and the Attorney General in Mexico. Though a mistake I failed to send copies however I feel the impact will be justified in just the letter.

Now in answer to your question. Yes I am most sure she is in the North Carolina State penitentiary. I do not know why Sunny would tell you something that could very easily be proved. When I wrote you in February, letter #5 I explained that she was there and that David Paul Aiken knew this "Sonny" in Atlanta. I am sure he is a capeable person and that he knows all about Creswell. In fact David said you could walk to Phelps Lake from Creswell. I think it's about five (5) miles. I really don't see what this has to do with me Mr. Bishop. I was only interested in Mexico and/or Central America as you know. I suggest you and David get together on this as he is well known in that area.

    Mr. Bishop I will not write you again until I transfer to North Dakota. I am really glad of this as I am fed up with the feds bs. it.

    Sincerely
    A. Ken Bankston
    93065-131

Credit Card Receipts

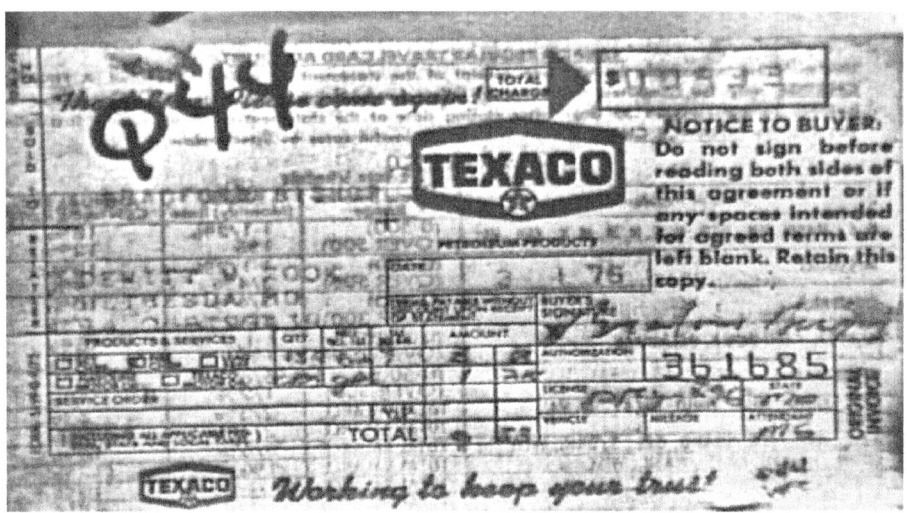

Works Cited

Introduction
Douglas, John. Anatomy of a Motive. New York: Simon and Schuster, 2012.

Beyond Shady Grove
Boerma, Jurgen, "The Bradford Bishop Mystery," *The Washington Daily News*, 10 April 2014.

Chang, Terrence C, Powdthavee, Nattavudh, and Oswald, Andrew J, "Longitudinal Evidence for a Midlife Nadir in Human Well-being: Results from Four Data Sets." Institute for the Study of Labor, Discussion Paper Series: *Forschungsinstitut zur Zukunft der Arbeit*, IZA DP No. 7942 February 2014.

Golian, Ed. Personal Interview. 8 December 2011.

Hockenos, Paul: (2003) *Homeland Calling*. Ithaca, New York: Cornell University Press

The Glittering Prize

Bishop, Bradford W. U.S. International Trade Commission Finding in Escape Clause Case Involving Non –Rubber Footwear. (Cable) US Department of State Washington DC,21 February, 1976.

Eagles. *Hotel California.* Rec. Feb. 1977. Bill Szymczyk, n.d. Vinyl recording.

Ingram, Eric Taylor. Personal Interview. 9 October 2016.

Pacepa, Mikai Ion. Red Horizons. Washington DC: Regnery Gateway. 1987.

Williams, Albert. Telephone Interview. 29 July, 2016

Only the UDBA Kills Like That

"5 slain linked to missing U. S. aide." *Chicago Tribune* pg. 11. 9 March 1976

Baker, Donald and Cynthia Goreney. "5 in Md. Family Found Slain," *The Washington Post* "pg. A1. 9 March 1976

Bayarri, Francesc Meeting in Sarajevo (Kindle Locations 2383-2384). Francesc Bayarri.Kindle Edition. 11 June, 2013

Cox, Kevin. "Marine Put in Prison for Espionage." *The Wilmington Morning Star.* Pg.1B. 9 January 1985.

Darei, Guy. "Auto Industry Layoffs Increase," *The Day,* (London Ct.) Pg. 40. 16 May 1089.

Duncan, John D. Jr. (US Department of State, Office of Inspector General) "Synopsis of the Bureau of Diplomatic Security File," Memo to John Cady. (Office of the State's Attorney) 18 May, 1994

Golian, Ed. Personal Interview. 9 August 2010

Gorney, Cynthia. "Neighbors Reassess Life After the Bishop Slayings.'" *The Washington Post"* pg. B1. 23 April 1976.

Harrell, Roy. Telephone Interview. 31 January 2011

"Legacy of Black Actions, The."

http://20committee.com/2013/06/29/the-legacy-of-black-actions The. XX Committee 29 June 2013

Weather 1 -- No Title. *The Washington Post,* pg. A1. Mar 1, 1976.

Balkan Revenge

CURRENT BIOGRAPHY, Who's News and Why, 1942. *Editor Maxine Block. Published* by: *H.W. Wilson Company, New York, N.Y. 1942 Quote: Pages 651, 652* and 653.

Francesc Bayarri and Isabel Tello (Translator): *Meeting in Sarajevo* Kindle Book, 2013

Morris, Joe Alex Jr. "City of Terror: Croat Exiles in Munich Fearful of Tito Agents Croatian Exiles." *Los Angeles Times,* Pg. 1. 13. May 1969.

The Great Smoky Mountains Search

Baldwin, Juanitta and Ester Grubb. Unsolved Disappearances in the Great Smoky Mountains. Suntop press, [Sevier County, Tennessee.] 1 September 1998.

"Car in Tennessee Identified as Suspect's in Slaying of 5," *New York Times,* pg. 10.19 March 1976.

"F.B.I. Searches in the Smokies for Suspect in Slaying of Family." *New York Times.* 23. 20 March 1976.

Grubisich, Thomas. "Healing After Horror of Murder: Healing Follows Horror of Murdersat Restaurant." *The Washington Post,* pg. 25, 6 March 1977

"Missing Government Aide Charged in Wife's Murder." *New York Times,* pg. 36.13 March 1976.

Nunes, Donald. "Search for Bishop is Widened." *The Washington Post,* pg. C1. 24 March 1976.

Telephone Book, US Department of State, Washington. Winter 1976, pg. 200.

The Golden Life

Brainerd, Edna. "Many in Pasadena Enjoy Vacations at Home." *Los Angeles Times.* B1. 4 August 1946.

"Charles Bishop." Obituaries. *Los Angeles Times,* pg. B 17. 2 March 1962.

Cordell, Hicks. "Children's Doll Fair Will Depict Events from California's Early History." *Los Angeles Times,* pg. B1. 22 November 1950.

Copp, James. "Skylarking." *Los Angeles Times,* pg. B3. 13 July 1953.

D'Amboise, Jacques. *I was a dancer: a memoir,* New York, New York: Alfred A. Knopf. 2011

"Dance will Climax Tennis Tourney," *Los Angeles Times,* pg. C9. 7 May 7 1953.

Douglas, John. *The Anatomy of a Motive.* New York, NY: A Lisa Drew Book/Scribner. 1999

"Germaine Haney, Mrs." Obituaries. *Los Angeles Times* pg. B3. 25 March 1961.

French, Tony: Telephone Interview. 18, May 2016

Goodland, Elizabeth. "Fall Parties Arrive in Dazzling Variety." *Los Angeles Times.* A1. 21 September 1959.

Hicks, Cordell. "Children's Doll Fair Will Depict Events from California's Early History." *Los Angeles Times,* pg. B1. 22 November 1950.

"Hospital Guild Staff to Meet at Pasadena." *Los Angeles Times.* pg. B2. 1 May 1950.

Kappa Sigma Dance (21 October 1917) Affairs in Society. *Colorado Springs Gazette* pg. 22

Kegley, Howard. California Oil News. *Los Angeles Times,* pg. 23. 31 May 1942.

Kegley, Howard. California Oil News. *Los Angeles Times,* pg. 14. 16 June 1942.

Kegley, Howard. California Oil News. *Los Angeles Times,* pg. 12, 21 April 1944.

Kuhn, Mary Ann. "Did his love letters hint of madness?" *Chicago*

Tribune. pg. 1. 3 April 1977.

Khun, Mary Ann. Telephone Interview. 19 March 2012.

Kappa Sigma Dance (21 October 1917) Affairs in Society. *Colorado Springs Gazette* pg. 22

Kegley, Howard. California Oil News. *Los Angeles Times,* pg. 23. 31 May 1942.

Kegley, Howard. California Oil News. *Los Angeles Times,* pg. 14. 16 June 1942.

Kegley, Howard. California Oil News. *Los Angeles Times,* pg. 12, 21 April 1944.

Kuhn, Mary Ann. "Did his love letters hint of madness?" *Chicago Tribune.* pg. 1. 3 April 1977.

Khun, Mary Ann. Telephone Interview. 19 March 2012.

Mills, Barney. Telephone Interview. 28 August 2015.

"Pasadena Guild to Have Noel Party Tomorrow." *Los Angeles Times,* pg. D17. 3 December 1950.

"Pasadena Kids Compete in Pet and Hobby Show" *Los Angeles Times,* Pg. A8. 3 May 1947.

"Philharmonic's New Members to be Honored." *Los Angeles Times,* pg. B6. 6 November 1952.

"School Pet Show Set." *Los Angeles Times*, pg. A 13. 2 May 1951.

"Sharps and Flats." *Los Angeles Times,* pg. C5. 21 September 1941.

Sullivan, Robert J. "Standard Reports Big Oil Find." *Los Angeles Times,* pg. 15. 28 May 1952.

"Supper Dance Will Follow Tennis Finals." *Los Angeles Times,* pg. B1. 15 May 1920.

Tallman, Douglas. Telephone Interview. 21 May 2013.

"Three Hundred Leases to Date." New from Fountain Field; Activities of the Oil

US Bureau of the Census. 1920 *Fourteenth Decennial Census of the US.* Decatur Township, Enumeration District 131, Sheet 1A, 15 March 1920.

US Bureau of the Census. *1940 Sixteenth Decennial Census of the US.* Pasadena Township, Ed 19-508, SD 12

US Bureau of the Census. 1930 *Fifteenth Decennial Census of the US.* Glendale Township,

World. *Colorado Springs Gazette* Pg. 5

US Bureau of the Census. 1930 *Fifteenth Decennial Census of the US.* Long Beach Township, ED 19-1067, Sheet 3A, pg. 283

US Draft Registration. Registrars Report 5-1-6-A. number 850/50.https://familysearch.org/ark:/61903/1:1:KZKX-XPW: 12 September 1918

US Draft Registration. Registration Card Serial Number 938, Order Number 1367 5-1-14 C

US Selective Service System [Draft Registration Cards, 1917-1918] Registration State: *Colorado*; Registration County: *El Paso*; Roll: *1561812*

Ward, Mary. "Pink Color Theme." *Los Angeles Times,* pg. C7. 2 July 1953.
Weddings 'Combes – Bishop' (18 August 1946) *Los Angeles Times* pg. B2

"WITH ALUMNAE" *Los Angeles Times,* pg. 15. 24 November 1956.

The Bitch Goddess Success

1955 Yale Yearbook, Calhoun by Richard Laurence Sassoon. Page 121, 1955.

1956 Yale Class book by Paul Nathan Zietlow. Page 118. 1956.

1957 Yale Class book. Calhoun, by Charles Farrington Leahy. Page 119. 1957.

"4,000 Disciplined at Yale because of a Snowball Riot," *New York Times*, Pg. 19, 10 January 1954.

Bridges, Rocky. "Quickly Quoted. Bridges Spent Winter Digging Ditches." *Milwaukee Journal*. Pg.18. 12 March 1958.

Burnham, Joan. "Pasadena Area Barbeque." Due. *Los Angeles Times* C-2. 6 September 1956.

California Department of Health and Welfare, [Marriage Index1949-1959] pg.102.

"Fire Hoses Halt Yale Student Riot." Page 1, *Lewiston Daily Sun*, Lewiston-Auburn, Maine 14 May, 1952

"Good Humor Starts Riot of 1500 at Yale." Page 1 *Chicago Daily Tribune*, 14 May 1952

Haggard, Merl Personal Interview: Rolling Stone Interview. October 2003. Reposted by *California Today*, 21 February 2015 and [Friends of the California Archives] "Bakersfield Boy Goes to the Big House, Comes Out a Man." February 21, 1958.

"In praise of Frank Baumer." Letter. alumninet.yale.edu/classes/yc1957/years.html

Yale University. 29 July 2009.

James, William. *The Bitch Goddess Success. Variation on American Theme,* New York: Steinhouse Press, (Binding Russell-Rutter Company) Reprint Eakins Press, 1968.

Kuhn. Mary Anne. Telephone Interview. 19 March 2012.

Nietzsche, Wilhelm F. The Antichrist, New York: AA Knopf, 1920

Nietzsche, Wilhelm F. Thus, Spoke Zarathustra, New York: Cambridge University Press, 2001

"Our Four Years." Letter. alumninet.yale.edu/classes/yc1957/years.html Yale University.16 January 1954

"Riot Vendors Appeal Fines," *New York Times*, pg.10B. 6 June 1952

Rosenbaum, Ron. The Great Ivy League Posture Photo Scandal. New York Times Sunday Magazine Section, *The New York Times*, 15 January 1995.

"Snow brings out Boy in Yale Men: 10 Arrested in Snowball War," *New York Times*, Pg. 8

16 January 1954

Steinhorn, Leonard. "The Gentleman's C. New York." *The New York Times*, Pg. A 38. 14December, 11 June 2001.

Williams, Linda. Nietzsche's Mirror: The World as Will to Power. [Lanham, Md.]: Rowman and Littlefield. 2001.

Wilson, Steven Child. Telephone Interview. 28 May 2011

Winks, Robin W. Cloak and Gown: Scholars in the Secret War, 1939-1961. New York: William Morrow. [Collins Harvill] 607 pages. 1987.

"Yale Sniffs Complacently," *Hartford Courant*, Pg. 2 16 May 1952.

"Yale University Announces $150 rise in Tuition Fees." *Columbia Daily Speculator* Volume CII, Number 77. 27 February 1958.

Sneaky Pete

Adorjan, Michael Herman. Lost Unconventional War Lessons from the Yugoslav Front, SAMSMonograph, *School of Advanced Military Studies*, [Fort Leavenworth, Kansas] [declassified] AY 2012-002. February 2012.

Adorjan, Michael Herman. U.S. Army School of Advanced Military Studies United States Army Command and General Staff College Fort Leavenworth, Kansas. 2012

Tracy, William R. "Army Intelligence School System," *The Phi Delta Kappan*, Vol. 44, No. 7, pp. 337-341. April 1963.

Army Special Operations Forces Unconventional Warfare, Field Manual No. 3-05.13. [declassified] Headquarters - Department of the Army, Washington, DC, 30 September 2008

"Bishop and Weis Rite Solemnized." *Los Angeles Times*, pg. A1. 5 August 1959.

Colley, David. Shadow Warriors: Intelligence operatives waged clandestine cold war." Kansas City: *VFW, Veterans of Foreign Wars Magazine*. Vol. 85 Issue 1, September, 1997

Janke, Peter. Guerrilla and Terrorist Organizations: A World Directory and Bibliography. Macmillan. 1983.

Koschade, Stuart. The Internal Dynamics of Terrorist Cells: A Social Network Analysis of Terrorist Cells in an Australian Context. Thesis, Queensland University of Technology. 2007

Phelan, Mark. Uncovering the History of Army Jeep No. 1, *Detroit Free Press,* (also *Tribune News Service/Stars and Stripes*) 20 December 2015.

Polmar, Norman and Allen, Thomas Allen, B. The Spy Book. New York: Random House, 1998

Shapley, Deborah. "Telecommunications Eavesdropping by NSA on Private Messages Alleged," Science AAS, New Series, Vol. 197, No. 4308. 9 September 1977, pp. 1061-1064

Specialized Training Program. US Army Security Agency, Recruitment Pamphlet circa 1960

The Incursion

"Croat 'Secret Army' in Australia" *The Manchester Guardian,* [London, UK] First Page 13. 6 September 1963.

De Launay, Jacques. *Les grandes controverses de l'histoire contemporaine 1914-1945.Edito-Service Histoire Secrete de Notre Temps. p. 568.*1974

Dragić, Marko University of Split, Croatia, Croatian Studies Review [Časopis za Hrvatske Studije] 87 Vol : 7, 2011.

Historical Facts Regarding the Croatian King Dmitar Zvonimir in Vladimir Nazor's Poetry,

Koschade, Stuart. Op. Cit.

Lummis, Dayton. Not Wanted. iUniverse. New York [Bloomington] pg. 83 – 91. 2010.

The Best and the Brightest

Baxter, Eric. Telephone Interview. 14 September 2016

Beach Party, William Asher. *American International Pictures (AIP).* 1963 Film

Coffee Ranks Tea

Barnes, Bart. "Edward M. Korry Dies; Diplomat and Journalist." *The Washington Post* B.06. 30 January 2003.

Beecroft, Mette. Telephone Interview. 11 March 2011.

Bishop, Bradford. Red Diary 1966

Edward Korry's testimony in the US Senate, *Ethiopia and the Horn of Africa.* p.36

Khayyam, Omar. Rubaiyat, Translation by Edward Fitzgerald Verse 7

"Kennedy begins trip to 4 African lands" *The New York Times,* pg. 3. 2 June, 1966.

"Kenyans Criticize Kennedy for Stand on South Africa" *New York Times;* pg. 9. 23 June 1966.

Lefebyre, Jeffrey A., *The United States, Ethiopia and the 1963 Somali-Soviet Arms Deal: Containment and the Balance of Power Dilemma in the Horn of Africa.* Source: The Journal of Modern African Studies, Vol. 36, No. 4. pp. 611-643 December 1998.

Lummis, Dayton. Telephone interview. 13 March, 2011.

Neimeier, Jerry. "U.S. base in Ethiopia has benefits but may be phased out." *Palo Alto Times* Palo Alto, California. 4 April 1970.

"Putting the aria into Somalia." *The Economist* pg. 72. 24 April 1993.

Rasmusen, John. *Remembering Kagnew Station.* Association of the US Army. Arlington. 2007.

Rosenthal, Eugene. Interview with Jack O'Brien. Association for Diplomatic Studies and Training, ADST, Foreign Affairs Oral History Project, 28 November 1989.

Larner, Steven. "Africa Goes to the Fair." *1966 Before Derg Time*, on line video clip, Youtube.by 'Addis 1625' United States National

Exhibition held in Addis Ababa, Film 1966.

"South Africa Bars Foreign Reporters on Kennedy's Tour." *The New York Times.* 10. 25 May 1966.

"South African Trip Begun by Kennedy; 1,000 Welcome Him." *The New York Times;* Pg. 6. 5 June 1966.

"South Africa Won't Admit Kennedy Again, Paper Says." *The New York Times;* pg. 8. 13 June 1966.

Stonehouse: First US Collector of Telemetry Signals. CIA, Author's name withheld. Pg. 20-23

Reproduced with permission of the copyright owner. Further reproduction prohibited without permission. Approved for Release by NSA on 09/18/2007.

"Tanzanian Town Greets Kennedy: Holiday Declared in Mbeya When Senator Flies In". *The New York Times,* Pg. 17. 12 June 1966,

Thompson, Karen. "Some connections last a lifetime: Local woman makes dreams come true in Ethiopia." *Fernandina Observer.* [Fernandina Beach, Florida.] 12 June 1966.

Taylor, Phillip. Global Communications, International Affairs, and the Media since 1945.Routledge, New York: p. 182. 1997.

Wilkerson, Alicia E. Telephone Interview. 15 March 2011.

Winkler, Gordon. Association for Diplomatic Studies and Training, by Dorothy Robins Mowry, ADST Foreign Affairs Oral History Project. 23 March 1989.

Milan
Biographic Register. *US Department of State* page 45. July 1967.

Bastiani, Carl A. Association for Diplomatic Studies and Training, by Charles Stuart Kennedy ADST Foreign Affairs Oral History Project (and also from "My Career as a US Consul and Diplomat" Xlibris Corporation, 2011) 25 February 2008.

Byington, Jane. Association for Diplomatic Studies and Training by

Margaret Sullivan. 8 March 1989.

Clarke, Ellis N. Association for Diplomatic Studies and Training by Charles Stuart Kennedy. ADST Foreign Affairs Oral History Project. 26 January 1998.

"Ex-French Envoy Takes Own Life; Killed wife, 2 Children in February" *The New York Times.* Pg. 9, 20 April 1977.

Holy See Brief. *The Guardian,* Pg. 8. 11 February 1977.

"Pope Canonizes Saint Elizabeth Ann." *The Guardian,* London. Pg. 2. 19 September 1975.

Murphy, Peter K. Interview. *Association for Diplomatic Studies and Training* by William D. Morgan. ADST Foreign Affairs Oral History Project. 4 April 1994.

STEYDLÉ, Gpourvu que le profit demeure [Paris] *Association pour l'Économie Distributive* Number 743. Février 1977.

Well, Martin. A Pretty Good Club. Norton, New York. 1978

Status Anxiety
Baker, Donald and Richard E. Prince. "Bishop had been seeing Psychiatrist. *"The Washington Post,* pg. B1. 1 March 1976.

De Botton, Alain. Status Anxiety. New York: Pantheon. 2004.

Mills, Barney. Telephone Interview. 4 May 2016.

Gaborone
"… and for Botswana?" *The Economist* [London, England] 18 June 1966: 1300. Also, *The Economist,* 14 Nov. 2015.

A Retrospective of US Peace Corps Service to Botswana, 1966-1970 Lynne Farmer

Botswana Notes and Records, Vol. 41, pp. 130-132. 2009.

Anderson, Jack. "Prison Site of Bird Hunt." *Tuscaloosa News.* [Tuscaloosa Alabama] Pg. 4. 10 September 1972.

Good, Barbara J. "Women in the Foreign Service: A Quiet Revolution." *Foreign Service Journal.* 47…51. January 1981.

Naude, Mauitz. Legacy of Rondavels and Rondavel houses in the Northern Interior of South Africa, Department of Agriculture, Tshwane University of Technology, [Pretoria] South Africa. 2007.

Nelson, Charles J. Association for Diplomatic Studies and Training by Celestine Tutt. ADST Foreign Affairs Oral History Project 31 October 1981.

The China Card

Hoagland, Jim. "Peking-Built Tanzam Railway Being Delayed by Money Snags." *The Washington Post, Olean Times Herald,* Pg. A9. 10 January 1970.[240]

The State Department on the Couch

Clarke, William Jr. Association for Diplomatic Studies and Training. By Thomas Stern, ADST Foreign Affairs Oral History Project. 11 January 1994.

Caprio, Frank. The Art of Sexual Lovemaking.: Fairview Book Company. 64 pages. 1967.

Caprio, Frank, and Berger, Joseph Healing yourself with Self Hypnosis. New York: Prentice Hall. 288 pages. 1998.

Caprio, Frank How to Avoid a Nervous Breakdown. New York: Meredith Press. 179 pages.1969.

Nietzsche, Friedrich. Beyond Good and Evil, The Free Spirit. [Chapter 2] Chicago: Gateway Editions; distributed by H. Regnery Co. 1955

Safire, William. The Right Word at the Right Place at the Right Time: Wit and Wisdom. New York. Simon and Schuster. 2004.

Stout, David. "John E. List, 82, Killer of 5 Family Members." *The New York Times,* New York Edition Pg. 86. 25 March 2008.

---

[240] In March 1954, the *Times-Herald* was purchased by Graham, owner of the more liberal *Post*. For a time, the combined paper was officially known as the *Washington Post and Times-Herald*. The *Times-Herald* portion of the nameplate became less and less prominent on a second line in ensuing years, however, and was dropped entirely in 1973.

The Corridor Reputation

Anonymous, Telephone Interview. 8 May 2016.

Davis, E. Philip. "Comparing bear markets – 1973 and 2000". National Institute Economic Review 183 (1): 78–89. doi:10.1177/0027950103183001464. January 2003. Retrieved 11 September 2007.

Woodard, Dustin. "1973 – 1974 Stock Market Crash". About.com.Archived from the original on 24 April 2009. Retrieved 11 September 2007.

"A Gilt-Edged Year for the Stock Market". *Time*, 8 January 1973. Retrieved 11 September 2007.

God as a Verb

"Anglican, Roman Catholic Statement Provides Setting for Recognition; No Present Change." *The Episcopal New Yorker*, Pg. 4. January 1974.

Bindle, Susan. Interview: Boston College Prof. Mary Daly 'Humanity should be 10% Male and 90% Female' *What is Enlightenment?* Issue 16. Fall/Winter 2002.

Campbell, Benjamin. "The Chicago Meeting of Bishops..." *The Episcopal New Yorker* Pg. 6. October 1974.

"Charges Refiled Against Ordaining Bishops." *The Episcopal New Yorker,* Volume XLVI pg. 1. October 1974.

Church News Items. *The Episcopal New Yorker,* Pg. 4. February 1974.

Kempton, Wayne H. Personal Interview. 8 June 2015.

Kerman, Peter. Comment: "Sex Discrimination in Help Wanted Advertising. "Volume 15 Number 1 *Santa Clara Lawyer* 183. 1974.

"N.Y. Reaffirms Support, Boost Ordination of Women Priests." *The Episcopal New Yorker,* Pg. 6. May 1974.

Wilkison, Jean. "Breaking out of the Patriarchal Past." *The Episcopal New Yorker,* Pg. 2. January 1994.

"Women Press for Ordination to Priesthood." *The Episcopal New Yorker,* Pg. 6. January 1974.

Molasses

Smith, Michael B. Interview. Association for Diplomatic Studies and Training by Charles Stuart Kennedy. ADST Foreign Affairs Oral History Project. 25 August 1993.

Smith, Joe. Personal Interview. 19 February 2016.

Smith, Judith A. Interview. Association for Diplomatic Studies and Training by Ruth Kahn. ADST Foreign Affairs Oral History Project. 13 July 1990.

Southwick, Michael A. Interview. Association for Diplomatic Studies and Training by Charles Stuart Kennedy. ADST Foreign Affairs Oral History Project. 4 May 2004.

The Hunt

Baker, Donald. "2nd Policeman in Shooting Dies." *The Washington Post* pg. A1. 30 March 1976.

Baker, Donald. "Five Years and No Progress Finding Mass Murder Suspect." *The Washington Post,* pg. B1. 2 March 1981.

"Former Diplomat Missing." *The Irish Times and The Weekly Irish Times,* [Dublin]Pg. 5. 3 April 1976.

Baker, Donald and Nunes, Donnel. "Slayings Laid to Bishop: Bethesda Man

'Only Suspect' In Death of 5 Bishop Charged with Killing." *The Washington Post,* Pg. A1. 13 March 1976.

"Bodies in Grave: Seek Missing Man." *Straits Times,* [Singapore] Pg. 3. 10 March 1976.

"General Doubts Fugitive Hides in S. Africa." *The Hartford Courant,* Pg. 4. 30 March 1976.

"Mass murderer 'hiding in UK." *The Guardian and The Observer,*

[London] page 2. 30October 1992.

Bishop Seen Everywhere

Grubisich, Thomas. "Clues in Roy Rogers Murders Are Few." *The Washington Post,* pg. E1. 20 March 1976.

Nunes, Donald. "Search for Bishop Is Widened." *The Washington Post* pg.C1. 24 March 1976.

"Roy Rogers Slaying Calls Flood Police," *The Washington Post* pg.C8. 16 March 1976

Szoldra, Paul. "How to Talk like a Spy." *Business Insider.* Military & Defense.3 September 2014.

The Migrant Trade

Larssen, Milene, "People Smuggling in Sicily: Europe or Die." Youtube.Vice Media LLC. video. August 2015. Accessed February 2016.

Prendergast, Dell. Interview. Association for Diplomatic Studies and Training by Charles Stuart Kennedy. ADST Foreign Affairs Oral History Project. 24 June 1999.

Smith, Joe, Personal Interview. 26 February 2016.

Petroleum

Crime and its Impact on the Balkans and affected countries. United Nations Office on Drugs and Crime. [Vienna, Austria] March 2008.

Smith, Joe. Personal Interview. 4 March 2016.

Westell, Dan. "Millions Lost to Fuel Bootleggers." *The Globe and Mail*, [Toronto] 19 May 2012.

Sightings

Baker, Donald. "The Elusive Mr. Bishop: Dead? Sweden? Italy"*? The Washington Post,* Pg. C. 19 June 1979.

Baker, Donald. "FBI Checking Brad Bishop Lead in Sweden." *The Washington Post,* pg. A1. 4 January 1979.

Baker, Donald. "No Reason to Believe Bishop Is Now in Sweden, Police Say: No New Sightings of Bishop Reported." *The Washington Post,* pg. A1. 5 January 1979.

Baker, Donald. "Police May Have Seen Bishop." *The Washington Post* Pg. D1. 6 January 1979.

Bruno, Karl. The Chilalo Agricultural Development Unit: Exporting Swedish agricultural knowledge to Haile Selassie's Ethiopia, 1967-1974, Division of Agrarian History, Swedish University of Agricultural Sciences. 22 January 2015.

Duncan, John. Personal Communication. Facsimile to John Cady. 1994 https://s3.amazonaws.com/s3.documentcloud.org/documents/1100589/bishop-state-dept-investigation.pdf. 18 May 1994.

Harrell, Roy Jr. Telephone Interview. 31 January 2011.

The Bankston Letter

Albert Kenneth Bankston v. United States of America, 433 – F.2nd 1294 (1970)

Albert Kenneth Bankston v. State of Mississippi, 236 So.2d 757 (June 1, 1970) Supreme Court of Mississippi

Albert Kenneth Bankston v. United States of America, 433 F.2d 1294 (5th Circuit November 11, 1980)

Cario, Phillip. The Iceman. New York, New York. St. Martin's Press. 2006.

Ellis, Bill. Cattle Mutilation: Contemporary Legends and Mythologies. Pages 39 - 80 of Contemporary Legend Volume 1. 1991.

Ellis, Bill. Raising the Devil. Lexington, Kentucky: (University of Kentucky Press) 2000

"Four Break Jail, Kidnap Sheriff. Two Others." *Chicago Tribune,* B13 January 3, 1969

Ivy, Jim. "Ranchers Enraged by Weird Deaths, 'Devil Cult' Sought in

Nebraska." *Washington Post,* 8 September 1974.

"Last Escapee Returns," *Tuscaloosa News*, p16 5 January 5, 1969

Lewis, James. Encyclopedia of Satanism. Create Space. p 287 16 June 2014

"Modern Building Far Cry from Ancient Log Jail" (9 June 1960) *Putnam County Herald*, Cookeville, TN

Nation, Nick P., and Williams, Elizabeth S. "Maggots, Mutilation and Myth: Patterns of Postmortem Scavenging of the Bovine Carcass." *The Canadian Veterinary Journal*, Can Vet J. 1989 Sep; 30(9): 742–747. PMCID: PMC1681190

O'Brien, Christopher. Stalking the Herd. Adventures Unlimited Press. [Kempton, Illinois] 15 March, 2014.

United States of America v. Albert Kenneth Bankston, 424 – F.2nd 714(5th Circuit, April 10, 1970)

"Three of Four Escapers Captured," *New York Times*, p14. January 4, 1969

"Three of Sheriff's Captors Seized in Mississippi." *Hartford Courant*, p7 January 8, 1969

United States of America v. Albert Kenneth Bankston, 424 – F.2nd 714(5th Circuit, April 10, 1970)

The Bankston Letter, Addenda
January 29, 1975, Federal Bureau of Investigation, Mutilations of Animals Minnesota, North and South Dakota Research Matter. Bureau Minneapolis, (Additional Comments by Richard Hilde (NA) Chief Agent, North Dakota Crime Bureau, Bismarck, ND.) 63-0-35659

To: SAC 62-0-14743

From: FBI sec 23 63-0-35659

Wheels Within Wheels
Albertini, Matteo. Mafia Links Between the Balkans and Scandinavia, State of Affairs. *Revista Română de Studii Baltice și*

Nordice / The Romanian Journal for Baltic and Nordic Studies, ISSN 2067-1725, Vol. 4, Issue 2: pp. 111-150. 2012.

Doder, Dusko, "Yugoslav Oil Pipeline to Serve E. Europe." *The Washington Post,* \Page A 16. 10 January 1974.

"Faltering Economy Spurs Unrest in Italy," *The Hartford Courant,* Pg. 2A. April 28, 1974.

"IMF Funds Oil Imports by Yugoslavia, Spain Under Special '75 Plan" (By a Staff Reporter) *Wall Street Journal,* Pg. 31, 24 Feb 1976

Kregar, Josip and Petričušić, Antonija. "Crime as a Business, Business as a Crime." (VARSTVOSLOVJE) *Journal of Criminal Justice and Security.* let. 12 št. 4 str. 367-377. 27 December 2010.

Posen, Barry. "Security Dilemma and Ethnic Conflict," *Survival*, vol. 35, no. 1.pg. 7-47. Spring 1993.

Smith, Colin. "Yugoslav Ethnic Splits Will Help the Russians After Tito Goes*." Los Angeles Times*, Page 13. 12 December 1976.

Taylor, Jerry and Van Doren, Peter. "Time to Lay the 1973 Oil Embargo to Rest." Cato Institute Commentary, Washington, DC. 17 October 2003.

Weeks, Albert. "Oil in the Soviet bloc's future**."** *The Christian Science Monitor,* page 16. 24 January 1974.

Legend, Myth and Brief Encounter Sightings
Banks, Carolyn. Darkroom. New York: Viking Adult Press. 1980.Rereleased as 'The Darkroom." 24 November 2014.

Banks, Carolyn Telephone Interview. 8 February 211.

"Media Fast Track," *The Washington Post,* p. SM2. 15 June 1980

Serna, Joseph. "FBI: Man suspected of brutally killing his family may be in L.A. area [Southern California]" *Los Angeles Times,* 14 April 2014.

Ralit, M. H. "Mind Altering." [Letters] *The Washington Post* Pg. 14.

13 July 1980.

Reeves, Pamela. "Scary past can spook homebuyers." *Cincinnati Post,* [Final Edition] Pg. 6D. 30 October 1994.

Gunrunning

"Croatia Acts as the Nexus of a New Arms Trade," GIS Special Topical Studies: Balkan Strategic Studies. International Securities Services Assn. [Zurich, Switzerland]31 October 1992.

Illegal German Weapons to Croatia and Bosnia Fuel the Balkan Conflict. GIS Special Topical Studies: Balkan Strategic Studies. International Securities Services Assn. [Zurich, Switzerland] 31 October 1992.

"Mass Murderer 'Hiding in UK'," *The Guardian* [Manchester (UK)]. 30 Oct 1992.

Schmetzer, Uli. Tribune Staff Writer, "How [the] West Let Croatia Sneak Arms." Chicago Tribune. 20 August 1995.

Weather 1 -- No Title (29 October 1992) *The Guardian* [Manchester] pg. A26

John Doe

Boerma, Jurgen. The Bradford Bishop Mystery, *The Scuppernong reminder* [Beaufort County, North Carolina] 26 September 2016. also see...*Washington Daily News,* 11 April 2014.

Goodwin, David and Santora, Marc. "3 Officers Shot in Greenwich Village; Fugitive is killed" *New York Times [N.Y/Region]* 28 July 2014.

Metcalf, Andrew. "Hunt for Bradford Bishop Led Authorities to Arrest of Different Fugitive." *Bethesda Magazine* [Bethesda Beat] 13 April 2015.

Morse, Dan. "Exhumed body in Alabama could be notorious Bethesda fugitive." *The Washington Post,* 9 October 2014.

Patterson, DeWayne. Who is Brad Bishop? *The Daily Sentinel* [Jackson County Alabama]11 October 2014.

Taylor, Victoria. "Florida fugitive arrested in Mexico after 37 years" *New York Daily News*, [also AP, Crimesider Staff] 11 January 2015.

The End Game

Actuarial Life Table, Social Security Administration, (2013) Washington DC

Ancestry Library Edition (ProQuest): Social Security Death Index

Geoghegan, Peter. "Welcome to Brčko, Europe's only free city and a law unto itself." *Manchester Guardian,* [Manchester, UK] 14 May 2014.

Lawrence, Steve. Telephone interview. 21 June 2017.

Remmert, Robert H. *Point of Contact* Kindle Book, 6 July 2015

Salo, Jackie. "Why Do Men Kill Their Wives and Family? Study Says New Information Can Prevent Murders." *International Business Times* [Pulse] 25 August 2015.

Epilogue

Association for Diplomatic Studies and Training, (22 July 2002) Coburn, Harry by Michael Mahoney ADST Foreign Affairs Oral History Project

Bruchi Susann, "A genetically distinct lion (Panthera leo) population from Ethiopia" *European Journal of Wildlife Research* 59:215–225. 2013.

Coburn, Harry. Association for Diplomatic Studies and Training. by Michael Mahoney ADST Foreign Affairs Oral History Project. 22 July 2002.

Coventry v Gladstone, Lord Justice Blackburn's definition of *Bill of Lading*

City Reports, Gaborone. Real Post Reports, *Talesmag.com.* March 2, 2015 Website. Referenced on May 1, 2016

Oberding, Janice. Haunted Lake Tahoe. Arcadia Publishing Pg. 86. 14 September 2015.

Seaberry, Jane and Knight, "Athelia Breeden's Life of Crime Began at 11." *Washington Post* Pg. A3. 4 November 1976.

Year: *1940*; Census Place: *Colorado Springs, El Paso, Colorado*; Roll: *T627_461*; Page: *5A*; Enumeration District: *21-21*

Allons![241] we must not stop here,
However sweet these laid-up stores, however convenient this dwelling we cannot remain here,
However shelter'd this port and however calm these waters we must not anchor here,
However welcome the hospitality that surrounds us we are permitted to receive it but a little while.

—Walt Whitman, Song of the Open Road from Leaves of Grass

---

[241] Allons is French for Let us go

An ideology of extreme personal freedom can be dangerous because it encourages people to leave homes, jobs, cities, and marriages in search of personal and professional fulfillment, thereby breaking the relationships that were probably their best hope for such fulfillment.

—Jonathan Haidt, The Happiness Hypothesis

FBI AGE ENHANCED SKETCH

Index

Acheson, Dean	132, 192
Aha Moment	219, 234, 301
Alabama	
Jackson County	272
Alexander, King	118, 119
Argentina	291
Eva Peron	102
Army Security Agency	107 - 109, 111 - 115, 126, 287
Amanrich, Gérard	164 - 166
Ambassador	
By age 50	73, 163, 296
Attack of the Crab Monsters	92
Australia	123-128, 140, 241, 242, 262, 285
Action Kangaroo	123, 124 – 126, 128
Canberra	123
Wodonga	123
Ballet	81, 84, 86, 160
André Eglevsky	84
Jacques d'Amboise	84
Banks, Carolyn	265
Bankston, Albert Kenneth	42, 43, 57, 58, 247 – 258, 221
Barthou, Louis	118
Bishop	
Annette	9, 23 – 27, 39, 44, 49, 52, 53, 62, 71, 86 – 88, 98 – 100, 102, 106 – 111, 134, 149, 152, 153, 157, 160, 181, 183, 198 – 200, 204, 206, 211, 216, 240, 241, 268, 276, 317
Brenton	5, 51, 52, 152
Charles	9, 79 – 81, 87, 88, 100, 129, 181
Geoffrey	5, 26, 38- 41, 50 – 53, 201, 230, 296
Helen	80, 87
Lobelia	9, 23, 25, 27, 36, 37, 44, 49, 52 –

352 | The Bradford Bishop Murders

	54, 70, 71, 81 – 88, 95, 98, 108, 110, 157, 160, 183, 185, 200 – 206, 209 – 211, 265, 280
William Bradford Sr.	9, 28, 79 – 86, 110, 120, 209
William Bradford III	9, 27, 37, 49, 50, 53, 110, 134, 163, 171, 152
Bechuanaland	171. 172
Bitch Goddess Success	89, 102, 208, 265, 286, 301, 302
Bloodhounds	72, 74, 231, 264
Botswana	25, 172 – 199, 207, 208, 212, 216, 243
Gaborone	174 – 179, 181-185, 201, 209, 216
Kazungula Bridge	191, 196, 202
Nelson, Charles J.	181, 185, 186, 192, 201
Okavango Delta	182, 192, 200
California	
Glendale	80
Griffith Park	84
Kern County	82
Mount Poso field	80, 82, 87, 105, 220
Newport Harbor	198, 270
Laguna Beach	86
Long Beach	80, 101, 237
San Marino	85, 160
South Pasadena	82 – 86, 91, 95 - 99, 110, 157, 160, 184, 200, 201, 270, 272, 283
University of California	88, 108, 109, 210
Camus, Albert	101, 226
Caprivi Strip	197, 191, 192, 292
Caprio, Frank	115, 204 – 209, 293, 318
China	181, 190, 192, 202, 223
Bamboo Railway	188
Tanzam Railway/Highway (See Tanzania)	
Beijing	188, 189
Taiwan	188, 189
CIA (Central Intelligence Agency)	43, 50, 55, 62, 112, 127, 265, 267

Class of 1954	86, 197, 198, 205, 268, 276, 277, 285, 293
Class of 1958	268, 280, 294
Colorado	
Colorado College	79
Manitou Springs	79
Croatia	110, 114, 115, 117, 118, 120, 121, 123 – 127, 214, 217, 236, 239, 244, 261 – 263, 267, 283
Currie, Ron	87, 108, 184
Daly, Mary	215, 217, 290
Detective Cady	23, 25, 50
Don Juanism	315, 316
Ethiopia	
Addis Ababa	135 – 139, 143, 147, 149, 150 – 153, 159, 161, 170, 171, 177, 178, 240, 244, 282
Hailie Selassie	135, 136, 143, 146, 149, 150, 153, 288
Lions	135, 136, 289
Italian Invasion	135
Kagnew Station	140, 142, 146 – 148, 157, 288
Existential Angst	306, 321
Existentialism	101, 322
Family Annihilator	17, 233, 322
FBI	17, 18, 60, 62, 69, 70, 74, 75, 205, 231, 241 – 249, 252 – 260, 268, 269, 272 – 277, 295
Flickinger, Donald E.	256, 257
Florida	68, 75, 229, 230
Atlantic Beach	230
Fort Lauderdale	229
Foord, Archibald	90, 101
Foreign Service Institute	131, 198, 205, 210, 211, 219, 220
Fuel Bootlegging	218, 224, 225
Gehlen, Reinhardt	111, 112, 130, 291
Golden Retriever	
Leo	27, 44, 50 – 61, 264, 282

Great Game	179, 187
Great Smoky Mountains National Park	17, 61, 62, 68, 71 – 76, 238, 241, 242, 245, 264, 269, 273, 280, 295,
Andrews Bald	71
Derrick Knob	75
Elkmont	59, 60, 272
Gatlinburg	60, 74, 75
Gibson, Trenny Lynn	71, 72, 269
Kuhlman Cabin	60, 76, 282
Jake's Creek Trail	60, 71, 76, 229, 238, 273, 282
Hitler	63 – 65, 111, 112, 120
Hong Kong	245
Italy	108, 109, 114, 118, 123 – 127, 160 – 163, 170, 217, 221, 223, 235, 243, 246, 257, 260, 262, 283
Bormio	160
Corriere della Sera	244
Courmayeur	221, 222, 260
Florence	127, 129, 160, 184
Holy See	165
Amanrich, Gérard	164-166
Naples	163, 164 198, 199, 243
Byington, Homer	163, 164, 176
Sicily	233
Catania	233
Sorrento	163, 243 – 245, 269
Venice	162, 262
Involutional Megalomania	208, 317, 318
Kennedy, Bobby	136, 139, 1433, 149, 153 – 157, 169
Khrushchev, Nikita	128, 129, 142, 146
Korry, Edward	139, 140, 143, 146, 147, 152, 161, 169, 171
LaVey, Anton	257, 259
Church of Satan, cults	247, 254 - 259
Dugan, Dan	255 - 258

List, John	293
Littorina railcar	141, 142, 145
Louisiana	248, 252, 253
New Orleans	248
Lummis, Dayton	14, 115, 266, 267
Maryland	
Annapolis	276, 278, 280
Montgomery County	14 – 16, 22, 24, 67, 70, 73, 216, 231, 245, 246, 250, 264, 265, 269, 273
Bethesda	23, 36, 69, 231
Caderock Springs	36, 44, 70, 71, 204, 211, 216, 231
Montgomery Mall	26, 51, 69
Poch's Hardware	25, 26, 50, 69
Montgomery County Police	15, 62, 67, 70, 245, 246, 250, 265, 273
Swim and Tennis Club	71
Minnesota	81, 247, 254
Yellow Medicine County	255, 290
Mississippi	
Bassville	249
Hazelhurst	249
Hopewell	250
Hinds County	249, 255
Plain	248
Missouri Monster	
Momo	251- 254
Mother Complex	39, 205, 209, 287, 315
Mozdir, Charles	274, 275
Mutilations (Mutes)	
Cattle	247, 251 - 257
Pigs and Hogs	55, 71, 254
Mussolini, Benito	119, 140
Narcissism	284, 314
National Security Agency	64, 114, 115, 208
Nay Theist	218, 310
New Haven	92 – 94, 276

Town and Gown	93, 94, 311
Yalies	93, 94
Nietzsche, Friedrich	102, 102, 106, 120, 142, 152, 285
Nihilism	102
North Carolina	
Columbia	43, 68, 270, 273
Creswell	43, 53
Phelps Lake	40, 42, 43
Jacksonville	56 – 59, 229, 272, 295
Hanover County	229, 230
Rutherford County	230
Spindale	230
Tyrell County	54, 56, 68, 69, 72, 270, 295
Pavelić, Ante	63 – 65, 119 – 121, 291
Peterson, Charles	129, 130
Polytechnic school	82, 83, 280
Portugal	
Angola	179, 196
Powers, Gary Francis	127, 128, 291
Serax	60, 96 – 99, 108, 142, 147, 193, 206, 283
Snippy the Horse	252, 292
South Africa	
Cape Town	154, 180 - 182
Luthuli, Albert	154
Mafeking	174, 182
Pretoria	14, 231, 241
Robben Island	180
John Hurd	179 – 181, 192
Status Anxiety	167, 208, 283, 319
Sweden	240, 241, 269, 283
Afton Bladet	243
Kungsträdgården	240
Police and sightings	239 - 242
Switzerland	38, 161, 221
Basel	239, 245 – 248, 260 – 263, 276
Lausanne	223

Tanzania
    Dar es Salaam   187
    Tanzam Railway/Highway   190, 191, 195, 289
Tennessee – See Great Smoky
Texas
    Fort Worth   256
    Kilgore Junior College   256
Tito, Josip Broz   64 – 67, 115, 122, 123, 130, 261, 262
Trailing Spouse   177, 183
Tobacco   137, 256
    Nigusu   137
    Nyala   137
UDBA   62, 64 – 67, 122, 125 – 127, 207, 267,
                                        312, 367
Ustaše   63 – 65, 114, 118 – 124, 214, 238
Virginia   24, 51, 70, 265
    Fairfax County   70, 231
Vjekoslav Luburić   63 – 66, 121 – 124, 130, 291
    Spain   13, 63, 65, 124, 179, 282
        Carcaixent   63, 65, 122
    Croatia   63, 65, 67, 110, 114 – 128, 207, 214,
                                        217, 236, 244, 261, 262, 263, 267, 283
        King Zvodomir   118
Wikileaks   19
Yale
    Calhoun College   89 – 93, 96 – 100, 106, 108, 266, 267
    Griswold, Whitney A.   92
    Ice Cream Riots   92 - 94
    Payne Whitney Gym   89
    Snowball Fight   94, 95
    Yale Record   91, 97
Yugoslavia
    Brčko   299, 347
    Kosovo   110
Zambia   186 – 191, 196
    Front Line States   188
    Kenneth Kaunda   186, 187

Made in the USA
Monee, IL
03 May 2026

49437535R00197